★  ★

"We hold these truths...

A DOCUMENTARY HISTORY
OF THE UNITED STATES

With Introduction by

HAROLD EARL HAMMOND
Professor of History,
New York University

D0925887

CAMBRIDGE BOOK CO., INC.

 **BRONXVILLE,
NEW YORK**

★   ★

INTRODUCTION

Documents constitute the foundation upon which the edifice of any people's history is constructed. Historical interpretations may vary according to the temper of the times, the emergence of new political or social or economic schools of thought, or the attitudes of people in a given section of the nation or of the nation as a whole. But the documentation upon which the variable of history is built remains essentially unchanged.

To illustrate, it is a well-recognized fact that such events as Secession, the Civil War, and Reconstruction are taught from entirely different points of view in different sections of the United States — with an identical general body of documentation available to all!

Further, schools of thought develop to suit the temper of the times or to accommodate a national attitude or need. Imbued with the chauvinism of a dynamic society reaching out across a vast continent, George Bancroft began his monumental *History of the United States* in the middle of the 19th century. This American patriot portrayed the British "Redbacks" in the same harsh tones that were used against the "Huns" of World War I or the "Yellow Japs" of World War II. Yet, even before Bancroft had completed his final volume, America's attitude toward the British nation had undergone a fundamental change, and his "historical interpretation" was already obsolete.

Sometimes a great or popular historian will develop a theory which will be seized upon by a group of disciples, and a "new viewpoint" will gain such popularity as to influence an entire generation of historical and textbook writers. For example, Frederick Jackson Turner's "safety-valve" theory on the effect of the seemingly endless American frontier upon the development of the American nation revolutionized historical thinking. Even more revolutionary to historical thinking and teaching was the thesis of Charles A. Beard, who let loose upon the country a school of "economic determinists" which may never die out!

How, then, is it possible for *factual* history to be so changeable and unstable — especially when it is drawn from essentially the same body of documents? This is a good question, and it is not easily answered.

The sin of omission, from the provincial, parochial or sectional point of view, may be greater than the sin of commission in order to develop an historical interpretation which is satisfying to a particular group of people. A writer may select the documents he wishes to use to suit a special purpose just as a salesman selects the arguments which present his product in the best possible light — and he may even do this with sincere conviction and an unintentional ignorance of some negative aspects of what he is trying to sell.

Just so, national problems or emergencies may raise previously despised historical figures to the highest pedestals, or reduce nations, treated earlier with tenderness by our historians, to nearly criminal status. Thus, men like Abraham Lincoln and Woodrow Wilson have grown in stature with each decade since their passing, while nations like Russia, Germany and Japan (fondly regarded by the American people during most of the last century) came to be regarded as monster-nations during our own century. These changes in national attitude cannot help but "reinterpret" history as events and the requirements of our times demand.

An historian of great stature and prestige sometimes rearranges the vast body of documentary evidence — constitutions, state papers, laws, proclamations, letters, diaries, judicial decisions, newspapers and magazine articles, and every other tangible evidence which casts light upon a given event — and forms a conclusion different from one currently held or never even thought of. When a group of this great historian's colleagues accepts his thesis, a "new viewpoint" of history requires a revision of previous thinking on the subject.

For all of these reasons, and because new documentary evidence is continually brought to light, history remains dynamic, and the facade of the structure is ever-changing. What does not change is the documentation itself, except for occasional additions. Therefore, we should review constantly the original sources — to do what Alfred E. Smith advised in his presidential campaign slogan: "Let's look at the record!"

The present collection of documents from American history has *not* been compiled with a view to helping the scholar distinguish between one historical viewpoint and another. On the contrary, it has been designed to acquaint the average layman and the pre-college student with some of the essential documents which bear upon the political and diplomatic highlights of our national life.

From this introductory "sampling" of some of the vital documents which helped to shape our nation's history, the editors and publishers hope to whet the appetite of as many Americans as possible for the exploration of further "original sources" in their search for truth. In this day of mass-media propaganda, it is especially important that citizens interested in the present and future of our nation search the past for its lessons and its wisdom. The best way to do this is to review the record; compare originals with the interpretations others have offered of the originals; and strengthen one's understanding of the most important events in our history with direct knowledge of those source materials which support the conclusions of the historians.

HAROLD EARL HAMMOND
Professor of History,
New York University

PREFACE

Any serious student of American history should investigate for himself the social and political documents which have had such a vital influence on the maturing institution of democracy in the United States.

The 70 documents included in this collection trace our nation's growth — from the simplest beginnings of colonial confederation for mutual protection to the dynamic constitution which melds fifty different states into a world power. These documents show the American love of liberty, and respect for the dignity and rights of human beings.

Dr. Milton Finkelstein and Professor Harold Earl Hammond have selected with great care the documents to be included in this book. Theirs was the task of "setting the stage" for each document, and making clear its social, political and intellectual importance in American history.

The documents follow each other in sequence of time and events. A brief, simple and strictly factual description of the events leading up to each specific document precedes the most pertinent excerpts from the document itself. The spelling in some of the old documents has been modernized for easier reading and for better understanding.

Each is followed by a quiz section to aid the reader in determining how much he has been able to extract and remember from his examination of the document. The thought questions can lead the student into allied fields of research.

This book is a valuable reference book — a source of information and a stimulating guide for those who seek a fuller understanding of the events which shaped American history. It is our hope that this book will find a useful and welcome place in the classroom, and in the school or home library. We hope it will be an inspiration for the further investigation of the development of the civil liberties which are our American heritage.

— THE EDITORS

CONTENTS

The Mayflower Compact 1620

* * * * *The group of colonists who are known* in American history as the Pilgrims had moved from England to Leyden, Holland. They then decided to attempt a colony in the New World. In 1619 they obtained the right to set up a private plantation from the Virginia Company — a trading company chartered by King James I to trade and make settlements in America. These 35 Pilgrims, plus 66 others from London, sailed from England. Their ship, the *Mayflower,* arrived off Cape Cod on November 21, 1620, with 102 passengers on board.

Much of our record of the first days of the colony they established comes from one of their leaders, William Bradford. Bradford tells us that there was much disagreement among the members of the group as to what rules, if any, they would have to follow in the New World. Some form of government was clearly necessary. The Pilgrim leaders prepared the Mayflower Compact, which was signed by 41 of the adult male passengers on November 11, 1620. They then went ashore to begin their new life.

The Mayflower Compact was the only constitution made by the Pilgrims. It was the first written agreement for self-government made in America. We should remember that the Pilgrims were really governed by their religious leaders. However, the Compact was an example of democratic decision as to how men should be ruled. As such, it set a pattern for later democratic agreements in other colonies.

In the name of God, Amen. We whose names are under-written, the loyal subjects of our dread sovereign Lord, King James, by the grace of God, of Great Britain, France, and Ireland king, defender of the faith, etc.

Having undertaken, for the glory of God, and advancement of the Christian faith, and honor of our king and country, a voyage to plant the first colony in the Northern parts of Virginia, do by these presents solemnly and mutually in the presence of God, and one of another, covenant and combine ourselves together into a civil body politic, for our better ordering and preservation and furtherance of the ends aforesaid; and by virtue hereof to enact, constitute, and frame such just and equal laws, ordinances, acts, constitutions, and offices, from time to time, as shall be thought most meet and convenient for the general good of the Colony, unto which we promise all due submission and obedience. In witness whereof we have hereunder subscribed our names at Cape Cod the 11 of November, in the year of the reign of our sovereign lord, King James, of England, France and Ireland the eighteenth, and of Scotland the fifty-fourth. Anno Dom. 1620.

TRUE OR FALSE?

Write the letter T *if the statement is correct; write* F *if it is false.*

_____1. The Pilgrims were forced to sign the Compact.

_____2. The Compact was similar to other such agreements that had already been made in other colonies.

_____3. The Pilgrims considered themselves subjects of King James.

_____4. The new laws were to be just and equal.

_____5. The Pilgrims later wrote a more complete constitution.

_____6. The Compact was a religious agreement for church rule.

_____7. A covenant is a religious book.

_____8. The Pilgrims promised to be obedient to William Bradford.

_____9. The Compact was our first democratic "constitution."

_____10. The Compact set the tone for later colonial thinking about self-government.

THOUGHT QUESTIONS

1. For what reasons did the Pilgrim leaders decide to draw up the Mayflower Compact?
2. Why was the Mayflower Compact important to:
   a. the Pilgrims;
   b. later colonists in other parts of New England?

Fundamental Orders
of Connecticut
1639

* * * * *There were several settlements in the* Connecticut Valley in the 1630's. In 1636, Puritans, dissatisfied with the autocratic rule of the Massachusetts Bay Colony, went to these settlements in groups, led by the Reverend Thomas Hooker. It was soon clear that these towns needed some form of government. Hooker's was the loudest voice among the colonists who argued that the government should be selected by the people. This was in contrast to the practice in other colonies of rule by a governor appointed by England.

The towns of Hartford, Windsor, and Wethersfield adopted a plan of government, which they called the *Fundamental Orders of Connecticut,* on January 24, 1639. Church members and property holders — the *freemen* — elected six magistrates and a governor. This charter proclaimed the independence of the colony and ignored the authority of King Charles I of England.

The Fundamental Orders was the first written constitution of a self-governing people in the New World. The Orders, excerpts of which are given here, continued in force until a charter was obtained from King Charles II in 1662.

Forasmuch as it hath pleased the Almighty God by the wise disposition of His divine providence so to order and dispose of things that we the inhabitants and residents of Windsor, Hartford, and Wethersfield are now cohabiting and dwelling in and upon the river of Connecticut and the lands thereunto adjoining; and well knowing where a people are gathered together the word of God requires that to maintain the peace and union of such a people there should be an orderly and decent government established according to God, to order and dispose of the affairs of the people at all seasons as occasion shall require; do therefore associate and conjoin ourselves to be as one public state or commonwealth; and do, for ourselves and our successors and such as shall be adjoined to us at any time hereafter, enter into combination and confederation together, to maintain and preserve the liberty and purity of the gospel of our Lord Jesus which we now profess, as also the discipline of the churches, which according to the truth of the said gospel is now practiced amongst us; as also in our civil affairs to be guided and governed according to such laws, rules, orders, and decrees as shall be made, ordered, and decreed, as followeth:

1. It is ordered that there shall be yearly two general assemblies or courts; . . . the first shall be called the court of election, wherein shall be yearly chosen . . . so many magistrates and other public officers as shall be found requisite: whereof one to be chosen governor for the year ensuing and until another be chosen, and no other magistrate to be chosen for more than one year; provided always there be six chosen beside the governor; which being chosen and sworn according to an oath recorded for that purpose shall have power to administer justice according to the laws here established, and for want thereof according to the rule of the word of God; which choice shall be made by all that are admitted freemen and have taken the oath of fidelity, and

do cohabit within this jurisdiction (having been admitted inhabitants by the major part of the town wherein they live), or the major part of such as shall be then present. . . .

4. It is ordered that no person be chosen governor above once in two years, and that the governor be always a member of some approved congregation, and formerly of the magistracy within this jurisdiction; and all the magistrates freemen of this commonwealth. . . .

5. It is ordered . . . that to the aforesaid Court of Election the several Towns shall send their deputies, and when the Elections are ended they may proceed in any public service as at other Courts. Also the General Court in September shall be for the making of Laws, and any other public occasion, which concerns the good of the Commonwealth.

7. It is ordered that after there are warrants given out for any of the said general courts, the constable . . . of each town shall forthwith give notice distinctly to the inhabitants of the same . . . that at a place and time by him or them limited and set, they meet and assemble themselves together to elect and choose certain deputies to be at the general court then following to agitate the affairs of the commonwealth; which said deputies shall be chosen by all that are admitted inhabitants in the several towns and have taken the oath of fidelity; provided that none be chosen a deputy for any general court which is not a freeman of this commonwealth. . . .

10. It is ordered that every general court . . . shall consist of the governor, or some one chosen to moderate the court, and four other magistrates at least, with the major part of the deputies of the several towns legally chosen; . . . in which said general courts shall consist the supreme power of the commonwealth, and they only shall have power to make laws or repeal them, to grant levies, to admit of freemen, dispose of lands undisposed of to several towns or persons; and also shall have power to call either court or magistrate or any other person whatsoever into question for any misdemeanor; and may for just causes displace or deal otherwise according to the nature of the offense; and also may deal in any other matter that concerns the good of this commonwealth, except election of magistrates, which shall be done by the whole body of freemen.

In which court the governor or moderator shall have power to order the court to give liberty of speech and [to] silence unseasonable and disorderly speakings, to put all things to vote, and in case the vote be equal to have the casting voice. But none of these courts shall be adjourned or dissolved without the consent of the major part of the court. . . .

11. It is ordered . . . that when any General Court upon the occasions of the Commonwealth have agreed upon any sum or sums of money to be levied upon the several towns within this Jurisdiction, that a Committee be chosen to set out and appoint what shall be the proportion of every Town to pay of the said levy, provided the Committee be made up of an equal number out of each Towne.

FILL IN THE ANSWERS

Write the word or phrase which best completes the statement.

1. The chief official under the Orders was the _____.
2. The Orders were written in the year _____. .
3. By "general courts" the Orders meant _____.
4. The governor held office for _____ year(s).
5. Laws were to be administered by local _____.
6. The chairman of the General Court was to be the _____.
7. The Orders were the constitution of the towns until _____.
8. The governor first had to be a _____.
9. According to the Fundamental Orders there were to be _____ general assemblies held each year.
10. Each general court was to consist of a governor and at least _____ magistrates.

THOUGHT QUESTIONS

1. Why was the decision of the three Connecticut towns to form their own government important to:
   a. the people of the towns;
   b. later American history?
2. How did the Orders contribute to New England town meetings?

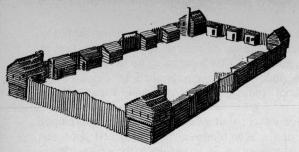

The
New England Confederation
1643

*   *   *   *   *On May 19, 1643, the four colonies*
of Massachusetts Bay, Connecticut, New Haven,
and Plymouth formed the New England Confederation for defense against the French in the north,
the Indians all around, and the Dutch of New Am-
sterdam. Though each colony handled its own internal affairs, each sent two commissioners to plan
military defense.

The Confederation's articles included rules for
the extradition of criminals, the return of runaway
indentured servants, and each colony's contribution
in men and material for defense. It settled boundary disputes and also collected money for Harvard
College and other causes.

Connecticut absorbed New Haven despite a guarantee of independence. Meetings of the commissioners ended in 1684 when the Massachusetts charter was revoked.

The New England Confederation was the first
union of independent colonies, and was a model
for the later Articles of Confederation.

Whereas we all came into these parts of America, with one
and the same end and aim, namely, to advance the Kingdom

of our Lord Jesus Christ, and to enjoy the liberties of the Gospel, in purity with peace; and whereas in our settling (by a wise providence of God) we are further dispersed upon the seacoasts and rivers than was at first intended, so that we cannot (according to our desire) with convenience communicate in one Government and jurisdiction; and whereas we live encompassed with people of several nations and strange languages, which hereafter may prove injurious to us and our posterity: And forasmuch as the natives have formerly committed sundry insolences and outrages upon several plantations of the English, and have of late combined against us. And seeing by reason of the sad distractions in England, which they have heard of, and by which they know we are hindered both from that humble way of seeking advice, and reaping those comfortable fruits of protection which, at other times, we might well expect; we therefore do conceive it our bounden duty, without delay, to enter into a present confederation amongst ourselves for mutual help and strength in all our future concerns, that, as in nation and religion, so in other respects, we be, and continue, One, according to the tenor and true meaning of the ensuing Articles.

1. Wherefore it is fully agreed and concluded by and between the parties or jurisdictions [of Massachusetts, Plymouth, Connecticut, and New Haven] That they all be, and henceforth be called by the name of, *The United Colonies of New-England.*

2. The said United Colonies for themselves and their posterities do jointly and severally hereby enter into a firm and perpetual league of friendship and amity, for offense and defense, mutual advice and succor, upon all just occasions, both for preserving and propagating the truth, and liberties of the Gospel, and for their own mutual safety and welfare.

3. . . . No other jurisdiction shall hereafter be taken in, as a distinct head, or member of this Confederation, nor shall any other either plantation, or jurisdiction in present being, and not already in combination, or under the jurisdiction of any of these Confederates, be received by any of them, nor shall any two of these Confederates, join in one Jurisdiction, without consent of the rest. . . .

4. It is also by these Confederates agreed, that the charge of all just wars, whether offensive or defensive, upon what part or member of this Confederation soever they fall, shall both in men, provisions, and all other disbursements be borne by all the parts of this Confederation, in different proportions, according to their different abilities, in manner following, namely, That the Commissioners for each jurisdiction, from time to time, as there shall be occasion bring a true account and number of all the males in each plantation, or any way belonging to, or under their several jurisdictions, of what quality, or condition soever they be, from sixteen years old, to three-score, being inhabitants there. And that according to the different numbers, which from time to time shall be found in each jurisdiction, upon a true and just account, the service of men, and all charges of the war, be borne by the poll: Each jurisdiction, or plantation, being left to their own just course, and custom, of rating themselves, and people, according to their different estates, with due respect to their qualities and exemptions among themselves, though the Confederation take no notice of any such privilege. And that, according to the different charge of each jurisdiction, and plantation, the whole advantage of the war (if it please God so to bless their endeavors) whether it be in lands, goods, or persons, shall be proportionately divided among the said Confederates.

5. It is further agreed, That if any of these jurisdictions, or any plantation under, or in combination with them, be invaded by any enemy whomsoever, upon notice, and request of any three magistrates of that jurisdiction so invaded, the rest of the Confederates, without any further meeting or expostulation, shall forthwith send aid to the Confederate in danger, but in different proportion, namely the Massachusetts one hundred men sufficiently armed, and provided for such a service and journey. And each of the rest five and forty men, so armed and provided, or any less number, if less be required, according to this proportion. . . . But in any such case of sending men for present aid, whether before or after such order or alteration, it is agreed, that at the meeting of the Commissioners for this Confederation, the cause of such war or invasion, be duly considered, and if it appear, that

the fault lay in the party so invaded, that then, that Jurisdiction, or Plantation, make just satisfaction, both to the invaders whom they have injured, and bear all the charges of the war themselves. . . .

And further, if any jurisdiction see any danger of an invasion approaching, and there be time for a meeting, that in such case, three magistrates of that jurisdiction may summon a meeting, at such convenient place, as themselves shall think meet, to consider, and provide against the threatened danger. . . .

6. It is also agreed, that for the managing and concluding of all affairs proper to, and concerning the whole Confederation, two Commissioners shall be chosen by, and out of the four jurisdictions, namely two for the Massachusetts, two for Plymouth, two for Connecticut, and two for New-Haven, being all in Church fellowship with us, which shall bring full power from their several general Courts respectively, to hear, examine, weigh, and determine all affairs of war, or peace, leagues, aides, charges, and numbers of men for war, division of spoils, or whatsoever is gotten by conquest, receiving of more confederates, or plantations into combination with any of these Confederates, and all things of like nature, which are the proper concomitants, or consequences of such a Confederation, for amity, offense, and defense, not intermeddling with the government of any of the jurisdictions, which by the third article, is preserved entirely to themselves. . . . It is further agreed, that these eight Commissioners shall meet once every year, besides extraordinary meetings, according to the fifth Article to consider, treat, and conclude of all affairs belonging to this Confederation. . . .

. . . .

8. It is also agreed, that the Commissioners for this Confederation hereafter at their meetings, whether ordinary or extraordinary, as they may have commission or opportunity, do endeavor to frame and establish agreements and orders in general cases of a civil nature, wherein all the plantations are interested, for preserving peace amongst themselves, and preventing (as much as may be) all occasions of war, or differences with others, as about the free and speedy

passage of justice in each jurisdiction, to all the Confederates equally, as to their own, receiving those that remove from one plantation to another, without due certificates, how all the jurisdictions may carry it towards the Indians, that they neither grow insolent, nor be injured without due satisfaction, lest war break in upon the Confederates, through such miscarriages. It is also agreed, that if any servant run away from his master, into any other of these Confederated Jurisdictions, that in such case, upon the certificate of one magistrate in the jurisdiction, out of which the said servant fled, or upon other due proof, the said servant shall be delivered either to his master, or any other that pursues, and brings such certificate, or proof. And that upon the escape of any prisoner whatsoever, or fugitive, for any criminal cause, whether breaking prison, or getting from the officer, or otherwise escaping, upon the certificate of two magistrates of the jurisdiction out of which the escape is made, that he was a prisoner or such an offender, at the time of the escape. . . .

9. And for that the justest wars may be of dangerous consequence, especially to the smaller plantations in these United Colonies, it is agreed, That neither the Massachusetts, Plymouth, Connecticut, nor New-Haven, nor any of the members of any of them, shall at any time hereafter begin, undertake or engage themselves or this Confederation, or any part thereof in any war whatsoever (sudden exigents with the necessary consequences thereof excepted, which are also to be moderated, as much as the case will permit) without the consent and agreement of the forenamed eight Commissioners, or at least six of them, as in the sixth article is provided. . . .

10. It is further agreed, that if any of the Confederates shall hereafter break any of these present articles, or be any other way injurious to any one of the other jurisdictions such breach of agreement, or injury, shall be duly considered, and ordered by the Commissioners for the other jurisdictions, that both peace, and this present Confederation, may be entirely preserved without violation. . . .

TRUE OR FALSE?

Write the letter T *if the statement is correct; write* F *if it is false.*

_____1. The New England Confederation included all the people of New England.

_____2. Should any of the colonies be attacked, all of the colonies would defend it.

_____3. Each of the four members had two commissioners with equal votes.

_____4. The commissioners met every month.

_____5. The agreement stated that runaway servants would be returned to their masters.

_____6. All the commissioners had to agree before any action could be taken.

_____7. The Confederation lasted for more than 40 years.

_____8. The Confederation was the first union of independent colonies in America.

_____9. The Confederation called itself the "United Colonies of New-England."

_____10. Massachusetts, the largest colony, was given the leadership of the New England Confederation.

THOUGHT QUESTIONS

1. In what ways did the New England Confederation affect the later history of the English colonies in America?

2. How did the people of New England use the Confederation to handle problems too big for any one town or colony to solve?

The Maryland Toleration Act 1649

* * * * *Cecil Calvert, the first Lord Balti-more* and Catholic proprietor of the colony of Maryland, hoped to make the colony a refuge for the Roman Catholics who were then greatly persecuted in England. Two problems arose: (1) Protestant settlers feared that they would be discriminated against in Maryland; (2) Catholics feared that they would be further persecuted by the Protestant majority in Maryland.

Lord Baltimore instructed the colony's leaders, whom he controlled, to pass the Toleration Act on April 21, 1649. It was the first document granting religious freedom in the New World, although it restricted this freedom to Christians. This act emphasized the supremacy of the government over the authority of the Church. It is important because it was the first step in the eventual separation of Church and State in American life. For these reasons the Toleration Act has been called the true beginning of religious freedom in America.

The punishments listed in the first paragraph were never enforced.

. . . whatsoever person or persons . . . shall from henceforth blaspheme God, . . . or shall deny our Saviour Jesus Christ to be the son of God, or shall deny the holy Trinity . . . shall be punished with death and confiscation and forfeiture of all his or her lands. . . .

Forasmuch as in a well Governed and Christian Commonwealth, matters concerning Religion and the Honor of God ought in the first place to be taken into serious consideration and endeavored to be settled . . . . And whereas the enforcing of the Conscience in matters of Religion has frequently fallen out to be of dangerous Consequence in those Commonwealths where it has been practiced, and for the more quiet and peaceable Government of this Province, and the better to preserve mutual love and unity amongst the Inhabitants here, Be it, . . . Ordained and Enacted, except as in this present Act is before declared and set forth, that no person or persons whatsoever within this Province or the Islands, Ports, Harbors, Creeks, or Havens thereunto belonging, professing to believe in Jesus Christ shall from henceforth be any ways troubled, molested or discountenanced, for or in respect of his or her Religion, nor in the free Exercise thereof within this Province or the Islands thereunto belonging, nor any way compelled to the belief or exercise of any other Religion against his or her consent, so as they be not unfaithful to the Lord Proprietary, or molest or conspire against the civil Government, established or to be established in this Province under him and his Heirs. And that all and every person and persons that shall presume contrary to this Act and the true intent and meaning thereof, directly or indirectly, either in person or estate, wilfully to wrong, disturb, or trouble, or molest any person or persons whatsoever within this Province professing to believe in Jesus Christ, for or in respect of his or her Religion, or the free Exercise thereof within this Province, otherwise than is provided for in this Act, That such person or persons so offending shall be compelled to pay treble damages to the party so wronged or molested, and for every such offence shall also forfeit 20 s. sterling in Money or the value thereof, . . . or if the party so offending as aforesaid, shall refuse or be unable to recompense the party so wronged or to satisfy such fine or forfeiture, then such offender shall be severely punished by public whipping and imprisonment during the pleasure of the Lord Proprietary or his Lieutenant or chief Governor of this Province for the time being, without Bail or Mainprise. . . .

FILL IN THE ANSWERS

Write the word or phrase which best completes the statement.

1. The proprietor of Maryland was Lord _____.
2. The two groups protected by the Maryland Toleration Act were the _____ and the _____.
3. Toleration was granted to all those believing in _____.
4. Persons breaking the law would pay _____ damages, or would be publicly _____.
5. The Toleration Act was passed on April _____, _____.
6. The Toleration Act emphasized the supremacy of the _____ _____ over the authority of the _____.
7. The Maryland Toleration Act was the first step in the eventual separation of _____ and _____ in American life.
8. The _____ had been persecuted in England.
9. Of the two faiths there were more _____ than _____ in Maryland.
10. The first Lord Baltimore was a _____.

THOUGHT QUESTIONS

1. How did the Toleration Act lead to a greater separation of Church and State?
2. Explain how religious freedom later grew in the colonies.

The British Navigation Acts 1660-1764

* * * *As the colonies developed economically,* British businessmen demanded that the colonies be forced to trade with Britain only.

To make colonial development a source of profit to the mother country, the British Parliament made laws regarding trade with the colonies. These laws would give British merchants and manufacturers a monopoly of the colonial market.

The restrictions on colonial trade ranged from the provision that all colonial goods must be shipped in colonial or English ships to the levying of duties on goods moving between colonial ports.

The colonists submitted to these restrictions when they found them profitable, or when they were forced to. But they resisted when they found them irritating. Smuggling became an honorable calling. In time, resistance to the Navigation Acts and other related laws became the watchword of colonial patriots — especially after England stepped up their enforcement after 1763.

It is important, in reading the following excerpts from the mercantile laws, to remember that their major purpose was to restrict the activities of the colonies to those which could best profit England.

First Navigation Act (1660)

I. For the increase of Shipping and encouragement of the Navigation of this Nation, wherein under the good providence and protection of God the Wealth, Safety and Strength of this Kingdom is so much concerned Be it Enacted . . . That from and after . . . [December I, I660] . . ., and from thence forward no Goods or Commodities whatsoever shall be Imported into or Exported out of any Lands, Islands, Plantations or Territories to his Majesty belonging or in his possession or which may hereafter belong unto or be in the possession of His Majesty His Heirs and Successors in Asia, Africa, or America in any other Ship or Ships, Vessel or Vessels whatsoever but in such Ships or Vessels as do truly and without fraud belong only to the people of England or Ireland, Dominion of Wales or Town of Berwick upon Tweed, or are of the built of, and belonging to any of the said Lands, Islands, Plantations or Territories as the Proprietors and right Owners thereof and whereof the Master and three fourths of the Mariners at least are English under the penalty of the Forfeiture and Loss of all the Goods and Commodities which shall be Imported into, or Exported out of, any the aforesaid places in any other Ship or Vessel, as also of the Ship or Vessel with all its Guns, Furniture, Tackle, Ammunition and Apparel. . . .

. . . .

Second Navigation Act (1663)

Be it enacted . . . That from and after . . . [March 25, 1664,] . . . no Commodity of the Growth, Production or Manufacture of Europe shall be imported into any Land, Island, Plantation, Colony, Territory or Place to His Majesty belonging, (or) . . . in the Possession of His Majesty . . . in Asia, Africa, or America (Tangier only excepted) but what shall be bona fide and without fraud laden and shipped in England Wales or the Town of Berwick upon Tweed and in English built Shipping, or which were bona fide bought before . . . [October 1, 1662,] . . . and had such Certificate thereof as is directed . . . [by the explanatory Navigation Act of 1662,] . . . and whereof the Master and three Fourths of the Mariners at least are English, and which shall be carried directly

PURPOSES OF ENGLAND'S MERCANTILE POLICY

To strengthen merchant marine and naval reserve

To make them agriculturally self-sufficient

To build up industry and put more people to work

HOW IT BENEFITED THE COLONIES

Encouraged colonies to build ships and a merchant marine

Forced merchants to seek new markets

A protected market forced colonies to develop natural resources

HOW IT HARMED THE COLONIES

Caused increase in shipping costs

Forced colonies to engage in smuggling

Prevented colonial industry from growing

thence to the said Lands, Islands, Plantations, Colonies, Territories or Places, and from no other place or places whatsoever, Any Law Statute or Usage to the contrary notwithstanding, under the Penalty of the loss of all such Commodities of the Growth, Production or Manufacture of Europe as shall be imported into any of them from any other Place whatsoever by Land or Water, and if by Water, of the Ship, or Vessel also in which they were imported with all her Guns, Tackle, Furniture, Ammunition and Apparel. . . .

The Tobacco Control Act (1672)

V. And whereas by . . . [the Navigation Act of 1660] . . ., and by several other Laws passed since that time it is permitted to ship, carry, convey and transport Sugar, Tobacco, Cotton-wool, Indigo, Ginger, Fustic and all other Dyeing wood of the Growth, Production and Manufacture of any of your Majesties Plantations in America, Asia or Africa from the places of their Growth, Production and Manufacture to any other of your Majesties Plantations in those Parts (Tangier only excepted) and that without paying of Customs for the same either at lading or unlading of the said Commodities by means whereof the Trade and Navigation in those Commodities from one Plantation to another is greatly increased, and the Inhabitants of diverse of those Colonies not contenting themselves with being supplied with those Commodities for their own use free from all Customs (while the Subjects of this your Kingdom of England have paid great Customs and Impositions for what of them has been spent here) but contrary to the express Letter of the aforesaid Laws have brought into diverse parts of Europe great quantities thereof, and do also daily vend great quantities thereof to the shipping of other Nations who bring them into diverse parts of Europe to the great hurt and diminution of your Majesties Customs and of the Trade and Navigation of this your Kingdom; For the prevention thereof . . . be it enacted . . . That from and after . . . [September 1, 1673,] . . . If any Ship or Vessel which by Law may trade in any of your Majesties Plantations shall come to any of them to ship and take on board any of the aforesaid Commodities, and that Bond shall not be first given with one sufficient

Surety to bring the same to England or Wales or the Town of Berwick upon Tweed and to no other place, and there to unload and put the same on shore (the danger of the Seas only excepted) that there shall be . . . paid to your Majesty . . . for so much of the said Commodities as shall be laded and put on board such Ship or Vessel these following Rates and Duties, That is to say

For Sugar White, the hundred Weight containing one hundred and twelve pounds, five shillings;

And Brown Sugar and Muscavados, the hundred Weight containing one hundred and twelve pounds, one shilling and six pence;

For Tobacco, the pound, one penny;

For Cotton-wool, the pound, one half-penny;

For Indigo, the pound, two pence;

For Ginger, the hundred Weight containing one hundred and twelve pounds, one shilling;

For Logwood, the hundred Weight containing one hundred and twelve pounds, five pounds;

For Fustic and all other Dyeing-wood, the hundred Weight containing one hundred and twelve pounds, six pence;

And also for every pound of Cacao-nuts, one penny . . .

Fourth Navigation Act (1696)

V. And for the more effectual preventing of Frauds and regulating Abuses in the Plantation Trade in America Be it further enacted . . . That all Ships coming into or going out of any of the said Plantations and lading or unlading any Goods or Commodities whether the same be His Majesties Ships of War or Merchants Ships and the Masters and Commanders thereof and their Ladings shall be subject and liable to the same Rules, Visitations, Searches, Penalties, and Forfeitures as to the entering, lading or discharging their respective Ships and Ladings as Ships and their Ladings and the Commanders and Masters of Ships are subject and liable unto in this Kingdom . . . [by virtue of the act 14 Chas. II., ch. II]. . . And that the Officers for collecting and managing His Majesties Revenue and inspecting the Plantation Trade in any of the said Plantations shall have the same Powers and Authorities for visiting and searching of Ships and taking their Entries and for seizing and securing or bringing on Shore any of the Goods prohibited to be imported or exported into or out of any of the said Plantations or for which any Duties are payable or ought to have been paid by any of the before mentioned Acts as are provided for the Officers of the Customs in England by the said last mentioned Act . . . [of 14 Chas. II., ch. II,] . . . and also to enter Houses or Warehouses to search for and seize any such Goods . . .

XV. Be it further enacted . . . That all Persons and their Assignees claiming any Right or Property in any Islands, or Tracts of Land upon the Continent of America by Charter or Letters Patents shall not at any time hereafter alien sell or dispose of any of the said Islands, Tracts of Land, or Properties other than to the Natural Born Subjects of England, Ireland, Dominion of Wales or Town of Berwick upon Tweed without the License and Consent of His Majesty . . . signified by His or Their Order in Council first had and obtained. . . .

XVI. And for a more effectual prevention of Frauds which may be used to elude the Intention of this Act by coloring Foreign Ships under English Names Be it further enacted . . . That from and after . . . [March 25, 1698,] . . . no Ship or Vessel whatsoever shall be deemed or pass as a Ship of the Built of England, Ireland, Wales, Berwick, Guernsey, Jersey or of any of His Majesties Plantations in America so as to be qualified to trade to, from, or in any of the said Plantations until the Person or Persons claiming Property in such Ship or Vessel shall register the same as followeth (that is to say) If the Ship at the time of such Register doth belong to any Port in England, Ireland, Wales, or to the Town of Berwick upon Tweed then Proof shall be made upon Oath of One or more of the Owners of such Ship or Vessel before the Collector and Comptroller of His Majesties Customs in such Port or if at the time of such Register the Ship belong to any of His Majesties Plantations in America or to the Islands of Guernsey or Jersey then the like Proof to be made before the Governor together with the Principal Officer of His Majesties Revenue residing on such Plantation or Island . . . .

The Molasses Act (1733)

WHEREAS the welfare and prosperity of your Majesty's sugar colonies in America are of the greatest consequence and importance to the trade, navigation and strength of this kingdom: and whereas the planters of the said sugar colonies have of late years fallen under such great discouragements, that they are unable to improve or carry on the sugar trade upon an equal footing with the foreign sugar colonies, without some advantage and relief be given to them from Great Britain: for remedy whereof . . . be it enacted . . ., That from and after . . . [December 25, 1733,] . . . there shall be raised, levied, collected and paid, unto and for the use of his Majesty . . ., upon all rum or spirits of the produce or manufacture of any of the colonies or plantations in America, not in the possession or under the dominion of his Majesty . . ., which at any time or times within or during the continuance of this act, shall be imported or brought into any of the colonies or plantations in America, which now are or hereafter may be in the possession or under the dominion of his Majesty . . ., the sum of nine pence, money of Great Britain, . . . for every gallon thereof, and after that rate for any greater or lesser quantity: and upon all molasses or syrups of such foreign produce or manufacture as aforesaid, which shall be imported or brought into any of the said colonies or plantations . . ., the sum of six pence of like money for every gallon thereof . . .; and upon all sugars and paneles of such foreign growth, produce or manufacture as aforesaid, which shall be imported into any of the said colonies or plantations . . ., a duty after the rate of five shillings of like money, for every hundred weight Avoirdupois. . . .

The Sugar Act (1764)

WHEREAS it is expedient that new provisions and regulations should be established for improving the revenue of this Kingdom, and for extending and securing the navigation and commerce between Great Britain and your Majesty's dominions in America, which, by the peace, have been so happily enlarged: and whereas it is just and necessary, that a revenue be raised, in your Majesty's said dominions in America, for defraying the expenses of defending, protecting and securing the same; . . . be it enacted . . ., That from and after . . . [September 29, 1764,] . . . there shall be raised, levied, collected, and paid, unto his Majesty . . ., for and upon all white or clayed sugars of the produce or manufacture of any colony or plantation in America, not under the dominion of his Majesty. . .; for and upon indigo, and coffee of foreign produce or manufacture; for and upon all wines (except French wine;) for and upon all wrought silks, bengals, and stuffs, mixed with silk or herba, of the manufacture of Persia, China, or East India, and all calico painted, dyed, printed, or stained there; and for and upon all foreign linen cloth called Cambrick and French Lawns, which shall be imported or brought into any colony or plantation in America, which now is, or hereafter may be, under the dominion of his Majesty . . ., the several rates and duties following; . . .

XVIII. And be it further enacted . . ., That from and after . . . [September 29, 1764] . . ., no rum or spirits of the produce or manufacture of any of the colonies or plantations in America, not in the possession or under the dominion of his Majesty . . ., shall be imported or brought into any of the colonies or plantations in America which now are, or hereafter may be, in the possession or under the dominion of his Majesty . . ., upon forfeiture of all such rum or spirits, together with the ship or vessel in which the same shall be imported, with the tackle, apparel, and furniture thereof. . . .

XXVIII. And it is hereby further enacted . . ., That from and after . . . [September 29, 1764] . . ., no iron, nor any sort of wood, commonly called Lumber, as specified in an act passed in the eighth year of the reign of King George the First, entitled, *An act for giving further encouragement for the importation of naval stores, and for other purposes therein mentioned,* of the growth, production, or manufacture, of any British colony or plantation in America, shall be there loaded on board any ship or vessel to be carried from thence, until sufficient bond shall be given, with one surety besides the master of the vessel, to the collector or other principal officer of the customs at the loading port, in a penalty of double the value of the goods, with condition, that the said goods shall not be landed in any part of Europe except Great Britain. . . .

CHOOSE THE CORRECT ANSWER

Write the letter that best completes the statement.

1. The Navigation Acts affected (*a*) shipping, (*b*) trade, (*c*) manufacturing, (*d*) all of these.　　　　　　1._____

2. The Navigation Acts were (*a*) approved by the colonial legislatures, (*b*) opposed by English merchants, (*c*) imposed on the colonies by England, (*d*) temporary tax laws. 2._____

3. All ships engaged in colonial trade had to be (*a*) built of British lumber, (*b*) manned by wholly British crews, (*c*) owned by Englishmen living in England, (*d*) captained by Englishmen.　　　　　　3._____

4. Goods could not be imported into the colonies in a ship belonging to a(n) (*a*) Irishman, (*b*) Frenchman, (*c*) New Yorker, (*d*) Scotsman.　　　　　　4._____

5. British officials in colonial ports had the power to (*a*) set taxes on cargoes, (*b*) search all ships, (*c*) execute those who broke the trade laws, (*d*) excuse British ships from taxes.　　　　　　5._____

6. The Sugar Act promised that England would use the money it raised through these special taxes to (*a*) defend and protect the colonies, (*b*) increase trade, (*c*) pay for new explorations, (*d*) buy more ships.　　　　　　6._____

7. A ship which was caught violating the Navigation Acts could be (*a*) sunk, (*b*) seized, (*c*) sent back home, (*d*) forced to pay a double tax.　　　　　　7._____

8. The Navigation laws affected all of the following *except* (*a*) goods, (*b*) land, (*c*) ownership of ships, (*d*) size of ships.　　　　　　8._____

9. The colonists found the Navigation Acts (*a*) necessary, (*b*) restrictive, (*c*) helpful, (*d*) unimportant.　　　　　　9._____

10. Of the following, the heaviest tax was placed on (*a*) sugar, (*b*) tobacco, (*c*) lumber, (*d*) coffee.　　　　　　10._____

THOUGHT QUESTIONS

1. Select ten specific regulations in these Acts. How was each one intended to benefit England's government, trade, or industry?

2. Select ten specific regulations in these laws and state what objections colonists might have had to each.

3. These Acts were intended to make the British Empire stronger. Explain how their final result was to weaken Great Britain and its empire.

COLONIAL REACTION TO ENGLISH CONTROL

STEPS TAKEN BY ENGLISH	COLONIAL REACTION

Navigation acts

Forced smuggling

Stamp Act

Fires, riots break out

Townshend program

Virginia resolves

The tea tax

Boston tea party

Writs of
Assistance
1755

* * * * *The colonists found the Navigation*
Acts very irritating. To evade the duties imposed
by the British, they resorted to smuggling. Goods
on which taxes had not been paid were stored and
hidden everywhere, and sometimes sold openly.
This situation was most acute in New England,
the center of colonial trade, especially in Massachusetts.

In order to prevent this smuggling, customs officials secured from the court writs of assistance
which gave them the general right to search for
and seize goods on which proper customs duties had
not been paid. Unlike a search warrant which
states that a specific place is to be searched for a
specific reason, the writs allowed customs officers
to search any home, ship or place of business at
any time.

The writs, which were issued and used only in Massachusetts and New Hampshire, were viewed by the colonists as another example of British tyranny. In 1755 the writ printed here was issued to Charles Paxton, the chief customs official in Boston. Paxton's use of this writ encouraged colonial merchants to support the growing move to break away from England.

Province of Massachusetts Bay

George the Third by the grace of God of Great Britain France & Ireland King Defender of the Faith etc.

To all & singular our Justices of the Peace Sheriffs Constables and to all other our Officers and Subjects within our said Province and to each of you Greeting.

Know ye that whereas in and by an Act of Parliament . . . it is declared to be the Officers of our Customs & their Deputies are authorized and impowered to go & enter aboard any Ship or Vessel outward or inward bound for the purposes in the said Act mentioned and it is also in & by the said Act further enacted & declared that it shall be lawful for any person or persons authorized by Writ of assistance under the seal of our Court of Exchequer to take a Constable Headborough or other public Officer inhabiting near unto the place and in the day time to enter & go into any House, Shop, Cellar, Warehouse or Room or other place and in case of resistance to break open doors, chests, trunks & other package there to seize and from thence to bring any kind of goods or merchandise whatsoever prohibited & uncustomed and to put and secure the same in His Majestys Storehouse in the port next to the place where such seizure shall be made.

And whereas in & by an Act of Parliament . . . there is granted to the Officers for collecting and managing our revenue and inspecting the plantation trade in any of our plantations the same powers & authority for visiting & searching of Ships & also to enter houses or warehouses to search for and seize any prohibited or uncustomed goods as are provided for the Officers of our Customs in England by the said last mentioned Act . . . and the like assistance is required to be given to the said Officers in the execution of their office as by the said last mentioned Act is provided for the Officers in England.

And whereas our Commissioners for managing and causing to be levied & collected our customs subsidies and other duties have by Commission or Deputation under their hands & seal dated at London the 22nd day of May in the first year of our Reign deputed and impowered Charles Paxton Esquire to be Surveyor & Searcher of all the rates and duties arising and growing due to us at Boston in our Province aforesaid and have given him power to enter into any Ship Bottom, Boat or other Vessel & also into any Shop, House, Warehouse, Hostlery or other place whatsoever to make diligent search into any trunk, chest, pack, case, truss, or any other parcel or package whatsoever for any goods, wares or merchandise prohibited to be imported or exported or whereof the Customs or other Duties have not been duly paid and the same to seize to our use, In all things proceeding as the Law directs.

Therefore we strictly Injoin & Command you & every one of you that, all excuses apart, you & every one of you permit the said Charles Paxton according to the true intent & form of the said commission or deputation and the laws & statutes in that behalf made & provided, as well by night as by day from time to time to enter & go on board any Ship, Boat or other Vessel riding, lying or being within or coming to the said port of Boston or any Place or Creeks thereunto appertaining such Ship, Boat or Vessel then & there found to search & oversee and the persons therein being strictly to examine, touching the premises aforesaid & also according to the form, effect and true intent of the said commission or deputation in the day time to enter & go into the vaults, cellars, warehouses, shops & other places where any prohibited goods, wares or merchandises or any goods, wares or merchandises for which the customs or other duties shall not have been duly & truly satisfied and paid lie concealed or are suspected to be concealed, according to the true intent of the law to inspect & oversee & search for the said goods, wares & merchandise. And further to do and execute all things which of right and according to the laws & statutes in this behalf shall be to be done. And we further strictly Injoin & Command you and every one of you that to the said Charles Paxton Esqr you & every one of you from time to time be aiding, assisting & helping in the execution of the premises as is meet. And this you or any of you in no wise omit at your perils.

TRUE OR FALSE?

Write T *if the statement is correct; Write* F *if it is false.*

_____1. New England merchants turned to smuggling to avoid the Navigation Acts.

_____2. Smuggled goods were quickly shipped to other colonies.

_____3. Writs of assistance were like modern search warrants.

_____4. The issuance of writs of assistance was approved by acts of Parliament.

_____5. Charles Paxton led the colonial merchants who opposed the writs of assistance.

_____6. All searches under the writs were made at night.

_____7. Paxton could search anywhere in Massachusetts.

_____8. The writs did not contain penalties for those who were found to have smuggled goods.

_____9. Writs were not issued in New York or Philadelphia.

_____10. The writs were issued by courts.

THOUGHT QUESTIONS

1. Explain how the writs of assistance were an important part of the plan to use the colonies to benefit Great Britain.
2. Imagine that you are a Boston merchant. Write a letter to another merchant in Philadelphia in which you explain the evils of the writs being used in Boston.

Resolutions of the Stamp Act Congress 1765

* * * * *The British government left about* 10,000 soldiers in the colonies after the French and Indian War for defense against the Indians, to help enforce the Navigation Acts and to act as police. It was decided that a stamp tax should be imposed on the colonists to assist in the support of these troops. The British Parliament enacted the Stamp Tax in 1765. Such a tax had long been paid by residents in Britain. The Stamp Tax provided that all colonial newspapers, legal documents and business papers should be stamped.

Colonial reaction was violent. Newspaper publishers announced that they were suspending publication rather than pay the tax of one penny per copy printed and sold. Mobs demonstrated before the homes of the colonists who had been named as special Stamp Tax agents. When the day came for the Act to go into effect, all the agents had given up their posts rather than face the fury of the mobs and the anger of their friends and associates.

It was agreed to hold an inter-colony Congress. Representatives of nine colonies met in New York to discuss and take action on the problems created by the Stamp Act. This Congress sent resolutions to Parliament stating colonial objections to this and similar tax laws. Parliament repealed the Stamp Act in 1776.

The Stamp Act Congress showed that the colonists were ready to unite against a law they felt to be unfair. It presented ideas which grew in meaning during the next ten years. The resolutions stated the "rights of Englishmen," and pointed out that England was taking those rights away from the colonists. Paragraphs III and V offered a new slogan to colonial patriots — *no taxation without representation!*

The members of this Congress, sincerely devoted, with the warmest sentiments of affection and duty to his Majesty's person and government, ... esteem it our indispensible duty to make the following declarations of our humble opinion, respecting the most essential rights and liberties of the colonists, and of the grievances under which they labor, by reason of several late acts of parliament.

I. That his Majesty's subjects in these colonies, owe the same allegiance to the crown of Great Britain, that is owing from his subjects born within the realm, and all due subordination to that august body the parliament of Great Britain.

II. That his Majesty's liege subjects in these colonies, are entitled to all the inherent rights and liberties of his natural born subjects, within the kingdom of Great Britain.

III. That it is inseparably essential to the freedom of a people, and the undoubted right of Englishmen, that no

Taxes be imposed on them but with their own consent, given personally, or by their representatives.

IV. That the people of these colonies are not, and, from their local circumstances, cannot be, represented in the House of Commons in Great Britain.

V. That the only representatives of the people of these colonies are persons chosen therein by themselves, and that no taxes ever have been, or can be constitutionally imposed on them, but by their respective legislatures.

VI. That all supplies to the crown being free gifts of the people, it is unreasonable and inconsistent with the principles and spirit of the British constitution, for the people of Great Britain to grant to his Majesty the property of the colonists.

VII. That trial by jury, is the inherent and invaluable right of every British subject in these colonies.

VIII. That . . . the Stamp Act . . ., by imposing taxes on the inhabitants of these colonies, and the said act, and several other acts, by extending the jurisdiction of the courts of admiralty beyond its ancient limits, have a manifest tendency to subvert the rights and liberties of the colonists.

IX. That the duties imposed by several late acts of parliament, from the peculiar circumstances of these colonies, will be extremely burdensome and grievous; and from the scarcity of specie, the payment of them absolutely impracticable.

X. That as the profits of the trade of these colonies ultimately center in Great Britain, to pay for the manufactures which they are obliged to take from thence, they eventually contribute very largely to all supplies granted there to the crown.

XI. That the restrictions imposed by several late acts of parliament on the trade of these colonies, will render them unable to purchase the manufactures of Great Britain.

XII. That the increase, prosperity and happiness of these colonies, depend on the full and free enjoyments of their rights and liberties, and an intercourse with Great Britain mutually affectionate and advantageous.

XIII. That it is the right of the British subjects in these colonies to petition the king, or either house of parliament.

Lastly, That it is the indispensible duty of these colonies, to the best of sovereigns, to the mother country, and to themselves, to endeavor by a loyal and dutiful address to his Majesty, and humble applications to both houses of parliament, to procure the repeal of the act for granting and applying certain stamp duties, of all clauses of any other acts of parliament, whereby the jurisdiction of the admiralty is extended as aforesaid, and of the other late acts or the restriction of American commerce.

CHOOSE THE CORRECT ANSWER

Write the letter or phrase which best completes the statement.

1. The Stamp Act Congress stated that it was (*a*) ready to call for a rebellion, (*b*) loyal to the king, (*c*) unable to petition Parliament, (*d*) going to advise colonists not to pay the Stamp Tax. 1._____

2. The Congress stated that no law should take away the right of the colonists to (*a*) vote for members of the House of Commons, (*b*) pay taxes, (*c*) trial by jury, (*d*) own property. 2._____

3. The Stamp Act was (*a*) never enforced, (*b*) in force for one day, (*c*) in force for one year, (*d*) given to the colonial legislatures to enforce. 3._____

4. The Stamp Act Congress represented (*a*) the businessmen of the colonies, (*b*) all of the colonies, (*c*) a majority of the colonies, (*d*) all of the colonial legislatures. 4._____

5. The Congress stated that the people of the colonies should have (*a*) special rights, (*b*) the rights given them by their own legislatures, (*c*) the rights promised in their colonial charters, (*d*) the same rights as Englishmen in Great Britain. 5._____

6. The Congress asked for the repeal of (*a*) only the Stamp Act, (*b*) all acts which restricted trade, (*c*) all English taxes, (*d*) English rule over the colonies. 6._____

7. The Stamp Tax would have been collected by (*a*) special tax agents, (*b*) British officers, (*c*) regular town tax officials, (*d*) colonial legislatures. 7._____

8. The Congress objected to (*a*) all English laws, (*b*) English courts, (*c*) the way Parliament was chosen, (*d*) the way England taxed the colonies. 8._____

THOUGHT QUESTIONS

1. Prepare an editorial for a colonial newspaper in 1765 in which you present reasons why people should oppose the Stamp Act.

2. Explain the statement: *The Stamp Act united the colonies as no other English law had done, and set in motion the forces which were to lead to revolution.*

Declaration of Rights — First Continental Congress 1774

* * * * *Colonial opposition to British tax* laws and the growing movement toward independence were led by a group whose guiding spirit was Samuel Adams of Massachusetts. In June, 1774, Adams moved, in the Massachusetts House of Representatives, to set up a special committee to arrange for a meeting to which all the colonies would be invited to send representatives.

All of the thirteen colonies, with the exception of Georgia, were represented at the meeting in Philadelphia in September and October, 1774. The First Continental Congress adopted a set of resolutions which summarized the rights the colonists felt were basic to their existence, and which they felt Great Britain had violated. This "Declaration of Rights," excerpts of which are given here, was sent to the King.

Among those at the First Continental Congress were such colonial leaders as Samuel and John Adams, Patrick Henry, and George Washington.

These men realized that a mere statement of their rights would have little effect. The Congress, therefore, passed a resolution by which they refused to trade with England or use British products at least until Parliament had repealed the laws which restricted colonial rights. This was the strongest united action the colonies had yet attempted. It was a sign of the break soon to come. These colonial leaders would no longer allow their people to be less justly treated than Englishmen should be. Many of them prepared for even more forceful action.

That the inhabitants of the English colonies in North America, by the immutable laws of nature, the principles of the English constitution, and the several charters or compacts, have the following RIGHTS:

1. That they are entitled to life, liberty and property: and they have never ceded to any foreign power whatever, a right to dispose of either without their consent.

2. That our ancestors, who first settled these colonies, were at the time of their emigration from the mother country, entitled to all the rights, liberties, and immunities of free and natural-born subjects, within the realm of England.

3. That by such emigration they by no means forfeited, surrendered, or lost any of those rights, but that they were, and their descendants now are, entitled to the exercise and enjoyment of all such of them, as their local and other circumstances enable them to exercise and enjoy.

4. That the foundation of English liberty, and of all free government, is a right in the people to participate in their legislative council: and as the English colonists are not represented, and from their local and other circumstances, cannot properly be represented in the British parliament, they are entitled to a free and exclusive power of legislation in their several provincial legislatures, where their right of representation can alone be preserved, in all cases of taxation and internal policy, subject only to the negative of their sovereign, in such manner as has been heretofore used and

accustomed: But, from the necessity of the case, and a regard to the mutual interest of both countries, we cheerfully consent to the operation of such acts of the British parliament, as are bona fide, restrained to the regulation of our external commerce, for the purpose of securing the commercial advantages of the whole empire to the mother country, and the every idea of taxation internal or external, for commercial benefits of its respective members; including raising a revenue on the subjects, in America, without their consent.

5. That the respective colonies are entitled to the common law of England, and more especially to the great and inestimable privilege of being tried by their peers of the vicinity, according to the course of that law.

6. That they are entitled to the benefit of such of the English statutes, as existed at the time of their colonization; and which they have, by experience, respectively found to be applicable to their several local and other circumstances.

7. That these, his majesty's colonies, are likewise entitled to all the immunities and privileges granted and confirmed to them by royal charters, or secured by their several codes of provincial laws.

8. That they have a right peaceably to assemble, consider of their grievances, and petition the king; and that all prosecutions, prohibitory proclamations, and commitments for the same, are illegal.

9. That the keeping a standing army in these colonies, in times of peace, without the consent of the legislature of that colony, in which such army is kept, is against law.

10. It is indispensably necessary to good government, and rendered essential by the English constitution, that the constituent branches of the legislature be independent of each other; that, therefore, the exercise of legislative power in several colonies, by a council appointed, during pleasure, by the crown, is unconstitutional, dangerous and destructive to the freedom of American legislation.

All and each of which the aforesaid deputies, in behalf of themselves, and their constituents, do claim, demand, and insist on, as their indubitable rights and liberties; which cannot be legally taken from them, altered or abridged by any power whatever, without their own consent, by their representatives in their several provincial legislatures.

To obtain redress of these grievances, which threaten destruction to the lives, liberty, and property of his majesty's subjects, in North America, we are of opinion, that a non-importation, non-consumption, and non-exportation agreement, faithfully adhered to, will prove the most speedy, effectual, and peaceable measure: And, therefore, we do, for ourselves, and the inhabitants of the several colonies, whom we represent, firmly agree and associate, under the sacred ties of virtue, honor and love of our country, as follows:

First, That from and after the first day of December next, we will not import, into British America, from Great Britain or Ireland, any goods, wares, or merchandise whatsoever, or from any other place, any such goods, wares, or merchandise, as shall have been exported from Great Britain or Ireland; nor will we, after that day, import any East India tea from any part of the world; nor any molasses, syrups, paneles, coffee, or pimento, from the British plantations or from Dominica; nor wines from Madeira, or the Western Islands; nor foreign indigo.

Second, We will neither import nor purchase, any slave imported after the first day of December next; after which time, we will wholly discontinue the slave trade, and will neither be concerned in it ourselves, nor will we hire our vessels, nor sell our commodities or manufactures to those who are concerned in it.

Third, As a non-consumption agreement, strictly adhered to, will be an effectual security for the observation of the non-importation, we, as above, solemnly agree and associate, that from this day, we will not purchase or use any tea, imported on account of the East India company, or any on which a duty hath been or shall be paid; and from and after the first day of March next, we will not purchase or use any East India tea whatever; nor will we, nor shall any person for or under us, purchase or use any of those goods, wares, or merchandise, we have agreed not to import, which we shall know, or have cause to suspect, were imported after the first day of December, except such as come under the rules and directions of the tenth article hereafter mentioned.

Fourth, The earnest desire we have not to injure our fellow subjects in Great Britain, Ireland, or the West Indies, induces us to suspend a non-exportation, until the tenth day of September, 1775; at which time, if the said acts and parts of acts of the British parliament herein after mentioned, are not repealed, we will not directly or indirectly, export any merchandise or commodity whatsoever to Great Britain, Ireland, or the West Indies, except rice to Europe.

Fifth, Such as are merchants, and use the British and Irish trade, will give orders, as soon as possible, to their factors, agents and correspondents, in Great Britain and Ireland, not to ship any goods to them, on any pretense whatsoever, as they cannot be received in America; and if any merchant, residing in Great Britain or Ireland, shall directly or indirectly ship any goods, wares or merchandise, for America, in order to break the said non-importation agreement, or in any manner contravene the same, on such unworthy conduct being well attested, it ought to be made public; and, on the same being so done, we will not, from thenceforth, have any commercial connection with such merchant.

Ninth, Such as are venders of goods or merchandise will not take advantage of the scarcity of goods, that may be occasioned by this association, but will sell the same at the rates we have been respectively accustomed to do, for twelve months last past. — And if any vender of goods or merchandise shall sell such goods on higher terms, or shall, in any manner, or by any device whatsoever, violate or depart from this agreement, no person ought, nor will any of us deal with any such person, or his or her factor or agent, at any time thereafter, for any commodity whatever.

Eleventh, That a committee be chosen in every county, city, and town, by those who are qualified to vote for representatives in the legislature, whose business it shall be attentively to observe the conduct of all persons touching this association; and when it shall be made to appear, to the satisfaction of a majority of any such committee, that any person within the limits of their appointment has violated this association, that such majority do forthwith cause the truth of the case to be published in the gazette; to the end, that all such foes to the rights of British America may be publicly known, and universally condemned as the enemies of American liberty; and thenceforth we respectively will break off all dealings with him or her.

Thirteenth, That all manufactures of this country be sold

at reasonable prices, so that no undue advantage be taken of a future scarcity of goods.

Fourteenth, And we do further agree and resolve, that we will have no trade, commerce, dealings or intercourse whatsoever, with any colony or province, in North America, which shall not accede to, or which shall hereafter violate this association, but will hold them as unworthy of the rights of freemen, and as inimical to the liberties of their country.

FILL IN THE ANSWERS

Write the word or phrase which best completes the statement.

1. The First Continental Congress held that the colonists had the same rights as _____.
2. The Congress objected to colonists being tried in _____ courts.
3. According to the Congress, councils appointed by the king should not have the right to _____ _____.
4. The Congress stated that British tax laws should not be placed on the colonists without the _____ of their legislatures.
5. The agreement suggested by the Congress stated that the colonists should not _____ or _____ English goods.
6. The Congress said the colonies would wait until _____ _____ before they stopped selling goods to Great Britain.
7. The Congress felt that businessmen in the colonies should not _____ prices.
8. The First Continental Congress represented _____ of the colonies.
9. The most important right, according to the Congress, had to do with _____.
10. The agreement not to trade with England would be enforced by _____ in each county, city, or town.

THOUGHT QUESTIONS

1. State three rights which the Congress claimed England was taking away; for each describe a specific British law or action which violated the right.
2. How did the two actions taken by the First Continental Congress try to convince Parliament to change its tax policies?.

CAUSES OF THE AMERICAN REVOLUTION

Stricter British enforcement of mercantile policy

Colonial resistance to British taxation

Opposition to keeping a British army in America

Weakening of ties through space and time barriers

Royal decree preventing sale of western land

Struggle for more colonial home rule

Many skilled colonial leaders emerge

Declaration of Independence 1776

*   *   *   *   *The British did nothing to correct* the injustices the colonists listed in their Declaration of Rights. In fact, they made it clear they intended to govern the colonies by force. The British military marched on Lexington and Concord where they were opposed by colonial Minute Men.

The Second Continental Congress pledged aid to Massachusetts, and took over the conduct of the war. George Washington of Virginia took command of the continental army. Victories followed at Ticonderoga and Bunker Hill, and the British were forced to evacuate Boston.

The idea of independence spread through the colonies. Richard Henry Lee's proposal of both independence and confederation was passed by the Congress, and a committee consisting of John Adams, Benjamin Franklin, Thomas Jefferson, Robert Livingston, and Roger Sherman was named to write the declaration. Jefferson did most of the actual writing, and his draft, with some changes, was signed by the members of Congress on August 2, 1776.

The Declaration is one of the most significant documents in the history of man's struggle for freedom.

1. It stated the reasons why men set up governments.
2. It listed the reasons why the colonies were driven to break away from Britain.
3. It is a "glossary of tyranny" in its listing of colonial rights violated by Britain.
4. It has become a model statement of human rights. As such, it has been important to other peoples who have broken away from foreign control since 1776, and to peoples who have tried to strengthen democracy in their own countries.

When in the Course of human events, it becomes necessary for one people to dissolve the political bands which have connected them with another, and to assume among the powers of the earth, the separate and equal station to which the Laws of Nature and of Nature's God entitle them, a decent respect to the opinions of mankind requires that they should declare the causes which impel them to the separation.

We hold these truths to be self-evident, that all men are created equal, that they are endowed by their Creator with certain unalienable Rights, that among these are Life, Liberty and the pursuit of Happiness; That to secure these rights, Governments are instituted among Men, deriving their just powers from the consent of the governed; That whenever any Form of Government becomes destructive of these ends, it is the Right of the People to alter or abolish it, and to institute new Government, laying its foundation on such principles and organizing its powers in such form, as to them shall seem most likely to effect their Safety and Happiness. Prudence, indeed, will dictate that Governments long established should not be changed for light and transient causes; and accordingly all experience hath shown, that mankind are more disposed to suffer, while evils are sufferable, than to right themselves by abolishing the forms to which they are accustomed. But when a long train of abuses and usurpations, pursuing invariably the same Object evinces a design to reduce them under absolute Despotism, it is their right, it is their duty, to throw off such Government, and to provide new Guards for their future security; Such has been the patient sufferance of these Colonies; and such is now the necessity which constrains them to alter their former Systems of Government. The history of the present King of Great Britain is a history of repeated injuries and usurpations, all having in direct object the establishment of an absolute Tyranny over these States. To prove this, let Facts be submitted to a candid world.

He has refused his Assent to laws, the most wholesome and necessary for the public good.

He has forbidden his Governors to pass Laws of immediate and pressing importance, unless suspended in their operation till his Assent should be obtained; and when so suspended, he has utterly neglected to attend to them.

He has refused to pass other Laws for the accommodation of large districts of people, unless those people would relinquish the right of Representation in the Legislature, a right inestimable to them and formidable to tyrants only.

He has called together legislative bodies at places unusual, uncomfortable, and distant from the depository of their public Records, for the sole purpose of fatiguing them into compliance with his measures.

He has dissolved Representative Houses repeatedly, for opposing with manly firmness his invasions on the rights of the people.

He has refused for a long time, after such dissolutions, to cause others to be elected; whereby the Legislative powers, incapable of Annihilation, have returned to the People at large for their exercise; the State remaining in the mean time exposed to all the dangers of invasion from without, and convulsions within.

He has endeavoured to prevent the population of these States; for that purpose obstructing the Laws for Naturalization of Foreigners; refusing to pass others to encourage their migration hither, and raising the conditions of new Appropriations of Lands.

He has obstructed the Administration of Justice, by refusing his Assent to Laws for establishing Judiciary powers.

He has made Judges dependent on his Will alone, for the tenure of their offices, and the amount and payment of their salaries.

He has erected a multitude of New Offices, and sent hither swarms of Officers to harrass our people, and eat out their substance.

He has kept among us, in times of peace, Standing Armies without the Consent of our legislatures.

He has affected to render the Military independent of and superior to the Civil power.

He has combined with others to subject us to a jurisdiction foreign to our constitution, and unacknowledged by our laws; giving his Assent to their Acts of pretended Legislation;

For quartering large bodies of armed troops among us;

For protecting them, by a mock Trial, from punishment for any Murders which they should commit on the Inhabitants of these States;

For cutting off our Trade with all parts of the world;

For imposing Taxes on us without our Consent;

For depriving us in many cases of the benefits of Trial by Jury;

For transporting us beyond Seas to be tried for pretended offences;

For abolishing the free System of English Laws in a neighboring Province, establishing therein an Arbitrary government, and enlarging its Boundaries so as to render it at once an example and fit instrument for introducing the same absolute rule into these Colonies;

For taking away our Charters, abolishing our most valuable Laws, and altering fundamentally the Forms of our Governments;

For suspending our own Legislatures, and declaring themselves invested with power to legislate for us in all cases whatsoever.

He has abdicated Government here, by declaring us out of his Protection and waging War against us.

He has plundered our seas, ravaged our Coasts, burnt our towns, and destroyed the Lives of our people.

He is at this time transporting large Armies of foreign Mercenaries to complete the works of death, desolation and tyranny, already begun with circumstances of Cruelty and perfidy scarcely parallelled in the most barbarous ages, and totally unworthy the Head of a civilized nation.

He has constrained our fellow Citizens taken Captive on the high Seas to bear Arms against their Country, to become

Freedom of Speech and Press

Freedom of Religion

Right to Assemble

Right to Trial by Jury

We the People

Freedom from Unreasonable Search

the executioners of their friends and Brethren, or to fall themselves by their Hands.

He has excited domestic insurrections amongst us, and has endeavoured to bring on the inhabitants of our frontiers, the merciless Indian Savages, whose known rule of warfare, is an undistinguished destruction of all ages, sexes and conditions.

In every stage of these Oppressions We have Petitioned for Redress in the most humble terms: Our repeated Petitions have been answered only by repeated injury. A Prince, whose character is thus marked by every act which may define a Tyrant, is unfit to be the ruler of a free people.

Nor have We been wanting in attention to our British brethren. We have warned them from time to time of attempts by their legislature to extend an unwarrantable jurisdiction over us. We have reminded them of the circumstances of our emigration and settlement here. We have appealed to their native justice and magnanimity, and we have conjured them by the ties of our common kindred to disavow these usurpations, which would inevitably interrupt our connections and correspondence. They too have been deaf to the voice of justice and of consanguinity. We must, therefore, acquiesce in the necessity, which denounces our separation, and hold them, as we hold the rest of mankind, Enemies in War, in Peace Friends.

We, therefore, the Representatives of the *United States of America,* in General Congress, Assembled, appealing to the Supreme Judge of the world for the rectitude of our intentions, do, in the Name, and by the authority of the good People of these Colonies, solemnly publish and declare, That these United Colonies are, and of Right ought to be *Free and Independent States;* that they are Absolved from all Allegiance to the British Crown, and that all political connection between them and the State of Great Britain, is and ought to be totally dissolved; and that as Free and Independent States, they have full Power to levy War, conclude Peace, contract Alliances, establish Commerce, and to do all other Acts and Things which Independent States may of right do.

And for the support of this Declaration, with a firm reliance on the protection of divine Providence, we mutually pledge to each other our Lives, our Fortunes, and our sacred Honor.

TRUE OR FALSE?

Write T *if the statement is correct; Write* F *if it is false.*

_____1. War with England began as soon as the Declaration was issued.

_____2. According to the Declaration, the powers of a government should be given to it by the people.

_____3. King George is called a *tyrant* in the Declaration of Independence.

_____4. Other countries have paid little attention to the Declaration of Independence.

_____5. The Declaration of Independence protested against British treatment of Canada.

_____6. The British were accused of forcing American sailors to fight against American ships.

_____7. The Declaration of Independence praised the British for making their soldiers act properly.

_____8. The Declaration of Independence claimed that England was responsible for Indian attacks on frontier settlers.

_____9. The Declaration of Independence was not concerned with British tax laws.

_____10. The English king had sent too many settlers to some of the colonies.

THOUGHT QUESTIONS

1. List and explain ten of the reasons for independence found in the Declaration of Independence.
2. How did the Declaration of Independence:
   (*a*) Help unite the colonies in support of the revolution?
   (*b*) Explain the democratic goals of the patriots who supported it?

Articles of Confederation—1777

* * * * *The Continental Congress, having*
declared its independence from England, had next
to set up a form of government for the new United
States of America. John Dickinson of Delaware
led a committee appointed in 1776 to draw up a
plan of confederation. His plan was debated for
more than a year before it was sent to the state
legislatures for their approval.

Serious differences of opinion kept the states
from ratifying the Articles at once. One group
wanted a strong central government, another
wanted all power in the hands of the states. Other
issues were representation in Congress, the basis
for taxation, and the control of western lands.

By the end of 1778, eleven states had signed the
Articles. Delaware did not approve them until 1779,
and Maryland not until March 1, 1781. On March
2, 1781, Congress met as the nation's governing
body under the Articles.

The Articles set up a weak central government
which lacked an executive and a national judiciary.
Articles II and III declare that the states were to
retain their powers. Although the Confederation
carried the war to final victory, it never had the
power to levy taxes, to enforce laws, to control
trade or settle differences between the states.

Why was such a weak government established?
The people who wrote the Articles had for years
been struggling against a strong central government — Great Britain. They were not willing to
let another strong central government take Brit-

ain's place! The Articles did, however, set up a national government which allowed the Americans to gain experience in governing themselves. When the Articles were replaced by the Constitution of 1787, new meaning was given to Jefferson's idea that the people of a free nation have the right to change their government when they find it best to do so. Note that much of the language of the Articles reappeared in the Constitution.

Whereas the Delegates of the United States of America in Congress assembled did on the fifteenth day of November in the year of our Lord One Thousand Seven Hundred and Seventy-seven, and in the Second Year of the Independence of America agree to certain articles of Confederation and perpetual Union between the States of Newhampshire, Massachusetts-bay, Rhodeisland and Providence Plantations, Connecticut, New York, New Jersey, Pennsylvania, Delaware, Maryland, Virginia, North-Carolina, South-Carolina and Georgia in the Words following, viz.

Article I. The style of this confederacy shall be "The United States of America."

Article II. Each State retains its sovereignty, freedom and independence, and every power, jurisdiction and right, which is not by this confederation expressly delegated to the United States, in Congress assembled.

Article III. The said States hereby severally enter into a firm league of friendship with each other, for their common defense, the security of their liberties, and their mutual and general welfare, binding themselves to assist each other, against all force offered to, or attacks made upon them, or any of them, on account of religion, sovereignty, trade, or any other pretense whatever.

Article .IV. The better to secure and perpetuate mutual friendship and intercourse among the people of the different States in this Union, the free inhabitants of each of these States, paupers, vagabonds and fugitives from justice excepted, shall be entitled to all privileges and immunities of free citizens in the several States; and the people of each State shall have free ingress and regress to and from any other

State, and shall enjoy therein all the privileges of trade and commerce, subject to the same duties, impositions and restrictions as the inhabitants thereof respectively, provided that such restrictions shall not extend so far as to prevent the removal of property imported into any State, to any other state of which the owner is an inhabitant; provided also that no imposition, duties or restriction shall be laid by any State, on the property of the United States, or either of them.

If any Person guilty of, or charged with treason, felony, or

CONFEDERATION VS. CONSTITUTION

WEAKNESSES			STRENGTHS
Loose union of states; no strong executive head.			Close-knit union of states; strong executive head.
Congress could levy, but not collect taxes.			Power to levy and collect taxes.
No power to regulate trade between states and foreign nations.			Power to regulate interstate and foreign commerce.

other high misdemeanor in any State, shall flee from justice, and be found in any of the United States, he shall upon demand of the Governor or Executive power, of the State from which he fled, be delivered up and removed to the State having jurisdiction of his offense.

Full faith and credit shall be given in each of these States to the records, acts and judicial proceedings of the courts and magistrates of every other State.

Article V. . . . No State shall be represented in Congress by less than two, nor by more than seven members; and no person shall be capable of being a delegate for more than three years in any term of six years; nor shall any person, being a delegate, be capable of holding any office under the United States, for which he, or another for his benefit receives any salary, fees or emolument of any kind. . . .

. . . .

In determining questions in the United States, in Congress assembled, each State shall have one vote.

Freedom of speech and debate in Congress shall not be impeached or questioned in any court, or place out of Congress, and the members of Congress shall be protected in their persons from arrests and imprisonments, during the time of their going to and from, and attendance on Congress, except for treason, felony, or breach of the peace.

Article VI. No State without the consent of the United States in Congress assembled, shall send any embassy to, or receive any embassy from, or enter into any conference, agreement, alliance or treaty with any king, prince or state; nor shall any person holding any office of profit or trust under the United States, or any of them, accept of any present, emolument, office or title of any kind whatever from any king, prince or foreign state; nor shall the United States in Congress assembled, or any of them, grant any title of nobility.

No two or more States shall enter into any treaty, confederation or alliance whatever between them, without the consent of the United States in Congress assembled, specifying accurately the purposes for which the same is to be entered into, and how long it shall continue.

No State shall lay any imposts or duties, which may interfere with any stipulations in treaties, entered into by the

United States in Congress assembled, with any king, prince or state, in pursuance of any treaties already proposed by Congress, to the courts of France and Spain.

No vessels of war shall be kept up in time of peace by any State, except such number only, as shall be deemed necessary by the United States in Congress assembled, for the defense of such State, or its trade; nor shall any body of forces be kept up by any State, in time of peace, except such number only, as in the judgment of the United States, in Congress assembled, shall be deemed requisite to garrison the forts necessary for the defense of such State; but every State shall always keep up a well regulated and disciplined militia, sufficiently armed and accoutered, and shall provide and constantly have ready for use, in public stores, a due number of field pieces and tents, and a proper quantity of arms, ammunition and camp equipage.

No State shall engage in any war without the consent of the United States in Congress assembled, unless such State be actually invaded by enemies, or shall have received certain advice of a resolution being formed by some nation of Indians to invade such State, and the danger is so imminent as not to admit of a delay, till the United States in Congress assembled can be consulted: nor shall any State grant commissions to any ships or vessels of war, nor letters of marque or reprisal, except it be after a declaration of war by the United States in Congress assembled, and then only against the kingdom or state and the subjects thereof, against which war has been so declared, and under such regulations as shall be established by the United States in Congress assembled, unless such State be infested by pirates, in which case vessels of war may be fitted out for that occasion, and kept so long as the danger shall continue, or until the United States in Congress assembled shall determine otherwise.

. . . .

Article VIII. All charges of war, and all other expenses that shall be incurred for the common defense or general welfare, and allowed by the United States in Congress assembled, shall be defrayed out of a common treasury, which shall be supplied by the several States, in proportion to the value of all land within each State, granted to or surveyed for any person, as such land and the buildings and improvements thereon shall be estimated according to such mode as the United States in Congress assembled, shall from time to time direct and appoint.

The taxes for paying that proportion shall be laid and levied by the authority and direction of the Legislatures of the several States within the time agreed upon by the United States in Congress assembled.

Article IX. The United States in Congress assembled, shall have the sole and exclusive right and power of determining on peace and war, except in the cases mentioned in the sixth article; of sending and receiving ambassadors; entering into treaties and alliances, provided that no treaty of commerce shall be made whereby the legislative power of the respective States shall be restrained from imposing such imposts and duties on foreigners, as their own people are subjected to, or from prohibiting the exportation or importation of any species of goods or commodities whatsoever; of establishing rules for deciding in all cases, what captures on land or water shall be legal, and in what manner prizes taken by land or naval forces in the service of the United States shall be divided or appropriated; of granting letters of marque and reprisal in times of peace; appointing courts for the trial of piracies and felonies committed on the high seas and establishing courts for receiving and determining finally appeals in all cases of captures, provided that no member of Congress shall be appointed a judge of any of the said courts.

The United States in Congress assembled shall also be the last resort on appeal in all disputes and differences now subsisting or that hereafter may arise between two or more States concerning boundary, jurisdiction or any other cause whatever; which authority shall always be exercised in the manner following. Whenever the legislative or executive authority or lawful agent of any State in controversy with another shall present a petition to Congress, stating the matter in question and praying for a hearing, notice thereof shall be given by order of Congress to the legislative or executive authority of the other State in controversy, and a day assigned for the appearance of the parties by their lawful agents, . . . and if either party shall neglect to attend at the day appointed, without showing reasons, which Congress shall judge sufficient, or being present shall refuse to strike, the Congress shall proceed to nominate three persons out of each State, and the Secretary of Congress shall strike in behalf of such party absent or refusing; and the judgment and sentence of the court to be appointed, in the manner before prescribed, shall be final and conclusive; and if any of the parties shall refuse to submit to the authority of such court, or to appear or defend their claim or cause, the court shall nevertheless proceed to pronounce sentence, or judgment, which shall in like manner be final and decisive, . . . provided also that no State shall be deprived of territory for the benefit of the United States.

All controversies concerning the private right of soil claimed under different grants of two or more States . . . shall on the petition of either party to the Congress of the United States, be finally determined as near as may be in the same manner as is before prescribed for deciding disputes respecting territorial jurisdiction between different States.

The United States in Congress assembled shall also have the sole and exclusive right and power of regulating the alloy and value of coin struck by their own authority, or by that of the respective States; fixing the standard of weights and measures throughout the United States; regulating the trade and managing all affairs with the Indians, not members of any of the States, provided that the legislative right of any State within its own limits be not infringed or violated; establishing and regulating post-offices from one State to another, throughout all the United States, and exacting such postage on the papers passing thro' the same as may be requisite to defray the expenses of the said office; appointing all officers of the land forces, in the service of the United States, excepting regimental officers; appointing all the officers of the naval forces, and commissioning all officers whatever in the service of the United States; making rules for the government and regulation of the said land and naval forces, and directing their operations.

The United States in Congress assembled shall have authority . . . to ascertain the necessary sums of money to be raised for the service of the United States, and to appropriate and apply the same for defraying the public expenses; to borrow money, or emit bills on the credit of the United States, transmitting every half year to the respective States an account of the sums of money so borrowed or emitted; to build and equip a navy; to agree upon the number of land forces, and to make requisitions from each State for its quota, in proportion to the number of white inhabitants in such State. . . .

The United States in Congress assembled shall never engage in a war, nor grant letters of marque and reprisal in time of peace, nor enter into any treaties or alliances, nor coin money, nor regulate the value thereof, nor ascertain the sums and expenses necessary for the defense and welfare of the United States, or any of them, nor emit bills, nor borrow money on the credit of the United States, nor appropriate money, nor agree upon the number of vessels of war, to be built or purchased, or the number of land or sea forces to be raised, nor appoint a commander in chief of the army or navy, unless nine States assent to the same; nor shall a question on any other point, except for adjourning from day to day be determined, unless by the votes of a majority of the United States in Congress assembled.

The Congress of the United States shall have power to adjourn to any time within the year, and to any place within the United States, so that no period of adjournment be for a longer duration than the space of six months, and shall publish the journal of their proceedings monthly, except such parts thereof relating to treaties, alliances or military operations, as in their judgment require secrecy; and the yeas and nays of the delegates of each State on any question shall be entered on the journal, when it is desired by any delegate; and the delegates of a State, or any of them, at his or their request shall be furnished with a transcript of the said journal, except such parts as are above excepted, to lay before the Legislatures of the several States.

Article XI. Canada acceding to this confederation, and joining in the measures of the United States, shall be admitted into, and entitled to all the advantages of this Union; but no other colony shall be admitted into the same, unless such admission be agreed to by nine States.

Article XII. All bills of credit emitted, monies borrowed and debts contracted by, or under the authority of Congress, before the assembling of the United States, in pursuance of the present confederation, shall be deemed and considered as a charge against the United States, for payment and satisfaction whereof the said United States, and the public faith are hereby solemnly pledged.

Article XIII. Every State shall abide by the determinations of the United States in Congress assembled, on all questions which by this confederation are submitted to them. And the articles of this confederation shall be inviolably observed by every State, and the Union shall be perpetual; nor shall any alteration at any time hereafter be made in any of them; unless such alteration be agreed to in a Congress of the United States, and be afterwards confirmed by the Legislatures of every State.

And whereas it hath pleased the Great Governor of the World to incline the hearts of the Legislatures we respectively represent in Congress, to approve of, and to authorize us to ratify the said articles of confederation and perpetual union. Know ye that we the undersigned delegates, by virtue of the power and authority to us given for that purpose, do by these presents, in the name and in behalf of our respective constituents, fully and entirely ratify and confirm each and every of the said articles of confederation and perpetual union, and all and singular the matters and things therein contained: and we do further solemnly plight and engage the faith of our respective constituents, that they shall abide by the determinations of the United States in Congress assembled, on all questions, which by the said confederation are submitted to them. And that the articles thereof shall be inviolably observed by the States we respectively represent, and that the Union shall be perpetual.

In witness whereof we have hereunto set our hands in Congress. Done at Philadelphia in the State of Pennsylvania the ninth day of July in the year of our Lord one thousand seven hundred and seventy-eight, and in the third year of the independence of America.

CHOOSE THE CORRECT ANSWER

Write the letter that best completes the statement or answers the question.

1. The Articles were largely the work of (*a*) George Washington, (*b*) John Dickinson, (*c*) Thomas Jefferson, (*d*) James Madison.   1._____

2. The Articles lacked (*a*) rules for voting by Congress, (*b*) a procedure by which Congress could declare war, (*c*) a bill of rights, (*d*) protection for the states against the central government.   2._____

3. According to the Articles, state taxes could not interfere with (*a*) the laws made by other states, (*b*) rules made for the states by Congress, (*c*) the right of people to use land as they pleased, (*d*) agreements made in treaties of the United States.
3._____

4. The number of states which had to agree before Congress could act was (*a*) 7, (*b*) 9, (*c*) 11, (*d*) 13.   4._____

5. The states agreed to (*a*) return persons charged with crimes by other states, (*b*) carry out laws made by other states, (*c*) help other states who needed money, (*d*) give their public lands to Congress.   5._____

6. Congress could raise money by (*a*) direct taxes, (*b*) asking states for help, (*c*) taking control of banks, (*d*) selling rights to be privateers to sea captains.   6._____

7. The number of votes each state had in Congress was (*a*) one vote for each state, (*b*) according to its size, (*c*) according to its population, (*d*) according to its wealth.   7._____

8. The men who wrote the Articles expected a new state to be formed from (*a*) Virginia, (*b*) Florida, (*c*) Maine, (*d*) Canada.   8._____

9. No change could be made in the Articles unless (*a*) the people of all of the states voted for the change, (*b*) Congress alone voted for the change, (*c*) nine states voted for the change, (*d*) Congress and all of the state legislatures approved the change.   9._____

10. The Congress did not have the right to (*a*) appoint a Supreme Court, (*b*) appoint army officers, (*c*) make treaties, (*d*) discuss differences between the states.   10._____

THOUGHT QUESTIONS

1. State and explain four provisions of the Articles of Confederation which helped the United States govern itself, and which needed change so that it could govern itself better.

2. Explain why you agree or disagree with each of the following:
   a. The Articles of Confederation proved that a free people could govern themselves successfully.
   b. The Articles were a rigid set of rules designed to lead to confusion and inaction.
   c. The Articles taught our people the value of a strong central government by proving the folly of a weak one.

The Northwest Ordinance 1787

* * * *The statute governing the organization* and law of the western lands was the greatest contribution made under the Articles of Confederation. The lands northwest of the Ohio River (the present states of Ohio, Indiana, Illinois, Michigan and Wisconsin) had been given to the national government by the states which had at first claimed them. This large area was surveyed and prepared for settlement. In 1785, land sales began, largely to land companies that were able to afford the cost of the large blocks of land into which the territory had been divided.

The Northwest Ordinance of 1787 set the pattern for the new states formed during the next 125 years. The settlers were to be allowed to govern themselves as soon as was practicable. The stages were clearly defined: from government by officials appointed by the national government, to territorial status, and finally to statehood on an equal basis with the original thirteen states.

The Ordinance guaranteed religious freedom, and provided a· bill of rights. It encouraged and supported public education. It prohibited slavery in the states to be formed out of the Northwest Territory, thus making the prohibition of slavery an issue for the first time. It guaranteed a democratic form of government to all those who settled in the West.

Section 1. Be it ordained by the United States in Congress assembled, That the said territory, for the purposes of temporary government, be one district, subject, however, to be divided into two districts, as future circumstances may, in the opinion of Congress, make it expedient.

.   .   .   .

Section 3. Be it ordained by the authority aforesaid, That there shall be appointed, from time to time, by Congress, a governor, whose commission shall continue in force for the term of three years, unless sooner revoked by Congress; he shall reside in the district, and have a freehold estate therein in one thousand acres of land, while in the exercise of his office.

Section 4. There shall be appointed from time to time, by Congress, a secretary, whose commission shall continue in force for four years, unless sooner revoked; he shall reside in the district, and have a freehold estate therein, in five hundred acres of land, while in the exercise of his office. It shall be his duty to keep and preserve the acts and laws passed by the legislature, and the public records of the district, and the proceedings of the governor in his executive department, and transmit authentic copies of such acts and proceedings every six months to the Secretary of Congress. There shall also be appointed a court, to consist of three judges, any two of whom to form a court, who shall have a common-law jurisdiction, and reside in the district, and have each therein a freehold estate, in five hundred acres of land, while in the exercise of their offices; and their commissions shall continue in force during good behavior.

Section 5. The governor and judges, or a majority of them, shall adopt and publish in the district such laws of the original States, criminal and civil, as may be necessary, and best suited to the circumstances of the district, and report them to Congress from time to time, which laws shall be in force in the district until the organization of the general assembly therein, unless disapproved of by Congress; but afterwards the legislature shall have authority to alter them as they shall think fit.

Section 6. The governor, for the time being, shall be commander-in-chief of the militia, appoint and commission all officers in the same below the rank of general officers; all general officers shall be appointed and commissioned by Congress.

Section 7. Previous to the organization of the general assembly the governor shall appoint such magistrates, and other civil officers, in each county or township, as he shall find necessary for the preservation of the peace and good order in the same. After the general assembly shall be organized the powers and duties of the magistrates and other civil officers shall be regulated and defined by the said assembly; but all magistrates and other civil officers, not herein otherwise directed, shall, during the continuance of this temporary government, be appointed by the governor.

Section 8. For the prevention of crimes and injuries, the laws to be adopted or made shall have force in all parts of the district, and for the execution of process, criminal and civil, the governor shall make proper divisions thereof; and he shall proceed, from time to time, as circumstances may require, to lay out the parts of the district in which the Indian titles shall have been extinguished, into counties and townships, subject, however, to such alterations as may thereafter be made by the legislature.

Section 9. So soon as there shall be five thousand free male inhabitants, of full age, in the district, upon giving proof thereof to the governor, they shall receive authority, with time and place, to elect representatives from their counties or townships, to represent them in the general assembly. *Provided,* That for every five hundred free male inhabitants there shall be one representative, and so on, progressively, with the number of free male inhabitants, shall the right of representation increase, until the number of representatives shall amount to twenty-five; after which the number and proportion of representatives shall be regulated by the legislature. *Provided,* That no person be eligible or qualified to act as a representative, unless he shall have been a citizen of one of the United States three years, and be a resident in the district, or unless he shall have resided in the district three years; and, in either case, shall likewise hold in his own right, in fee-simple, two hundred acres of land within the same. *Provided, also,* That a freehold in fifty acres of land in the district, having been a citizen of one of the States, and being resident in the district, or the like freehold and two years' residence in the district, shall be necessary to qualify a man as an elector of a representative.

Section 10. The representatives thus elected shall serve for the term of two years; and in case of the death of a representative, or removal from office, the governor shall issue a writ to the county or township, for which he was a member, to elect another in his stead, to serve for the residue of the term.

Section 11. The general assembly, or legislature, shall consist of the governor, legislative council, and a house of representatives. The legislative council shall consist of five members, to continue in office five years, unless sooner removed by Congress; any three of whom to be a quorum; and the members of the council shall be nominated and appointed in the following manner, to wit: As soon as representatives shall be elected the governor shall appoint a time and place for them to meet together, and when met they shall nominate ten persons, residents in the district, and each possessed of a freehold in five hundred acres of land, and return their names to Congress, five of whom Congress shall appoint and commission to serve as aforesaid; and whenever a vacancy shall happen in the council, by death or removal from office, the house of representatives shall nominate two persons, qualified as aforesaid, for each vacancy, and return their names to Congress, one of whom Congress shall appoint and commission for the residue of the term; and every five years, four months at least before the expiration of the time of service of the members of council, and said house shall nominate ten persons, qualified as aforesaid, and return their names to Congress, five of whom Congress shall appoint and commission to serve as members of the council five years, unless sooner removed. And the governor, legislative council, and house of representatives shall have authority to make laws in all cases for the good government of the district, not repugnant to the principles and articles in this ordinance established and declared. And all bills, having passed by a majority in the house, and by a majority in the council, shall be referred to the governor for his assent; but no bill, or legislative act whatever, shall be of any force without his assent. The governor shall have power to convent, prorogue, and dissolve the general assembly when, in his opinion, it shall be expedient.

Section 12. [The governor and other officers to take an oath]. As soon as a legislature shall be formed in the district, the council and house assembled, in one room, shall have authority, by joint ballot, to elect a delegate to Congress who shall have a seat in Congress, with a right of debating, but not of voting, during this temporary government.

Section. 13. And for extending the fundamental principles of civil and religious liberty, which form the basis whereon these republics, their laws and constitutions, are erected; to fix and establish those principles as the basis of all laws, constitutions, and governments, which forever hereafter shall be formed in the said territory; to provide, also, for the establishment of States, and permanent government therein, and for their admission to a share in the Federal councils on an equal footing with the original States, at as early periods as may be consistent with the general interest.

Section 14. It is hereby ordained and declared, by the authority aforesaid, that the following articles shall be considered as articles of compact, between the original States and the people and States in the said territory, and forever remain unalterable, unless by common consent, to wit:

Article I. No person, demeaning himself in a peaceable and orderly manner, shall ever be molested on account of his mode of worship, or religious sentiments, in the said territories.

Article II. The inhabitants of the said territory shall always be entitled to the benefits of the writs of *habeas corpus,* and of the trial by jury; of a proportionate representation of the people in the legislature, and of judicial proceedings according to the course of common law. All persons shall be bailable, unless for capital offenses, where the proof shall be evident, or the presumption great. All fines shall be moderate; and no cruel or unusual punishments shall be inflicted. No man shall be deprived of his liberty or property, but by the judgment of his peers, or the law of the land, and should the public exigencies make it necessary, for the common preservation, to take any person's property, or to demand his particular services, full compensation shall be made for the same. And, in the just preservation of rights and property, it is understood and declared, that no law ought ever to be made or have force in the said territory, that shall, in any manner whatever, interfere with or affect private contracts, or engagements, *bona fide,* and without fraud previously formed.

WRIT OF HABEAS CORPUS

1. Petition to Judge or Court

2. Writ of Habeas Corpus issued

3. Prisoner must be produced by person who holds him. Judge or Court passes on legality of imprisonment

Article III. Religion, morality, and knowledge being necessary to good government and the happiness of mankind, schools and the means of education shall forever be encouraged. The utmost good faith shall always be observed towards the Indians; their lands and property shall never be taken from them without their consent; and in their property, rights, and liberty they never shall be invaded or disturbed, unless in just and lawful wars authorized by Congress; but laws founded in justice and humanity shall, from time to time, be made, for preventing wrongs being done to them, and for preserving peace and friendship with them.

Article IV. The said territory, and the states which may be formed therein, shall forever remain a part of this confederacy of the United States of America, subject to the Articles of Confederation, and to such alterations therein as shall be constitutionally made; and to all the acts and ordinances of the United States in Congress assembled, conformable thereto. The inhabitants and settlers in the said territory shall be subject to pay a part of the Federal debts, contracted, or to be contracted, and a proportional part of the expenses of government to be apportioned on them by Congress, according to the same common rule and measure by which apportionments thereof shall be made on the other States; and the taxes for paying their proportion shall be laid and levied by the authority and direction of the legislatures of the district, or districts, or new States, as in the original States, within the time agreed upon by the United States in Congress assembled. The legislatures of those districts, or new States, shall never interfere with the primary disposal of the soil by the United States in Congress assembled, nor with any regulations Congress may find necessary for securing the title in such soil to the *bona fide* purchasers. No tax shall be imposed on lands the property of the United States; and in no case shall non-resident proprietors be taxed higher than residents. The navigable waters leading into the Mississippi and Saint Lawrence, and the carrying places between the same, shall be common highways, and forever free, as well to the inhabitants of the said territory as to the citizens of the United States, and those of any other States that may be admitted into the confederacy, without any tax, impost, or duty therefor.

Article V. There shall be formed in the said territory not less than three nor more than five States; and the boundaries of the States, as soon as Virginia shall alter her act of cession and consent to the same, shall become fixed and established as follows, to wit: The western State, in the said territory, shall be bounded by the Mississippi, the Ohio, and the Wabash Rivers; a direct line drawn from the Wabash and Post Vincents, due north, to the territorial line between the United States and Canada; and by the said territorial line to the Lake of the Woods and Mississippi. The middle State shall be bounded by the said direct line, the Wabash from Post Vincents to the Ohio, by the Ohio, by a direct line drawn due north from the mouth of the Great Miami to the said territorial line, and by the said territorial line. The eastern State shall be bounded by the last-mentioned direct line, the Ohio, Pennsylvania, and the said territorial line. *Provided, however,* And it is further understood and declared, that the boundaries of these three States shall be subject so far to be altered, that, if Congress shall hereafter find it expedient, they shall have authority to form one or two States in that part of the said territory which lies north of an east and west line drawn through the southerly bend or extreme of Lake Michigan. And whenever any of the said States shall have sixty thousand free inhabitants therein, such State shall be admitted, by its delegates, into the Congress of the United States, on an equal footing with the original States, in all respects whatever; and shall be at liberty to form a permanent constitution and State government. *Provided,* The constitution and government, so to be formed, shall be republican, and in conformity to the principles contained in these articles, and, so far as it can be consistent with the general interest of the confederacy, such admission shall be allowed at an earlier period, and when there may be a less number of free inhabitants in the State than sixty thousand.

Article VI. There shall be neither slavery nor involuntary servitude in the said territory, otherwise than in the punishment of crimes, whereof the party shall have been duly convicted. *Provided always,* That any person escaping into the same, from whom labor or service is lawfully claimed in any one of the original States, such fugitive may be lawfully reclaimed, and conveyed to the person claiming his or her labor or service as aforesaid.

TRUE OR FALSE?

Write T *if the statement is correct; Write* F *if it is false.*

_____1. The number of states to be formed from the Northwest Territory was to be at least 2 but not more than 5.

_____2. The first officials of the Northwest Territory were appointed by Congress.

_____3. A territorial government could be set up as soon as a territory contained 60,000 people.

_____4. The Ordinance provided that any slave who escaped to the Northwest Territory would be forever free.

_____5. Representatives to territorial legislatures had to be citizens and landowners.

_____6. The people of the new territories were guaranteed trial by jury.

_____7. The Ordinance permitted settlers to take Indian lands if they paid for them.

_____8. The legislatures of the new states were given control of all rivers in their states.

_____9. The people of the Northwest Territory would have to pay taxes levied by Congress.

_____10. The governor of a territory could veto any law passed by a territorial legislature.

THOUGHT QUESTIONS

1. State and explain three ways in which the Northwest Ordinance furthered democracy in the United States.
2. Trace the steps by which settlers moving into the Northwest Territory could set up a state.

The Constitution 1787

* * * * *The Constitution of the United States* is a familiar part of most American history textbooks, and it is not reprinted in its entirety in this book. Those sections, however, which show how the rights of individuals are defined and protected by the Constitution are included here.

These excerpts explain the reasons for the growth of freedom under law in the United States. Individual rights are respected and protected by law. Governments are prevented by the courts from interfering with those rights. The decisions of courts are obeyed by all citizens and all officials at every level of government.

The Constitution has been a growing governing instrument. As ideas of human rights have changed through the years, its amendments have become part of American governmental and civilian life.

Preamble

We the People of the United States, in order to form a more perfect Union, establish justice, insure domestic tranquillity, provide for the common defense, promote the general welfare, and secure the blessings of liberty to ourselves and our posterity, do ordain and establish this Constitution for the United States of America.

Article I
Section 6

1. The Senators and Representatives shall receive a compensation for their services to be ascertained by law, and paid out of the Treasury of the United States. They shall in all cases except treason, felony and breach of the peace, be privileged from arrest during their attendance at the session of their respective Houses, and in going to and returning from the same; and for any speech or debate in either House they shall not be questioned in any other place.

2. No Senator or Representative shall, during the time for which he was elected, be appointed to any civil office under the authority of the United States which shall have been created, or the emoluments whereof shall have been increased during such time; and no person holding any office under the United States shall be a member of either House during his continuance in office.

Section 8

The Congress shall have power:

8. To promote the progress of science and useful arts by securing for limited times to authors and inventors the exclusive right to their respective writings and discoveries.

18. To make all laws which shall be necessary and proper for carrying into execution the foregoing powers, and all other powers vested by this Constitution in the Government of the United States, or in any department or officer thereof.

Section 9

2. The privilege of the writ of habeas corpus shall not be suspended unless when in cases of rebellion or invasion the public safety may require it.

3. No bill of attainder or ex post facto law shall be passed.

6. No preference shall be given by any regulation of com-

merce or revenue to the ports of one State over those of another; nor shall vessels bound to or from one State be obliged to enter, clear, or pay duties in another.

7. No money shall be drawn from the Treasury but in consequence of appropriations made by law; and a regular statement and account of the receipts and expenditures of all public money shall be published from time to time.

8. No title of nobility shall be granted by the United States. And no person holding any office of profit or trust under them shall, without the consent of the Congress, accept any present, emolument, office, or title of any kind whatever from any king, prince, or foreign state.

Section 10

1. No State shall enter into any treaty, alliance, or confederation, grant letters of marque and reprisal, coin money, emit bills of credit, make anything but gold and silver coin a tender in payment of debts, pass any bill of attainder, ex post facto law, or law impairing the obligation of contracts, or grant any title of nobility.

Article II

Section 1

7. The President shall, at stated times, receive for his services a compensation which shall neither be increased nor diminished during the period for which he shall have been elected, and he shall not receive within that period any other emolument from the United States or any of them.

8. Bef ● he enter on the execution of his office, he shall take the following oath or affirmation: "I do solemnly swear (or affirm) that I will faithfully execute the office of President of the United States, and will, to the best of my ability, preserve, protect and defend the Constitution of the United States."

Section 2

2. (The President) . . . shall have power, by and with the advice and consent of the Senate, to make treaties, provided two-thirds of the Senators present concur; and he shall nominate, and by and with the advice and consent of the Senate, shall appoint ambassadors, other public ministers and consuls, judges of the Supreme Court, and all other officers of

the United States whose appointments are not herein otherwise provided for, and which shall be established by law; but the Congress may by law vest the appointment of such inferior officers as they think proper in the President alone, in the courts of law, or in the heads of departments.

Section 3

He shall from time to time give to the Congress information of the state of the Union, and recommend to their consideration such measures as he shall judge necessary and expedient; he may, on extraordinary occasions, convene both Houses, or either of them, and in case of disagreement between them, with respect to the time of adjournment, he may adjourn them to such time as he shall think proper; he shall receive ambassadors and other public ministers; he shall take care that the laws be faithfully executed, and shall commission all officers of the United States.

Section 4

The President, Vice President, and all civil officers of the United States shall be removed from office on impeachment for and conviction of treason, bribery, or other high crimes and misdemeanors.

Article III
Section 1

The judicial power of the United States shall be vested in one Supreme Court, and in such inferior courts as the Congress may from time to time ordain and establish. The judges, both of the Supreme and inferior courts, shall hold their offices during good behavior, and shall at stated times receive for their services a compensation which shall not be diminished during their continuance in office.

Section 2

The trial of all crimes, except in cases of impeachment, shall be by jury, and such trial shall be held in the State where the said crimes shall have been committed; but when not committed within any State, the trial shall be at such place or places as the Congress may by law have directed.

Section 3

1. Treason against the United States shall consist only in levying war against them, or in adhering to their enemies, giving them aid and comfort. No person shall be convicted of treason, unless on the testimony of two witnesses to the same overt act, or on confession in open court.

2. The Congress shall have power to declare the punishment of treason, but no attainder of treason shall work corruption of blood or forfeiture except during the life of the person attained.

Article IV
Section 2

1. The citizens of each State shall be entitled to all privileges and immunities of citizens in the several States.

2. A person charged in any State with treason, felony, or other crime, who shall flee from justice, and be found in

OUR SYSTEM OF CHECKS AND BALANCES

PRESIDENT	CONGRESS	SUPREME COURT
Powers	**Powers**	**Powers**
1. Enforces laws. 2. Can veto bills. 3. Can appoint judges and other officials.	1. Makes the laws. 2. By a two-thirds vote of members Congress can pass a law over President's veto. 3. Can impeach President. 4. Must approve President's appointment of judges and other officials.	1. Interprets the laws. 2. Can declare laws unconstitutional.
Controls	**Controls**	**Controls**
1. Can be removed by Congress. 2. Congress can override veto. 3. Appointments must first be approved by Congress.	1. President can veto a bill passed by Congress. 2. Laws passed by Congress can be declared unconstitutional by Supreme Court.	1. Judges appointed for life by the President. 2. Appointments must first be approved by Congress. 3. Judges can be removed by Congress for improper behavior.

another State, shall, on demand of the Executive authority of the State from which he fled, be delivered up, to be removed to the State having jurisdiction of the crime.

Section 4

The United States shall guarantee to every State in this Union a Republican form of government, and shall protect each of them against invasion, and, on application of the Legislature, or of the Executive (when the Legislature cannot be convened), against domestic violence.

Article V

The Congress, whenever two-thirds of both Houses shall deem it necessary, shall propose amendments to this Constitution, or, on the application of the Legislatures of two-thirds of the several States, shall call a convention for proposing amendments, which, in either case, shall be valid to all intents and purposes, as part of this Constitution, when ratified by the Legislatures of three-fourths of the several States, or by conventions in three-fourths thereof, as the one or the other mode of ratification may be proposed by the Congress; . . . and that no State, without its consent, shall be deprived of its equal suffrage in the Senate.

Article VI

1. All Debts contracted and Engagements entered into before the Adoption of this Constitution shall be as valid against the United States under this Constitution as under the Confederation.

2. This Constitution and the Laws of the United States which shall be made in Pursuance thereof and all Treaties made, or which shall be made, under the Authority of the United States, shall be the supreme Law of the Land, and the Judges in every State shall be bound thereby, any Thing in the Constitution or Laws of any State to the Contrary notwithstanding.

3. The Senators and Representatives before mentioned, and the Members of the several State Legislatures, and all executive and judicial Officers, both of the United States and of the several States, shall be bound by Oath or Affirmation to support this Constitution; but no religious Test shall ever be required as a Qualification to any Office or public Trust under the United States.

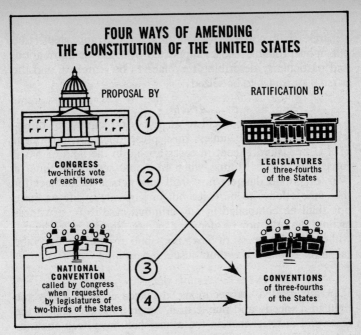

FOUR WAYS OF AMENDING THE CONSTITUTION OF THE UNITED STATES

PROPOSAL BY

RATIFICATION BY

CONGRESS
two-thirds vote
of each House

LEGISLATURES
of three-fourths
of the States

**NATIONAL
CONVENTION**
called by Congress
when requested
by legislatures of
two-thirds of the States

CONVENTIONS
of three-fourths
of the States

Amendments
Article I

Congress shall make no law respecting an establishment of religion, or prohibiting the free exercise thereof; or abridging the freedom of speech, or of the press; or the right of the people peaceably to assemble, and to petition the Government for a redress of grievances.

Article II

A well regulated Militia being necessary to the security of a free State, the right of the people to keep and bear Arms, shall not be infringed.

Article III

No Soldier shall, in time of peace be quartered in any house, without the consent of the Owner, nor in time of war but in a manner to be prescribed by law.

Article IV

The right of the people to be secure in their persons, houses, papers, and effects, against unreasonable searches and seizures, shall not be violated, and no Warrants shall issue but upon probable cause, supported by Oath or affirmation, and particularly describing the place to be searched, and the persons or things to be seized.

Article V

No person shall be held to answer for a capital, or otherwise infamous crime, unless on a presentment or indictment of a Grand Jury, except in cases arising in the land or naval forces, or in the Militia, when in actual service in time of War or public danger; nor shall any person be subject for the same offense to be twice put in jeopardy of life or limb; nor shall be compelled in any criminal case to be a witness against himself, nor be deprived of life, liberty, or property, without due process of law; nor shall private property be taken for public use without just compensation.

Article VI

In all criminal prosecutions, the accused shall enjoy the right to a speedy and public trial, by an impartial jury of the State and district wherein the crime shall have been committed, which district shall have been previously ascertained by law, and to be informed of the nature and cause of the accusation; to be confronted with the witnesses against him; to have compulsory process for obtaining witnesses in his favor, and to have the assistance of counsel for his defense.

Article VII

In suits at common law, where the value in controversy shall exceed twenty dollars, the right of trial by jury shall be preserved, and no fact tried by a jury shall be otherwise re-examined in any court of the United States than according to the rules of the common law.

Article VIII

Excessive bail shall not be required, nor excessive fines imposed, nor cruel and unusual punishments inflicted.

Article IX

The enumeration in the Constitution of certain rights shall not be construed to deny or disparage others retained by the people.

Article X

The powers not delegated to the United States by the Constitution, nor prohibited by it to the States, are reserved to the States respectively, or to the people.

Article XI (1798)

The judicial power of the United States shall not be construed to extend to any suit in law or equity, commenced or prosecuted against one of the United States by citizens of another State, or by citizens or subjects of any foreign state.

NOTE: Article XII deals with the order of succession on the death of the President while in office. This order was passed in 1792, changed in 1886, 1947 and 1955. The order of succession is now: Vice-President, Speaker of the House, President *pro tempore* of the Senate, and the Cabinet, in this order: State, Treasury, Defense, Attorney General, Interior, Agriculture, Commerce, Labor, and Health, Education and Welfare. With the death of President Kennedy on November 22, 1963, the Vice-President, Lyndon B. Johnson, became President. Since there is no provision for the order of succession to the Vice Presidency, the office of Vice President was not occupied.

Article XIII (1865)

Neither slavery nor involuntary servitude, except as punishment for crime whereof the party shall have been duly convicted, shall exist within the United States, or any place subject to their jurisdiction.

Article XIV (1868)

All persons born or naturalized in the United States, and subject to the jurisdiction thereof, are citizens of the United States and of the State wherein they reside. No State shall make or enforce any law which shall abridge the privileges or immunities of citizens of the United States; nor shall any State deprive any person of life, liberty, or property, without due process of law; nor deny to any person within its jurisdiction the equal protection of the laws.

Article XV (1870)

The right of citizens of the United States to vote shall not be denied or abridged by the United States or by any State on account of race, color, or previous condition of servitude.

Article XIX (1920)

The right of citizens of the United States to vote shall not be denied or abridged by the United States or by any State on account of sex.

Article XXIII (1961)

The District constituting the seat of Government of the United States shall appoint ... a number of electors ... for the purpose of the election of President and Vice President. ...

THOUGHT QUESTIONS

HOW MUCH DO YOU KNOW ABOUT TERMS USED IN THE CONSTITUTION?

An understanding of the vocabulary of the Constitution is basic to an understanding of the American government and the rights Americans enjoy under the Constitution. You should be able to:

a. define each of the terms listed below;
b. state what the Constitution says in reference to it;
c. explain the importance of what the Constitution says about it.

1. Amendment
2. Appropriation
3. Assistance of counsel
4. Bill of attainder
5. Citizenship
6. Cruel and unusual punishments
7. Domestic tranquillity
8. Delegated powers
9. Double jeopardy
10. Due process of law
11. Enumerated powers
12. Equal protection of the laws
13. Establishment of religion
14. Excessive bail
15. Excessive fines
16. Ex post facto law
17. Freedom of the press
18. Freedom of religion
19. Freedom of speech
20. General welfare
21. Good behavior
22. Grand jury
23. Habeas corpus
24. Impeachment
25. Involuntary servitude
26. Just compensation
27. Letters of marque and reprisal
28. Militia
29. "Necessary and proper"
30. Posterity
31. Presidential oath of office
32. Privileges and immunities
33. Quartering of soldiers
34. Redress of grievances
35. Religious test
36. Republican form of government
37. Right to assemble
38. Right to call witnesses
39. Right to petition
40. Right to vote
41. Rights of authors and inventors
42. Slavery
43. Speedy and public trial by jury
44. State of the Union
45. Supreme law of the land
46. Title of nobility
47. Treason
48. Tribunal
49. Unreasonable searches and seizures
50. Witness against self

Washington Documents 1793-1796

* * * * *News came to the United States in* April, 1793, that France had declared war on Great Britain and its allies. The French king had been killed, and the Reign of Terror had begun. Citizen Genet was on his way to President Washington as a special French minister to try to recruit Americans and raise money for the French Revolution.

The United States had been allied with France since their treaty of 1778, and had promised to defend the French islands in the West Indies. Britain's superior navy was about to attack them. Keeping the promises that the United States had made in its treaty with France meant war with England and its allies.

President George Washington was determined to keep the United States out of this new European war. Although he knew that many Americans still hated England, and that many people, including such important national leaders as Thomas Jefferson, thought that the United States should support the French Revolution, he decided to announce his country's neutrality to the world without delay. His cabinet agreed with his plan, and Attorney-General Randolph drew up a proclamation of neutrality which the President issued on April 22, 1793.

The proclamation gained time for the United States, a new country, to continue its development. It showed Americans that they could avoid becoming involved in European wars. It was the beginning of the century-long American foreign policy of isolation from the wars and revolutions of Europe.

Proclamation of Neutrality (1793)

Whereas it appears that a state of war exists between Austria, Prussia, Sardinia, Great Britain and the United Netherlands, on the one part, and France on the other; and the duty and interest of the United States require that they should with sincerity and good faith adopt and pursue a conduct friendly and impartial toward the belligerent Powers:

I have, therefore, thought fit by these presents to declare the disposition of the United States to observe the conduct aforesaid towards those Powers respectively; and to exhort and warn the citizens of the United States carefully to avoid all acts and proceedings whatsoever, which may in any manner tend to contravene such disposition.

And I do hereby also make known, that whosoever of the citizens of the United States shall render himself liable to punishment or forfeiture under the law of nations, by committing, aiding, or abetting hostilities against any of the said

Powers, or by carrying to any of them those articles which are deemed contraband by the modern usage of nations, will not receive the protection of the United States, against such punishment or forfeiture; and further, that I have given instructions to those officers, to whom it belongs, to cause prosecutions to be instituted against all persons, who shall, within the cognizance of the courts of the United States, violate the law of nations, with respect to the Powers at war, or any of them. . . .

Geo. Washington

FILL IN THE ANSWERS

Write the word or phrase which best completes the statement.

1. The two important nations at war in 1793 were _____ and _____.
2. The member of Washington's cabinet who wanted to help France was _____.
3. A belligerent is a country which is _____.
4. The proclamation was made even though the United States had a treaty with _____.
5. American ships were not permitted to carry _____ to either side.
6. The Proclamation of Neutrality was drawn up by _____.
7. The Proclamation of Neutrality helped the United States continue its _____.
8. The Proclamation of Neutrality was the beginning of an American policy of isolation which lasted for about _____.
9. The Proclamation of Neutrality was issued on _____, 1783.
10. According to Washington it was the duty and interest of the United States to pursue a conduct _____ and _____ toward the belligerent powers.

THOUGHT QUESTIONS

1. (*a*) Why was the United States able to keep out of war in 1793?
   (*b*) Why would such a proclamation of neutrality be impossible today?
2. How did Washington's proclamation of neutrality affect United States history during the time it was in effect and in later years?

Washington's Farewell Address (1796)

* * * * *George Washington decided to retire* from public life at the end of his second term as President. He felt that his continuing personal popularity might keep others from running for the presidency. He did not want, however, just to decline to be a candidate for a third term. He chose to make a statement to the American people containing his convictions on a variety of important public questions.

This statement was published in the *American Daily Advertiser* of Philadelphia on September 19, 1796. It was never delivered as a public speech. The Farewell Address was based on a rough draft which Washington had written. He consulted Hamilton, Jay, and Madison on its phrasing, and accepted many of their suggestions. It is probable that the final form of the Address was largely Hamilton's work.

The Farewell Address publicly took Washington out of politics. It also permitted him to advise future political leaders and all American citizens of the directions in which he felt his country should move. Important among his ideas were: (1) the distrust of political and sectional divisions in national life; (2) the need for the country to concentrate its energies upon its domestic development; (3) the importance of avoiding permanent alliances or enmities with the countries of Europe.

Friends and Fellow-Citizens:

The period for a new election of a citizen to administer the executive government of the United States being not far distant, and the time actually arrived when your thoughts must be employed in designating the person who is to be clothed with that important trust, it appears to me proper, especially as it may conduce to a more distinct expression of the public voice that I should now apprise you of the resolution I have formed to decline being considered among the number of those out of whom a choice is to be made. . . .

. . . a solicitude for your welfare, which cannot end but with my life, and the apprehension of danger natural to that solicitude, urge me on an occasion like the present to offer to your solemn contemplation, and to recommend to your frequent review, some sentiments which are the result of much reflection, of no inconsiderable observation, and which appear to me all important to the permanency of your felicity as a people. . . .

The unity of government which constitutes you one people is also now dear to you. It is justly so, for it is a main pillar in the edifice of your real independence, the support of your tranquillity at home, your peace abroad, of your safety, of your prosperity, of that very liberty which you so highly prize. But as it is easy to foresee that from different causes and from different quarters much pains will be taken, many artifices employed, to weaken in your minds the conviction of this truth, as this is the point in your political fortress against which the batteries of internal and external enemies will be most constantly and actively (though often covertly and insidiously) directed, it is of infinite moment that you should properly estimate the immense value of your national union to your collective and individual happiness; that you should cherish a cordial, habitual, and immovable attachment to it; accustoming yourselves to think and speak of it as of the palladium of your political safety and prosperity; watching for its preservation with jealous anxiety; discountenancing whatever may suggest even a suspicion that it can in any event be abandoned; and indignantly frowning upon the first dawning of every attempt to alienate any portion of our country from the rest, or to enfeeble the sacred ties which now link together the various parts.

For this you have every inducement of sympathy and interest. Citizens by birth or choice of a common country, that country has a right to concentrate your affections. The name of American, which belongs to you in your national capacity, must always exalt the just pride of patriotism more than any appellation derived from local discriminations. With slight shades of difference, you have the same religion, manners, habits, and political principles. You have in a common cause fought and triumphed together. The independence and liberty you possess are the work of joint councils and joint efforts, of common dangers, sufferings, and successes.

But these considerations, however powerfully they address themselves to your sensibility, are greatly outweighed by those which apply more immediately to your interest. Here every portion of our country finds the most commanding motives for carefully guarding and preserving the union of the whole.

. . . .

. . . every part of our country thus feels an immediate and particular interest in union, all the parts combined cannot fail to find in the united mass of means and efforts greater strength, greater resource, proportionably greater security from external danger, and less frequent interruption of their peace by foreign nations; and, what is of inestimable value, they must derive from union an exemption from those broils and wars between themselves, which so frequently afflict neighboring countries not tied together by the same government, which their own rivalships alone would be sufficient to produce, but which opposite foreign alliances, attachments, and intrigues would stimulate and embitter. Hence, likewise, they will avoid the necessity of those overgrown military establishments which, under any form of government, are inauspicious to liberty, and which are to be regarded as particularly hostile to republican liberty. In this sense it is that your union ought to be considered as a main prop of your liberty, and that the love of the one ought to endear to you the preservation of the other. . . .

In contemplating the causes which may disturb our Union, it occurs as matter of serious concern that any ground should have been furnished for characterizing parties by geographical discriminations—Northern and Southern, Atlantic and Western—whence designing men may endeavor to excite a belief that there is a real difference of local interests and views. One of the expedients of party to acquire influence within particular districts is to misrepresent the opinions and aims of other districts. You cannot shield yourselves too much against the jealousies and heartburnings which spring from these misrepresentations. They tend to render alien to each other those who ought to be bound together by fraternal affection. . . .

The basis of our political systems is the right of the people to make and to alter their constitutions of government. But the constitution which at any time exists, till changed by an explicit and authentic act of the whole people, is sacredly obligatory upon all. The very idea of the power and the right of the people to establish government presupposes the duty of every individual to obey the established government.

All obstructions to the execution of the laws, all combinations and associations, under whatever plausible character, with the real design to direct, control, counteract, or awe the regular deliberation and action of the constituted authorities are destructive of this fundamental principle and of fatal tendency. They serve to organize faction; to give it an artificial and extraordinary force; to put in the place of the delegated will of the nation the will of a party, often a small but artful and enterprising minority of the community; and, according to the alternate triumphs of different parties, to make the public administration the mirror of the ill-concerted and incongruous projects of faction, rather than the organ of consistent and wholesome plans, digested by common counsels and modified by mutual interests.

However combinations or associations of the above description may now and then answer popular ends, they are likely, in the course of time and things, to become potent engines by which cunning, ambitious, and unprincipled men will be enabled to subvert the power of the people, and to usurp for themselves the reins of government, destroying afterward the very engines which have lifted them to unjust dominion.

Toward the preservation of your government and the permanency of your present happy state, it is requisite not only that you steadily discountenance irregular oppositions to its acknowledged authority, but also that you resist with care the spirit of innovation upon its principles, however specious the pretexts. One method of assault may be to effect in the forms of the Constitution alterations which will impair the energy of the system, and thus to undermine what cannot be directly overthrown. In all the changes to which you may be invited, remember that time and habit are at least as necessary to fix the true character of governments as of other human institutions; that experience is the surest standard by which to test the real tendency of the existing constitution of a country; that facility in changes upon the credit of mere hypotheses and opinion exposes to perpetual change, from the endless variety of hypotheses and opinion; and remember, especially, that for the efficient management of your common interests in a country so extensive as ours, a government of as much vigor as is consistent with the perfect security of liberty is indispensable. Liberty itself will find in such a government, with powers properly distributed and adjusted, its surest guardian. It is, indeed, little else than a name where the government is too feeble to withstand the enterprises of faction, to confine each member of the society within the limits prescribed by the laws, and to maintain all in the secure and tranquil enjoyment of the rights of person and property.

I have already intimated to you the danger of parties in the state, with particular reference to the founding of them on geographical discriminations. Let me now take a more comprehensive view, and warn you in the most solemn manner against baneful effects of the spirit of party generally. . . .

There is an opinion that parties in free countries are useful checks upon the administration of the government and serve to keep alive the spirit of liberty. This within certain limits is probably true; and in governments of a monarchical cast patriotism may look with indulgence, if not with favor, upon the spirit of party. But in those of the popular character, in governments purely elective, it is a spirit not to be encouraged. From their natural tendency it is certain there will always be enough of that spirit for every salutary purpose. And there being constant danger of excess, the effort ought to be, by force of public opinion, to mitigate and assuage it. A fire not to be quenched, it demands a uniform vigilance to prevent its bursting into a flame, lest, instead of warming, it should consume. . . .

The necessity of reciprocal checks in the exercise of political power, by dividing and distributing it into different depositories, and constituting each the guardian of the public weal against invasions by the others, has been evinced by experiments ancient and modern, some of them in our country and under our own eyes. To preserve them must be as necessary as to institute them.

Of all the dispositions and habits which lead to political prosperity, religion and morality are indispensable supports. In vain would that man claim the tribute of patriotism who should labor to subvert these great pillars of human happiness, these firmest props of the duties of men and citizens. . . .

As a very important source of strength and security, cherish public credit. One method of preserving it is to use it as sparingly as possible, avoiding occasions of expense by cultivating peace, but remembering also that timely disbursements to prepare for danger frequently prevent much greater disbursements to repel it; avoiding likewise the accumulation of debt, not only by shunning occasions of expense, but by vigorous exertions in time of peace to discharge the debts which unavoidable wars have occasioned, not ungenerously throwing upon posterity the burthen which we ourselves ought to bear. . . . It is essential that you should practically bear in mind that toward the payment of debts there must be revenue; that to have revenue there must be taxes; that no taxes can be devised which are not more or less inconvenient and unpleasant; that the intrinsic embarrassment inseparable from the selection of the proper objects (which is always a choice of difficulties) ought to be a decisive motive for a candid construction of the conduct of the government in making it, and for a spirit of acquiescence in the measures for obtaining revenue which the public exigencies may at any time dictate.

Observe good faith and justice toward all nations. Cultivate peace and harmony with all. Religion and morality enjoin this conduct; and can it be that good policy does not equally enjoin it? It will be worthy of a free, enlightened, and at no distant period, a great nation, to give to mankind the magnanimous and too novel example of a people always guided by an exalted justice and benevolence. Who can doubt that in the course of time and things the fruits of such a plan would richly repay any temporary advantages which might be lost by a steady adherence to it? Can it be that Providence has not connected the permanent felicity of a nation with its virtues? The experiment, at least, is recommended by every sentiment which ennobles human nature. Alas! is it rendered impossible by its vices?

In the execution of such a plan nothing is more essential than that permanent, inveterate antipathies against particular nations and passionate attachments for others should be excluded, and that in place of them just and amicable feelings toward all should be cultivated. The nation which indulges toward another an habitual hatred, or an habitual fondness, is in some degree a slave. It is a slave to its animosity or to its affection, either of which is sufficient to lead it astray from its duty and its interest. Antipathy in one nation against another disposes each more readily to offer insult and injury, to lay hold of slight causes of umbrage, and to be haughty and intractable when accidental or trifling occasions of dispute occur. . . .

Against the insidious wiles of foreign influence (I conjure you to believe me, fellow-citizens) the jealousy of a free people ought to be constantly awake, since history and experience prove that foreign influence is one of the most baneful foes of republican government. But that jealousy, to be useful, must be impartial, else it becomes the instrument of the very influence to be avoided, instead of a defense against it. Excessive partiality for one foreign nation and excessive dislike for another, cause those whom they actuate to see danger only on one side and serve to veil and even second the arts of influence on the other. Real patriots, who may resist the intrigues of the favorite, are liable to become suspected and odious, while its tools and dupes usurp the applause and confidence of the people to surrender their interests.

The great rule of conduct for us in regard to foreign nations is, in extending our commercial relations, to have with them as little political connection as possible. So far as we have already formed engagements, let them be fulfilled with perfect good faith. Here let us stop.

Europe has a set of primary interests which to us have

none, or a very remote relation. Hence she must be engaged in frequent controversies, the causes of which are essentially foreign to our concerns. Hence, therefore, it must be unwise in us to implicate ourselves by artificial ties in the ordinary vicissitudes of her politics, or the ordinary combinations and collisions of her friendships or enmities.

Our detached and distant situation invites and enables us to pursue a different course. If we remain one people, under an efficient government, the period is not far off when we may defy material injury from external annoyance; when we may take such an attitude as will cause the neutrality we may at any time resolve upon to be scrupulously respected; when belligerent nations, under the impossibility of making acquisitions upon us, will not lightly hazard the giving us provocation; when we may choose peace or war, as our interest, guided by justice, shall counsel.

Why forego the advantages of so peculiar a situation? Why quit our own to stand upon foreign ground? Why, by interweaving our destiny with that of any part of Europe, entangle our peace and prosperity in the toils of European ambition, rivalship, interest, humor, or caprice?

It is our true policy to steer clear of permanent alliances with any portion of the foreign world, so far, I mean, as we are now at liberty to do it; let me not be understood as capable of patronizing infidelity to existing engagements. (I hold the maxim no less applicable to public than to private affairs, that honesty is always the best policy.) I repeat it, therefore, let those engagements be observed in their genuine sense. But in my opinion it is unnecessary and would be unwise to extend them.

Taking care always to keep ourselves by suitable establishments on a respectable defensive posture, we may safely trust to temporary alliances for extraordinary emergencies. . . .
. . . .
Relying on its kindness in this as in other things, and actuated by that fervent love toward it which is so natural to a man who views in it the native soil of himself and his progenitors for several generations, I anticipate with pleasing expectation that retreat in which I promise myself to realize, without alloy, the sweet enjoyment of partaking, in the midst of my fellow-citizens, the benign influence of good laws

under a free government—the ever favorite object of my heart and the happy reward, as I trust, of our mutual cares, labors, and dangers.

TRUE OR FALSE?

Write T if the statement is correct; write F if it is false.

_____1. Washington delivered his Farewell Address at his last press conference.

_____2. Washington felt people should think of themselves as Americans first and as citizens of their State later.

_____3. Washington felt that the Union of our states benefitted all sections.

_____4. Washington felt that the political parties of the North and the South should make alliances.

_____5. Washington believed that the United States should learn to hate its enemies, and avoid peaceful actions toward them.

_____6. Washington believed we should do everything possible to show friendship to a very friendly nation rather than to others.

_____7. Washington believed that people should follow their religious beliefs.

_____8. Washington thought it proper for a government to borrow money, for a public debt could always be paid in the future.

_____9. Washington warned the people to be on guard against political leaders who might try to take too much power.

_____10. Washington warned that the liberties of the people were safe only so long as the people watched over them.

THOUGHT QUESTIONS

1. Explain the advice Washington gave in his Farewell Address relating to:
   (*a*) political parties
   (*b*) sectionalism
   (*c*) relations with other countries.
2. Discuss the statement: Washington's Farewell Address tried to place his nation on a path which, if strictly followed, would create as many problems as it could solve.
   (*a*) In what respects do you agree with the statement?
   (*b*) In what respects do you disagree with the statement?

The Alien
and Sedition Acts
1798

* * * *The Federalist Party controlled Congress*
and President John Adams in 1798 when the
nation was threatened by war with France. Thomas
Jefferson's strong pro-French opposition party was
led in Congress by Albert Gallatin, an immigrant
from Switzerland. Visiting French officials were
busy trying to defeat the Federalists and replace
them with the pro-French Jeffersonians. A movement grew among Federalists to expel the many
French and other Europeans, including Irish and
English immigrants, who had come to the United
States and then devoted themselves to opposing
Federalist policies.

Congress passed four laws in 1798 intended to
control or end opposition to the Federalists.

(1) The Naturalization Act required residence of 14 years before an alien who had arrived after 1795 could become a citizen.

(2) The Alien Act gave the President power to deport any aliens dangerous to the country's peace and safety.

(3) The Alien Enemies Act gave the President power in time of war to deport or restrain aliens.

(4) The Sedition Act was directed against those who conspired to overthrow the government. It authorized heavy fines and imprisonment for those who spoke, acted or wrote against the government, the President, or the Congress.

The Federalists' use of the Alien and Sedition Acts to prevent political opposition at home caused a great reaction. The Sedition Act violated the guarantees of free speech and press in the first Amendment to the Constitution. The country turned against the Federalists, and the chief result was Jefferson's election in 1800. The Federalists never recovered as a national political party. The Alien and Sedition Acts ended when Jefferson and his party came into power.

Naturalization Act

Section 1. Be it enacted . . . That no alien shall be admitted to become a citizen of the United States, or of any state, unless in the manner prescribed by the act, entitled "An act to establish a uniform rule of naturalization; and to repeal the act heretofore passed on that subject," he shall have declared his intention to become a citizen of the United States, five years, at least, before his admission, and shall, at the time of his application to be admitted, declare and prove, to the satisfaction of the court having jurisdiction in the case, that he has resided within the United States fourteen years, at least, and within the state or territory where, or for which such court is at the time held, five years, at least, besides conforming to the other declarations, renunciations and proofs, by the said act required, any thing therein to the contrary hereof notwithstanding. *Provided,* that any alien, who was residing within the limits, and under the jurisdiction of the United States, before . . . [January 29, 1795,] . . . may within one year after the passing of this act — and any alien who shall have made the declaration of his intention to become a citizen of the United States, in conformity to the provisions of the act [of Jan. 29, 1795], may, within four years after having made the declaration aforesaid, be admitted to become a citizen, in the manner prescribed by the said act, upon his making proof that he has resided five years, at least, within the limits, and under the jurisdiction of the United States. *And provided also,* that no alien, who shall be a native, citizen, denizen or subject of any nation or state with whom the United States shall be at war, at the time of his application, shall be then admitted to become a citizen of the United States.

. . . .

Section 4. And be it further enacted, That all white persons, aliens, (accredited foreign ministers, consuls, or agents, their families and domestics, excepted) who, after the passing of this act, shall continue to reside, or who shall arrive, or come to reside in any port or place within the territory of the United States, shall be reported, if free, and of the age of twenty-one years, by themselves, or being under the age of twenty-one years, or holden in service, by their parent, guardian, master or mistress in whose care they shall be, to the clerk of the district court of the district, if living within ten miles of the port or place, in which their residence or arrival shall be, and otherwise, to the collector of such port or place, or some officer or other person there, or nearest thereto, who shall be authorized by the President of the United States, to register aliens. . . .

Section 5. And be it further enacted, That every alien who shall continue to reside, or who shall arrive, as aforesaid, of whom a report is required as aforesaid, who shall refuse or neglect to make such report, and to receive a certificate thereof, shall forfeit and pay the sum of two dollars; and any justice of the peace, or other civil magistrate, who has authority to require surety of the peace, shall and may, on complaint to him made thereof, cause such alien to be brought before him, there to give surety of the peace and good behavior during his residence within the United States, or for such term as the justice or other magistrate shall deem reasonable, and until a report and registry of such alien shall be made, and a certificate thereof, received as aforesaid; and in failure of such surety, such alien shall and may be committed to the common goal, and shall be there held, until the order which the justice or magistrate shall and may reasonably make, in the premises, shall be performed. And every person, whether alien, or other, having the care of any alien or aliens, under the age of twenty-one years, or of any white alien holden in service, who shall refuse and neglect to make report thereof, as aforesaid, shall forfeit the sum of two dollars, for each and every such minor or servant, monthly, and every month, until a report and registry, and a certificate thereof, shall be had, as aforesaid.

. . . .

Alien Act

Section 1. Be it enacted . . . That it shall be lawful for the President of the United States at any time during the continuance of this act, to *order* all such *aliens* as he shall judge dangerous to the peace and safety of the United States, or shall have reasonable grounds to suspect are concerned in any treasonable or secret machinations against the government thereof, to depart out of the territory of the United States, within such time as shall be expressed in such order, which order shall be served on such alien by delivering him a copy thereof, or leaving the same at his usual abode, and returned to the office of the Secretary of State, by the marshal or other person to whom the same shall be directed. And in case any alien, so ordered to depart, shall be found at large within the United States after the time limited in such order for his departure, and not having obtained a *license* from the President to reside therein, or having obtained such *license* shall not have conformed thereto, every such alien shall, on conviction thereof, be imprisoned for a term not exceeding three years, and shall never after be admitted to become a citizen of the United States. *Provided always, and be it further enacted,* that if any alien so ordered to depart shall prove to the satisfaction of the President, by evidence to be taken before such person or persons as the President shall direct, who are for that purpose hereby authorized to administer oaths, that no injury or danger to the United States will arise from suffering such alien to reside therein, the President may grant a *license* to such alien to remain within the United States for such time as he shall judge proper, and at such place as he may designate. And the President may also require of such alien to enter into a bond to the United States, in such penal sum as he may direct, with one or more sufficient sureties to the satisfaction of the person authorized by the President to take the same, conditioned for the good behavior of such alien during his residence in the United States, and not violating his license, which license the President may revoke, whenever he shall think proper.

Section 2. And be it further enacted, That it shall be lawful for the President of the United States, whenever he may deem it necessary for the public safety, to order to be removed out of the territory thereof, any alien who may or shall be in prison in pursuance of this act; and to cause to be arrested and sent out of the United States such of those aliens as shall have been ordered to depart therefrom and shall not have obtained a license as aforesaid, in all cases where, in the opinion of the President, the public safety requires a speedy removal. And if any alien so removed or sent out of the United States by the President shall voluntarily return thereto, unless by permission of the President of the United States, such alien on conviction thereof, shall be imprisoned so long as, in the opinion of the President, the public safety may require.

. . . .

Section 5. And be it further enacted, That it shall be lawful for any alien who may be ordered to be removed from the United States, by virtue of this act, to take with him such part of his goods, chattels, or other property, as he may find convenient; and all property left in the United States by any alien, who may be removed, as aforesaid, shall be, and remain subject to his order and disposal, in the same manner as if this act had not been passed.

. . . .

Alien Enemies Act

Be it enacted . . . That whenever there shall be a declared war between the United States and any foreign nation or government, or any invasion or predatory incursion shall be perpetrated, attempted, or threatened against the territory of the United States, by any foreign nation or government, and the President of the United States shall make public proclamation of the event, all natives, citizens, denizens, or subjects of the hostile nation or government, being males of the age of fourteen years and upwards, who shall be within the United States, and not actually naturalized, shall be liable to be apprehended, restrained, secured and removed, as alien enemies. And the President of the United States shall be, and he is hereby authorized, in any event, as aforesaid, by his proclamation thereof, or other public act, to direct the conduct to be observed, on the part of the United States, towards the aliens who shall become liable, as aforesaid; the manner and degree of the restraint to which they shall be subject, and in what cases, and upon what security their residence shall be permitted, and to provide for the removal of those, who, not being permitted to reside within the United States, shall refuse or neglect to depart therefrom; and to establish any other regulations which shall be found necessary in the premises and for the public safety. Provided, that aliens resident within the United States, who shall become liable as enemies, in the manner aforesaid, and who shall not be chargeable with actual hostility, or other crime against the public safety, shall be allowed, for the recovery, disposal, and removal of their goods and effects, and for their departure, the full time which is, or shall be stipulated by any treaty, where any shall have been between the United States, and the hostile nation or government, of which they shall be natives, citizens, denizens or subjects; and when no such treaty shall have existed, the President of the United States may ascertain and declare such reasonable time as may be consistent with the public safety, and according to the dictates of humanity and national hospitality.

. . . .

Sedition Act

Section 1. Be it enacted . . . That if any persons shall unlawfully combine or conspire together, with intent to oppose any measure or measures of the government of the United States, which are or shall be directed by proper authority, or to impede the operation of any law of the United States, or to intimidate or prevent any person holding a place or office in or under the government of the United States, from undertaking, performing or executing his trust or duty; and if any person or persons, with intent as aforesaid, shall counsel, advise or attempt to procure any insurrection, riot, unlawful assembly, or combination, whether such conspiracy, threatening, counsel, advice, or attempt shall have the proposed effect or not, he or they shall be deemed guilty of a high misdemeanor, and on conviction, before any court of the United States having jurisdiction thereof, shall be punished by a fine not exceeding five thousand dollars, and by imprisonment during a term not less than six months nor exceeding five years; and further, at the discretion of the court may be holden to find sureties for his good behavior in such sum, and for such time, as the said court may direct.

Section 2. And be it further enacted, That if any person shall write, print, utter or publish, or shall cause or procure to be written, printed, uttered or published, or shall knowingly and willingly assist or aid in writing, printing, uttering or publishing any false, scandalous and malicious writing or writings against the government of the United States, or either house of the Congress of the United States, or the President of the United States, with intent to defame the said government, or either house of the said Congress, or the said President, or to bring them, or either of them, into contempt or disrepute; or to excite against them, or either or any of them, the hatred of the good people of the United States, or to stir up sedition within the United States, or to excite any unlawful combinations therein, for opposing or resisting any law of the United States, or any act of the President of the United States, done in pursuance of any such law, or of the powers in him vested by the constitution of the United States, or to resist, oppose, or defeat any such law or act, or to aid, encourage or abet any hostile designs of any foreign nation against the United States, their people or government, then such person, being thereof convicted before any court of the United States having jurisdiction thereof, shall be punished by a fine not exceeding two thousand dollars, and by imprisonment not exceeding two years.

Section 3. And be it further enacted and declared, That if any person shall be prosecuted under this act, for the writing or publishing any libel aforesaid, it shall be lawful for the defendant, upon the trial of the cause, to give in evidence in his defense, the truth of the matter contained in the publication charged as a libel. And the jury who shall try the cause shall have the right to determine the law and the fact, under the direction of the court as in other cases.

CHOOSE THE CORRECT ANSWER

Write the letter that best completes the statement or answers the question.

1. An alien is a person who (*a*) is a traitor, (*b*) cannot become a citizen, (*c*) is not yet a citizen, (*d*) must leave the United States.   1._____

2. Under the Alien Act, a person could not become a citizen until he had lived in the United States (*a*) 2 years, (*b*) 5 years, (*c*) 9 years, (*d*) 14 years.   2._____

3. Each alien had to have (*a*) a job, (*b*) a license to remain in the United States, (*c*) a return ticket to his own country, (*d*) two citizens who would be responsible for him.
                                                                       3._____

4. An alien could be forced to leave the country at the orders of (*a*) the President, (*b*) any court, (*c*) Congress, (*d*) a petition signed by his neighbors.   4._____

5. Sedition is best defined as (*a*) disobeying laws, (*b*) trying to defeat the political party in power, (*c*) treason, (*d*) attempted murder of an official.   5._____

6. The Sedition Act could punish those who (*a*) voted against a member of Congress, (*b*) made a speech criticizing Congress, (*c*) wrote a letter of complaint to a Congressman, (*d*) bought a newspaper that criticized Congress.   6._____

7. A person accused under the Sedition Act (*a*) could defend himself in court, (*b*) was held in jail for five years, (*c*) could be excused if he paid a fine, (*d*) was forced to leave the United States.   7._____

8. The Sedition Act was really directed against (*a*) the French, (*b*) gossip, (*c*) organized rebellion, (*d*) political opposition.

8._____

9. The Sedition Act prevented people from (*a*) running for political office, (*b*) writing for newspapers, (*c*) trying to amend the Constitution, (*d*) opposing any law of the United States.

9._____

10. Under the Alien Act, all aliens had to (*a*) leave the country, (*b*) register, (*c*) become citizens, (*d*) pay a monthly fee of two dollars.

10._____

THOUGHT QUESTIONS

1. (*a*) For what reasons did the Federalists pass the Alien and Sedition Acts?

   (*b*) State the chief provisions of the four laws passed in 1798.

2. *The Sedition Act violated the rights guaranteed by the Constitution.* Explain this statement in specific detail.

The Kentucky and Virginia Resolutions 1798-1799

* * * * *The political nature of the Alien and* Sedition Acts soon became clear. There were a number of convictions under the Sedition Act, which was being used to crush the growing opposition to the Federalists. Jefferson's followers, who controlled the state legislatures of Virginia and Kentucky, determined to make a public attack on the Acts. In Kentucky, John Breckenridge prepared a set of resolutions which Jefferson himself had drafted. In Virginia, James Madison, Jefferson's close friend, neighbor, and second-in-command, prepared a similar set of resolutions.

The resolutions described the Constitution as a compact between equal states to form a common government with definitely prescribed powers. All powers not specifically given to the federal government were reserved for the states.

The resolutions protested against the government's obvious violation of the First Amendment's guarantee of free speech and free press in the Sedition Act. They protested against the dictatorial and discriminatory powers given to the President to act as he saw fit against critics of the government. They insisted that when Congress took to itself more authority than the states meant it to have, the individual states had the right to decide whether its laws should be obeyed.

Copies of the resolutions were sent to the governors of the other states in the hope that their legislatures would favor them. Seven Northern states replied unfavorably. However, a great deal of publicity had been given to the Federalists' abuse of civil rights. The doctrine of states' rights became an important part of the presidential campaign which elected Jefferson in 1800. The Federalist Party disappeared as the nation's dominant political group.

Kentucky Resolutions (1798)

I. *Resolved,* that the several States composing the United States of America, are not united on the principle of unlimited submission to their general government; but that by compact under the style of title of a Constitution for the United States and of amendments thereto, they constituted a general government for special purposes, delegated to that government certain definite powers, reserving each State to itself, the residuary mass of right to their own self-govern-

THE GOVERNMENT IS TOO STRONG

THE GOVERNMENT IS NOT STRONG ENOUGH

ANTI-FEDERALISTS

JEFFERSON

HAMILTON

FEDERALISTS

THE UNITED STATES CONSTITUTION

Conflicting Groups	Disagreements	Compromises
Large States vs. **Small States**	1. Virginia Plan wanted representation in Congress to be based on population. 2. New Jersey Plan wanted equal representation of states.	The *Great Compromise*, or *Connecticut Compromise*, provided for a 2-house legislature, the upper house, or Senate, to be based on equal representation for all the states, and a lower house, of Representatives, to be based on population.
Southern States vs. **Northern States**	1. Southern states wanted slaves to be counted as part of the population. 2. Northern states objected to this plan.	The *Three-Fifths Compromise* provided that five slaves would be counted for three whites for purposes of representation and taxation.
Slave States vs. **Free States**	1. Slave states wanted to bring in as many slaves as they wanted. 2. Free states objected to this and wanted to limit the importation of slaves.	The *Slave Trade Compromise* permitted the importation of slaves with no interference for 20 years, but a head tax of $10 per slave could be levied.
Agricultural States vs. **Manufacturing States**	1. Agricultural states were against giving Congress the power to tax imports and exports. 2. Manufacturing states favored giving Congress the power to levy tariffs.	The *Commerce Compromise* stated that Congress, by a majority vote, could tax imports but could not tax exports.
Aristocracy vs. **Democrats**	1. Aristocrats favored indirect election of the President, some wanting him elected for life. 2. Democrats favored his direct election for a single term.	The President was to be elected by an Electoral College for a 4-year term and was eligible for re-election; the Senate was to be elected indirectly by state legislatures; the House directly by the people.

ment; and that whensoever the general government assumes undelegated powers, its acts are unauthoritative, void, and of no force. That to this compact each State acceded as a State, and is an integral party, its co-States forming, as to itself, the other party. That the government created by this compact was not made the exclusive or final judge of the extent of the powers delegated to itself; since that would have made its discretion, and not the Constitution, the measure of its powers; but that as in all other cases of compact among parties having no common Judge, each party has an equal right to judge for itself, as well of infractions as of the mode and measure of redress.

II. *Resolved*, that the Constitution of the United States having delegated to Congress a power to punish treason, counterfeiting the securities and current coin of the United States, piracies and felonies committed on the high seas, and offenses against the laws of nations, and no other crimes whatever, and it being true as a general principle, and one of the amendments to the Constitution having also declared "that the powers not delegated to the United States by the Constitution, nor prohibited by it to the States, are reserved to the States respectively, or to the people," therefore also . . . their acts which assume to create, define, or punish crimes other than those enumerated in the Constitution, are altogether void and of no force, and that the power to create, define, and punish such other crimes is reserved, and of right appertains solely and exclusively to the respective States, each within its own Territory.

III. *Resolved,* that it is true as a general principle, and is also expressly declared by one of the amendments to the Constitution that "the powers not delegated to the United States by the Constitution, nor prohibited by it to the States, are reserved to the States respectively or to the people;" and that no power over the freedom of religion, freedom of speech, or freedom of the press being delegated to the United States by the Constitution, nor prohibited by it to the States, all lawful powers respecting the same did of right remain, and were reserved to the States, or to the people. That thus was manifested their determination to retain to themselves the right of judging how far the licentiousness of speech and of the press may be abridged without lessening their useful freedom, and how far those abuses which cannot be separated from their use should be tolerated rather than the use be destroyed; and thus also they guarded against all abridgment by the United States of the freedom of religious opinions and exercises, and retained to themselves the right of protecting the same, as this State, by a law passed on the general demand of its citizens, had already protected them from all human restraint or interference. And that in addition to this general principle and express declaration, another and more special provision has been made by one of the amendments to the Constitution which expressly declares, that "Congress shall make no law respecting an establishment of religion, or prohibiting the free exercise thereof, or abridging the freedom of speech, or of the press," thereby guarding in the same sentence, and under the same words, the freedom of religion, of speech, and of the press, insomuch, that whatever violates either, throws down the sanctuary which covers the others, and that libels, falsehoods, defamation equally with heresy and false religion, are withheld from the cognizance of Federal tribunals. That therefore . . . [the Sedition Act] . . . which does abridge the freedom of the press, is not law, but is altogether void and of no effect.

IV. *Resolved,* that alien friends are under the jurisdiction and protection of the laws of the State wherein they are; that no power over them has been delegated to the United States, nor prohibited to the individual States distinct from their power over citizens; and it being true as a general principle, and one of the amendments to the Constitution having also declared that "the powers not delegated to the United States by the Constitution, nor prohibited by it to the States, are reserved to the States respectively, or to the people," the . . . [Alien Act of June 22, 1798] . . . which assumes power over alien friends not delegated by the Constitution, is not law, but is altogether void and of no force.

V. *Resolved,* that in addition to the general principle as well as the express declaration, that powers not delegated are reserved, another and more special provision inserted in the Constitution from abundant caution has declared, "that the migration or importation of such persons as any of the States now existing shall think proper to admit, shall not be prohibited by the Congress prior to the year 1808." That this Commonwealth does admit the migration of alien friends described as the subject of the said act concerning aliens; that a provision against prohibiting their migration is a provision against all acts equivalent thereto, or it would be nugatory; that to remove them when migrated is equivalent to a prohibition of their migration, and is therefore contrary to the said provision of the Constitution, and void.

VI. *Resolved,* that the imprisonment of a person under the protection of the laws of this Commonwealth on his failure to obey the simple order of the President to depart out of the United States, as is undertaken by the said act entitled "An act concerning aliens," is contrary to the Constitution, one amendment to which has provided, that "no person shall be deprived of liberty without due process of law," and that another having provided "that in all criminal prosecutions, the accused shall enjoy the right to a public trial by an impartial jury, to be informed of the nature and cause of the accusation, to be confronted with the witnesses against him, to have compulsory process for obtaining witnesses in his favor, and to have the assistance of counsel for his defense," the same act undertaking to authorize the President to remove a person out of the United States who is under the protection of the law, on his own suspicion, without accusation, without jury, without public trial, without confrontation of the witnesses against him, without having witnesses in his favor, without defense, without counsel, is contrary to these provisions also of the Constitution, is therefore not law, but utterly void and of no force. That transferring the power of judging any person who is under the protection of the laws, from the courts to the President of the United States, as is undertaken by the same act concerning aliens, is against the article of the Constitution which provides, that "the judicial power of the United States shall be vested in courts, the judges of which shall hold their offices during good behavior," and that the said act is void for that reason also; and it is further to be noted, that this transfer of judiciary power is to that magistrate of the general government who already possesses all the executive, and a qualified negative in all the legislative powers.

. . . .

VIII. *Resolved,* that the preceding Resolutions be transmitted to the Senators and Representatives in Congress from this Commonwealth, who are hereby enjoined to present the same to their respective Houses, and to use their best endeavors to procure, at the next session of Congress, a repeal of the aforesaid unconstitutional and obnoxious acts.

IX. *Resolved,* lastly, that the Governor of this Commonwealth be, and is hereby authorized and requested to communicate the preceding Resolutions to the Legislatures of the several States, to assure them that this Commonwealth considers Union for specified National purposes, and particularly for those specified in their late Federal Compact, to be friendly to the peace, happiness, and prosperity of all the States; that faithful to that compact according to the plain intent and meaning in which it was understood and acceded to by the several parties, it is sincerely anxious for its preservation; that it does also believe, that to take from the States all the powers of self-government, and transfer them to a general and consolidated government, without regard to the special delegations and reservations solemnly agreed to in that compact, is not for the peace, happiness, or prosperity of these States. And that, therefore, this Commonwealth is determined, as it doubts not its co-States are, tamely to submit to undelegated and consequently unlimited powers in no man or body of men on earth; that if the acts before specified should stand, these conclusions would flow from them; that the general government may place any act they think proper on the list of crimes and punish it themselves, whether enumerated or not enumerated by the Constitution as cognizable by them; that they may transfer its cognizance to the President or any other person, who may himself be the accuser, counsel, judge, and jury, whose suspicions may be the evidence, his order the sentence, his officer the executioner, and his breast the sole record of the transaction; that a very numerous and valuable description of the inhabitants of these States being by this precedent reduced as outlaws to the absolute dominion of one man, and the barrier of the Constitution thus swept away from us all, no rampart now remains against the passions and the powers of a majority of Congress, to protect from a like exportation or other more grievous punishment the minority of the same body, the legislatures, judges, governors, and counselors of the States, nor their other peaceable inhabitants who may venture to reclaim the constitutional rights and liberties of the State and people, or who for other causes, good or bad, may be obnoxious to the views or marked by the suspicions of the President, or be thought dangerous to his or their elections or other interests, public or personal; that the friendless alien has indeed been selected as the safest subject of a first experiment, but the citizen will soon follow, or rather has already followed; for, already has a sedition act marked him as its prey; that these and successive acts of the same character, unless arrested on the threshold, may tend to drive these States into revolution and blood, and will furnish new calumnies against Republican governments, and new pretexts for those who wish it to be believed, that man cannot be governed but by a rod of iron; that it would be a dangerous delusion were a confidence in the men of our choice to silence our fears for the safety of our rights; that confidence is everywhere the parent of despotism; free government is founded in jealousy and not in confidence; it is jealousy and not confidence which prescribes limited Constitutions to bind down those whom we are obliged to trust with power; that our Constitution has accordingly fixed the limits to which and no further our confidence may go; and let the honest advocate of confidence read the alien and sedition acts, and say if the Constitution has not been wise in fixing limits to the government it created, and whether we should be wise in destroying those limits; let him say what the government is if it be not a tyranny, which the men of our choice have conferred on the President, and the President of our choice has assented to and accepted over the friendly strangers, to whom the mild spirit of our country and its laws had pledged hospitality and protection; that the men of our choice have more respected the bare suspicions of the President than the solid rights of innocence, the claims of justification, the sacred force of truth, and the forms and substance of law and justice. In questions of power then let no more be heard of confidence in man, but bind him down from mischief by the claims of the Constitution. That this Commonwealth does, therefore, call on its co-States for an expression of their sentiments on the acts concerning aliens, and for the punishment of certain crimes herein before specified, plainly declaring whether these acts are or are not authorized by the Federal Compact. And it doubts not that their sense will be so announced as to prove their attachment unaltered to limited government, whether general or particular, and that the rights and liberties of their co-States will be exposed to no dangers by remaining embarked on a common bottom with their own. That they will concur with this Commonwealth in considering the said acts so palpably against the Constitution as to amount to an undisguised declaration, that the compact is not meant to be the measure of the powers of the general government, but that it will proceed in the exercise over these States of all powers whatsoever. That they will view this as seizing the rights of the States and consolidating them in the hands of the general government with a power assumed to bind the States (not merely in cases made Federal) but in all cases whatsoever, by laws made, not with their consent, but by others against their consent. That this would be to surrender the form of government we have chosen, and to live under one deriving its powers from its own will, and not from our authority; and that the co-States, recurring to their natural right in cases not made Federal, will concur in declaring these acts void and of no force, and will each unite with this Commonwealth in requesting their repeal at the next session of Congress.

Virginia Resolutions (1789)

Resolved, That the General Assembly of Virginia doth unequivocally express a firm resolution to maintain and defend the Constitution of the United States, and the Constitution of this State, against every aggression either foreign or domestic; and that they will support the Government of the United States in all measures warranted by the former.

That this Assembly most solemnly declares a warm attachment to the Union of the States, to maintain which it pledges all its powers; and that, for this end, it is their duty to watch over and oppose every infraction of those principles which constitute the only basis of that Union, because a faithful observance of them can alone secure its existence and the public happiness.

That this Assembly doth explicitly and peremptorily declare that it views the powers of the Federal Government as resulting from the compact to which the States are parties, as limited by the plain sense and intention of the instrument constituting that compact; as no further valid than they are authorized by the grants enumerated in that compact; and that, in case of a deliberate, palpable, and dangerous exercise of other powers not granted by the said compact, the States, who are parties thereto, have the right and are in duty bound to interpose for arresting the progress of the evil, and for maintaining within their respective limits the authorities, rights, and liberties appertaining to them.

That the General Assembly doth also express its deep regret, that a spirit has in sundry instances been manifested by the Federal Government to enlarge its powers by forced constructions of the constitutional charter which defines them; and that indications have appeared of a design to expound certain general phrases (which, having been copied from the very limited grant of powers in the former Articles of Confederation, were the less liable to be misconstrued) so as to destroy the meaning and effect of the particular enumeration which necessarily explains and limits the general phrases; and so as to consolidate the States, by degrees, into one sovereignty, the obvious tendency and inevitable consequence of which would be to transform the present republican system of the United States into an absolute, or, at best, a mixed monarchy.

That the General Assembly doth particularly protest against the palpable and alarming infractions of the Constitution in the two late cases of the "Alien and Sedition Acts," passed at the last session of Congress; the first of which exercises a power nowhere delegated to the Federal Government, and which, by uniting legislative and judicial powers to those of [the] executive, subvert the general principles of free government, as well as the particular organization and positive provisions of the Federal Constitution; and the other of which acts exercises, in like manner, a power not delegated by the Constitution, but, on the contrary, expressly and positively forbidden by one of the amendments thereto, — a power which, more than any other, ought to produce universal alarm, because it is levelled against the right of freely examining public characters and measures, and of free communication among the people thereon, which has ever been justly deemed the only effectual guardian of every other right.

That this State having by its Convention which ratified the Federal Constitution expressly declared that, among other essential rights, "the liberty of conscience and of the press cannot be cancelled, abridged, restrained or modified by any authority of the United States," and from its extreme anxiety to guard these rights from every possible attack of sophistry or ambition, having, with other States, recommended an amendment for that purpose, which amendment was in due time annexed to the Constitution, — it would mark a reproachful inconsistency and criminal degeneracy, if an indifference were now shown to the palpable violation of one of the rights thus declared and secured, and to the establishment of a precedent which may be fatal to the other.

That the good people of this Commonwealth, having ever felt and continuing to feel the most sincere affection for their brethren of the other States, the truest anxiety for establishing and perpetuating the union of all and the most scrupulous fidelity to that Constitution, which is the pledge of mutual friendship, and the instrument of mutual happiness, [the General Assembly doth solemnly appeal to the like dispositions of the other States, in confidence that they will concur with this Commonwealth in declaring, as it does hereby declare, that the acts aforesaid are unconstitutional; and that the necessary and proper measures will be taken by each for co-operating with this State, in maintaining unimpaired the authorities, rights, and liberties reserved to the States respectively, or to the people.

.   .   .   .

Kentucky Resolutions (1799)

.   .   .   .

The representatives of the good people of this Commonwealth, in General Assembly convened, having maturely considered the answers of sundry States in the Union, to their resolutions passed the last session, respecting certain unconstitutional laws of Congress, commonly called the Alien and Sedition Laws, would be faithless, indeed, to themselves and to those they represent, were they silently to acquiesce in the principles and doctrines attempted to be maintained in all those answers, that of Virginia only excepted.

Resolved, That this Commonwealth considers the Federal Union, upon the terms and for the purposes specified in the late compact, conducive to the liberty and happiness of the several States; that it does now unequivocally declare its attachment to the Union, and to that compact, agreeably to its obvious and real intention, and will be among the last to seek its dissolution; that if those who administer the General Government be permitted to transgress the limits fixed by that compact, by a total disregard to the special delegations of power therein contained, an annihilation of the State Governments, and the creation upon their ruins of a General Consolidated Government, will be the inevitable consequence; that the principle and construction contended for by sundry of the state legislatures, that the General Government is the exclusive judge of the extent of the powers delegated to it, stop nothing [short] of *despotism* — since the discretion of those who administer the government, and not the *Constitution,* would be the measure of their powers; that the several states who formed that instrument being sovereign and independent, have the unquestionable right to judge of the infraction; and, *that a Nullification by those sovereignties, of all unauthorized acts done under color of that instrument is the rightful remedy;* that this Commonwealth does, under the most deliberate reconsideration, declare, that the said Alien and Sedition Laws are, in their opinion, palpable violations of the said Constitution; and, however cheerfully it may be disposed to surrender its opinion to a majority of its sister states, in matters of ordinary or doubtful policy, yet, in no momentous regulations like the present, which so vitally wound the best rights of the citizen, it would consider a silent acquiescence as highly criminal; that although this Commonwealth, as a party to the federal compact, will bow to the laws of the Union, yet, it does, at the same [time] declare, that it will not now, or ever hereafter, cease to oppose in a constitutional manner, every attempt at what quarter soever offered, to violate that compact. And, finally, in order that no pretext or arguments may be drawn from a supposed acquiescence, on the part of this Commonwealth in the constitutionality of those laws, and be thereby used as precedents for similar future violations of the Federal compact — this Commonwealth does now enter against them its solemn PROTEST.

TRUE OR FALSE?

Write T *if the statement is correct; write* F *if it is false.*

_____1. The Kentucky and Virginia Resolutions were prepared by Jefferson and Madison.

_____2. Every one of the other state legislatures supported the ideas expressed in the Resolutions.

_____3. One of the Kentucky Resolutions favored the nullification of laws which gave the federal government too much power.

_____4. The Resolutions held that the Constitution was a compact.

_____5. According to the Resolutions, the federal government had the power to control aliens in whatever way it decided.

_____6. The Resolutions held that Congress could not limit freedom of speech unless the states approved.

_____7. The Resolutions agreed that Congress could define all crimes which should be punished by the federal government.

_____8. The Resolutions argued that the Alien and Sedition Acts gave too much power to the President.

_____9. The political party responsible for the Alien and Sedition Acts was the Federalist Party led by Thomas Jefferson.

_____10. The Virginia Resolutions stated the fear that laws such as the Alien and Sedition Acts could change our country into a monarchy.

THOUGHT QUESTIONS

1. Explain the reasons for which the Kentucky and Virginia Resolutions were written.

2. How were the Resolutions important:
   (*a*) at the time they were written?
   (*b*) in the later history of our country?

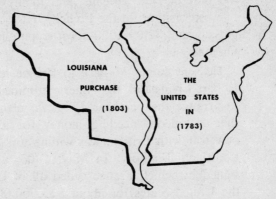

LOUISIANA

PURCHASE

(1803)

THE

UNITED STATES

IN

(1783)

The

Louisiana Purchase

1803

* * * * *The vast region called "Louisiana,"* now the west central section of the United States, was under French control as late as 1763. Then the French gave it to Spain. The Spanish held the land west of the Mississippi until 1800, when Napoleon took it back for France by the secret treaty of St. Idelfonso. Spanish officials continued in charge at the key city of New Orleans, which controlled all ocean-bound trade on the Mississippi. President Jefferson learned of this secret treaty and of Napoleon's plans to reestablish a great French empire in North America.

In 1802 the Spanish commander of New Orleans took away the right of Americans to store goods there until they were shipped abroad. To insure the right of Americans to use the Mississippi and the port of New Orleans, and to prevent the loss of western states to the French, Jefferson had Congress grant $2,000,000 for the purchase of New Orleans.

He sent James Monroe to France to work with Robert Livingston, the American minister in Paris, to arrange the purchase. The two men discovered that Napoleon, needing money for a threatened new war with Britain, was willing to sell all of the Louisiana Territory. In May, 1803, a treaty was signed by which France ceded all of Louisiana to the United States for about $15,000,000.

The acquisition of this enormous tract of land doubled the size of the United States. The people of Louisiana were given American citizenship, and the right to form states.

Jefferson's constitutional misgivings were settled 25 years later when the Supreme Court held the Louisiana Purchase constitutional.

Article I. Whereas, by the article the third of the treaty concluded at St. Idelfonso, the 9th Vendémiaire, an. 9 (1st October, 1800) between the First Consul of the French Republic and his Catholic Majesty, it was agreed as follows: "His Catholic Majesty promises and engages on his part, to cede to the French Republic, six months after the full and entire execution of the conditions and stipulations herein relative to his royal highness the duke of Parma, the colony or province of Louisiana with the same extent that it now has in the hands of Spain, and that it had when France possessed it; and such as it should be after the treaties subsequently entered into between Spain and other states." And *whereas,* in pursuance of the treaty, and particularly of the third article, the French Republic has an incontestible title to the domain and to the possession of the said territory.

The First Consul of the French Republic desiring to give to the United States a strong proof of his friendship, doth hereby cede to the said United States, in the name of the French Republic, forever and in full sovereignty, the said territory with all its rights and appurtenances, as fully and in the same manner as they have been acquired by the French Republic, in virtue of the above-mentioned treaty, concluded with his Catholic Majesty.

Article II. In the cession made by the preceding article are included the adjacent islands belonging to Louisiana, all public lots and squares, vacant lands, and all public buildings, fortifications, barracks, and other edifices which are not private property. The archives, papers, and documents relative to the domain and sovereignty of Louisiana, and its dependencies, will be left in the possession of the commissaries of the United States. . . .

Article III. The inhabitants of the ceded territory shall be incorporated in the Union of the United States, and admitted as soon as possible, according to the principles of the Federal constitution, to the enjoyment of all the rights, advantages and immunities of citizens of the United States; and in the mean time they shall be maintained and protected in the free enjoyment of their liberty, property, and the religion which they profess.

Article VI. The United States promise to execute such treaties and articles as may have been agreed between Spain and the tribes and nations of Indians, until, by mutual consent of the United States and the said tribes or nations, other suitable articles shall have been agreed upon.

Article VII. As it is reciprocally advantageous to the commerce of France and the United States to encourage the communication of both nations for a limited time in the country ceded by the present treaty, until general arrangements relative to the commerce of both nations may be agreed on; it has been agreed between the contracting parties, that the French ships coming directly from France or any of her colonies, loaded only with the produce and manufactures of France or her said colonies; and the ships of Spain coming directly from Spain or any of her colonies, loaded only with the produce or manufactures of Spain or her colonies, shall be admitted during the space of twelve years in the ports of New Orleans, and in all other legal ports of entry within the ceded territory, in the same manner as the ships of the United States coming directly from France or Spain, or any of their colonies, without being subject to any other or greater duty on merchandise, or other or greater tonnage than that paid by the citizens of the United States.

During the space of time above mentioned, no other nation shall have a right to the same privileges in the ports of the ceded territory. . . . it is however well understood that the object of the above article is to favor the manufactures, commerce, freight and navigation of France and of Spain, so far as relates to the importations that the French and Spanish shall make into the said ports of the United States, without in any sort affecting the regulations that the United States may make concerning the exportation of the produce and merchandise of the United States, or any right they may have to make such regulations.

Article VIII. In future and forever after the expiration of the twelve years, the ships of France shall be treated upon the footing of the most favored nations in the ports above mentioned.

FILL IN THE ANSWERS

Write the word or phrase which best completes the statement.

1. In 1803, the country that controlled Louisiana was _____.
2. This country had taken Louisiana from _____.
3. The total cost of Louisiana was approximately _____.
4. Napoleon's title in 1803 was _____.
5. The treaty protected the citizens of Louisiana, as well as the _____ who lived there.
6. The inhabitants of Louisiana were given the right to form _____.
7. French ships were given the right to trade freely in _____.
8. The country which received the same trading rights as France was _____.
9. The American minister to France in 1803 was _____.
10. Jefferson had at first intended to buy only _____.

THOUGHT QUESTIONS

1. Explain why the Louisiana Purchase has been called the greatest land bargain in history.
2. Select four aspects of our later history that were affected by the Louisiana Purchase, and show the effect of the Purchase on each.

Marbury vs Madison 1803

* * * * *Jefferson had won the election of* 1800, and the Federalist Party was being retired from national power. In the last days of his presidency, President Adams placed as many Federalists as he could in long-term government positions. A number of his so-called "midnight appointments" were for judges.

William Marbury was one of these judges. He waited for the Secretary of State to prepare and deliver his official commission as justice of the peace of the District of Columbia. But James Madison, an anti-Federalist, was appointed Secretary of State before Marbury was to receive his commission. Madison, with Jefferson's approval, refused to honor Adams' last-minute appointment of Marbury.

Marbury thereupon asked the Supreme Court for a "writ of mandamus," a court order compelling a public official (the Secretary of State) to carry out one of his duties.

Chief Justice Marshall, himself a Federalist, wrote the opinion in the case, which was not decided until 1803. He denied Marbury's request for the writ on the grounds that the Supreme Court did not have the power to issue it. He further declared that the law under which Marbury had been appointed was unconstitutional. He firmly believed that the Supreme Court alone had the power to decide on the constitutionality of laws passed by Congress.

The Supreme Court did not hold any other act of Congress unconstitutional until the Dred Scott decision, fifty years later.

(MARSHALL, C. J.) . . . In the order in which the Court has viewed this subject, the following questions have been considered and decided: 1st. Has the applicant a right to the commission he demands? 2d. If he has a right, and that right has been violated, do the laws of this country afford him a remedy? 3d. If they do afford him a remedy, is it a *mandamus* issuing from this Court? . . .

It is, then, the opinion of the Court: 1st. That by signing the commission of Mr. Marbury, the President of the United States appointed him a justice of peace for the county of Washington, in the district of Columbia; and that the seal of the United States, affixed thereto by the secretary of state, is conclusive testimony of the verity of the signature, and of the completion of the appointment; and that the appointment conferred on him a legal right to the office for the space of five years.

2d. That, having this legal title to the office, he has a consequent right to the commission; a refusal to deliver which is a plain violation of that right, for which the laws of his country afford him a remedy.

3. It remains to be inquired whether he is entitled to the remedy for which he applies? This depends on—1st, The nature of the writ applied for; and, 2d, The power of this Court.

[*Answering the first question, the court held it to be "a plain case for a* mandamus, *either to deliver the commission, or a copy of it from the record."*] . . . it only remains to be inquired, whether it can issue from this Court.

The act to establish the judicial courts of the United States authorizes the Supreme Court "to issue writs of *mandamus,* in cases warranted by the principles and usages of law, to any courts appointed, or persons holding office, under the authority of the United States."

The secretary of state, being a person holding an office under the authority of the United States, is precisely within the letter of the description; and if this court is not authorized to issue a writ of *mandamus* to such an officer, it must be because the law is unconstitutional, and therefore absolutely incapable of conferring the authority, and assigning the duties which its words purport to confer and assign.

The constitution vests the whole judicial power of the United States in one supreme court, and such inferior courts as congress shall, from time to time, ordain and establish. This power is expressly extended to all cases arising under the laws of the United States; and, consequently, in some form, may be exercised over the present case; because the right claimed is given by a law of the United States.

In the distribution of this power it is declared that "the supreme court shall have original jurisdiction, in all cases affecting ambassadors, other public ministers and consuls, and those in which a state shall be a party. In all other cases, the supreme court shall have appellate jurisdiction." . . .

If it had been intended to leave it in the discretion of the legislature to apportion the judicial power between the supreme and inferior courts, according to the will of that body, it would certainly have been useless to have proceeded further than to have defined the judicial power, and the tribunals in which it should be vested. The subsequent part of the section is mere surplusage—is entirely without meaning, if such is to be the construction. If congress remains at liberty to give this court appellate jurisdiction, where the constitution has declared their jurisdiction shall be original; and original jurisdiction where the constitution has declared it shall be appellate; the distribution of jurisdiction, made in the constitution, is form without substance.

Affirmative words are often, in their operation, negative of other objects than those affirmed; and in this case, a negative or exclusive sense must be given to them, or they have no operation at all.

It cannot be presumed, that any clause in the constitution is intended to be without effect; and, therefore, such a construction is inadmissible, unless the words require it. . . .

The authority, therefore, given to the supreme court, by the act establishing the judicial courts of the United States, to issue writs of *mandamus* to public officers, appears not to be warranted by the constitution; and it becomes necessary to inquire, whether a jurisdiction so conferred can be exercised.

The question, whether an act, repugnant to the constitution, can become the law of the land, is a question deeply interesting to the United States; but, happily, not of an intricacy proportioned to its interest. It seems only necessary to recognize certain principles supposed to have been long and well established, to decide it.

That the people have an original right to establish, for their future government, such principles, as, in their opinion, shall most conduce to their own happiness, is the basis on which the whole American fabric has been erected. The exercise of this original right is a very great exertion; nor can it, nor ought it, to be frequently repeated. The principles, therefore, so established, are deemed fundamental; and as the authority from which they proceed is supreme, and can seldom act, they are designed to be permanent.

This original and supreme will organizes the government, and assigns to different departments their respective powers. It may either stop here, or establish certain limits not to be transcended by those departments.

The government of the United States is of the latter description. The powers of the legislature are defined and limited; and that those limits may not be mistaken, or forgotten, the constitution is written. To what purpose are powers limited, and to what purpose is that limitation committed to writing, if these limits may, at any time, be passed by those intended to be restrained? The distinction between a government with limited and unlimited powers is abolished, if those limits do not confine the person on whom they are imposed, and if acts prohibited and acts allowed, are of equal obligation. It is a proposition too plain to be contested, that the constitution controls any legislative act repugnant to it; or, that the legislature may alter the constitution by an ordinary act.

Between these alternatives there is no middle ground. The constitution is either a superior paramount law, unchangeable by ordinary means, or it is on a level with ordinary legislative acts, and, like other acts, is alterable when the legislature shall please to alter it. If the former part of the alternative be true, then a legislative act, contrary to the constitution, is not law; if the latter part be true, then written constitutions are absurd attempts, on the part of the people, to limit a power, in its own nature, illimitable.

Certainly all those who have framed written constitutions contemplate them as forming the fundamental and paramount law of the nation, and consequently, the theory of every such government must be, that an act of the legislature, repugnant to the constitution, is void. This theory is essentially attached to a written constitution, and is, consequently, to be considered, by this court, as one of the fundamental principles of our society. It is not, therefore, to be lost sight of in the further consideration of this subject.

If any act of the legislature, repugnant to the constitution, is void, does it, notwithstanding its invalidity, bind the courts, and oblige them to give it effect? Or, in other words, though it be not law, does it constitute a rule as operative as if it was a law? This would be to overthrow in fact what was established in theory; and would seem, at first view, an absurdity too gross to be insisted on. It shall, however, receive a more attentive consideration.

It is emphatically the province and duty of the judicial department to say what the law is. Those who apply the rule to particular cases, must of necessity expound and interpret that rule. If two laws conflict with each other, the courts must decide on the operation of each.

So, if a law be in opposition to the constitution; if both the law and the constitution apply to a particular case, so that the court must either decide that case conformable to the law, disregarding the constitution; or conformable to the constitution, disregarding the law; the court must determine which of these conflicting rules governs the case. This is of the very essence of judicial duty. If, then, the courts are to regard the constitution, and the constitution is superior to any ordinary act of the legislature, the constitution, and not such ordinary act, must govern the case to which they both apply. . . .

There are many other parts of the constitution which serve to illustrate this subject. It is declared, that "no tax or duty shall be laid on articles exported from any state." Suppose a duty on the export of cotton, of tobacco, or of flour; and a suit instituted to recover it. Ought judgment to be rendered in such a case? Ought the judges to close their eyes on the constitution, and only see the law?

The constitution declares "that no bill of attainder or *ex post facto* law shall be passed." If, however, such a bill should be passed, and a person should be prosecuted under it; must the court condemn to death those victims whom the constitution endeavors to preserve?

"No person," says the constitution, "shall be convicted of treason, unless on the testimony of two witnesses to the same overt act, or on confession in open court." Here the language of the constitution is addressed especially to the courts. It prescribes, directly for them, a rule of evidence not to be departed from. If the legislature should change that rule, and declare one witness, or a confession out of court, sufficient for conviction, must the constitutional principle yield to the legislative act?

From these, and many other selections which might be made, it is apparent that the framers of the constitution contemplated that instrument as a rule for the government of courts, as well as of the legislature.

Why otherwise does it direct the judges to take an oath to support it? This oath certainly applies in an especial manner to their conduct in their official character. How immoral to impose it on them, if they were to be used as the instruments, and the knowing instruments, for violating what they swear to support!

The oath of office, too, imposed by the legislature, is completely demonstrative of the legislative opinion on this subject. It is in these words: "I do solemnly swear, that I will administer justice without respect to persons, and do equal right to the poor and to the rich; and that I will faithfully and impartially discharge all the duties incumbent on me as . . ., according to the best of my abilities and understanding, agreeably to the constitution and laws of the United States." Why does a judge swear to discharge his duties agreeably to the constitution of the United States, if that constitution forms no rule for his government? If it is closed upon him, and cannot be inspected by him? If such be the

CHIEF JUSTICE JOHN MARSHALL'S DECISIONS

1 Court should set aside Federal laws it considers unconstitutional.

2 Court should set aside State laws it considers unconstitutional.

3 Court should reverse State court decisions it thinks incorrect.

CONSTITUTION OF THE UNITED STATES

U.S. BANK

4 Constitution should be interpreted broadly.

real state of things, this is worse than solemn mockery. To prescribe, or to take this oath, becomes equally a crime.

It is also not entirely unworthy of observation, that in declaring what shall be the supreme law of the land, the constitution itself is first mentioned; and not the laws of the United States, generally, but those only which shall be made in pursuance of the constitution, have that rank.

Thus, the particular phraseology of the constitution of the United States confirms and strengthens the principle, supposed to be essential to all written constitutions, that a law repugnant to the constitution is void; and that courts, as well as other departments, are bound by that instrument.

The rule must be discharged [i.e., Marbury's request for a writ of *mandamus* is denied].

CHOOSE THE CORRECT ANSWER

Write the letter that best completes the statement or answers the question.

1. The decision in this case was written by (a) John Adams, (b) John Marshall, (c) William Marbury, (d) James Madison.

    1._____

2. Marbury asked for (a) damages, (b) back pay, (c) a court order, (d) his position on the Supreme Court.   2._____

3. This was the first case in which a federal law was held (a) unnecessary, (b) unfair, (c) unclear, (d) unconstitutional.

    3._____

4. A court which reviews the decisions of other courts is (a) a peace court, (b) a court of original jurisdiction, (c) an appellate court, (d) a national court.   4._____

5. The decision of a court is also called (a) a conviction, (b) an appeal, (c) a judgment, (d) a charge.   5._____

6. A defendant is protected by the rules of (a) evidence, (b) court debate, (c) judicial power, (d) police power.   6._____

7. The highest court of the land is (a) the President, (b) Congress, (c) the Supreme Court, (d) the Constitution. 7._____

THOUGHT QUESTIONS

1. Explain how *Marbury vs Madison* placed the Supreme Court on equal footing with the Executive and the Legislature.
2. The Supreme Court did not hold another act of Congress unconstitutional for more than 50 years. Why then was the *Marbury vs Madison* decision so important?

TROUBLE SPOTS LEADING TO WAR OF 1812

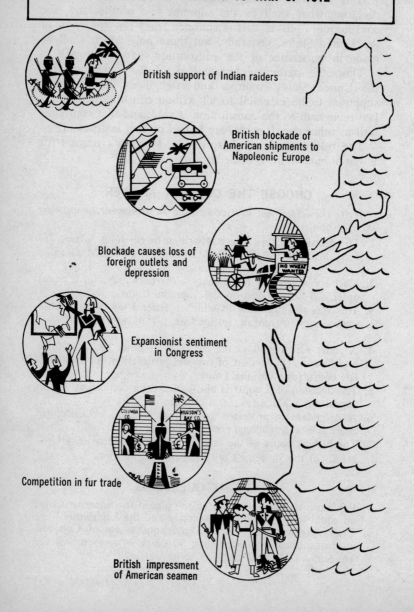

British support of Indian raiders

British blockade of American shipments to Napoleonic Europe

Blockade causes loss of foreign outlets and depression

Expansionist sentiment in Congress

Competition in fur trade

British impressment of American seamen

Madison's Declaration of War 1812

* * * *James Madison, who succeeded Jefferson* as President in 1809, found it increasingly difficult to avoid the pressure of war with England. On June 1, 1812, he sent a message to Congress listing the following major grounds for war: (1) impressment of American seamen; (2) violation of United States neutral rights; (3) blockade of American ports; (4) incitement of Indian attacks upon American settlements.

Congress approved a bill, which was signed by the President on June 18, declaring war upon Great Britain.

The language used by the United States in declaring war was established by Madison's declaration which marked the official beginning of the

War of 1812. Later declarations of war do not include references to letters of marque and reprisal which gave American privateers the right to seize enemy property. The growth of the United States Navy made such letters unnecessary.

An Act declaring War between the United Kingdom of Great Britain and Ireland and the Dependencies Thereof, and the United States of America and Their Territories.

Be it enacted . . . , That war be and the same is hereby declared to exist between the United Kingdom of Great Britain and Ireland and the dependencies thereof, and the United States of America and their territories; and that the President of the United States is hereby authorized to use the whole land and naval force of the United States to carry the same into effect, and to issue to private armed vessels of the United States commissions or letters of marque and general reprisal, in such form as he shall think proper, and under the seal of the United States, against the vessels, goods, and effects of the said United Kingdom of Great Britain and Ireland, and the subjects thereof.

FILL IN THE ANSWERS

Write the word or phrase which best completes the statement.

1. A war can be declared only by the American _____.
2. The declaration of war is issued by the _____.
3. The armed forces of the United States are under the command of the _____.
4. Letters of marque and reprisal were issued to ships which were called _____.
5. The War of 1812 was fought against _____.

THOUGHT QUESTIONS

1. Explain the role played in the second war between the United States and England by each of the following:
   (*a*) Tecumseh;
   (*b*) Captain Oliver Hazard Perry;
   (*c*) Henry Clay.
2. The War of 1812 gave us a national anthem. Explain this statement.

McCulloch vs Maryland 1819

BANK OF THE UNITED STATES

Provision of a sound paper currency

Safe place for public funds

Source of credit for business loans

TAX COLLECTOR

Financial agent for U.S. Government

* * * * *The First Bank of the United States,* though bitterly opposed, was established to assure a sound and uniform currency. When its charter expired in 1811, there were 88 state-chartered banks in the country. President Madison asked Congress to charter a Second Bank of the United States.

Many states opposed a strong national bank, preferring the easier money and credit policies of state-chartered banks. The State of Maryland, wanting to raise revenue to help its state banks and to weaken the Bank of the United States, passed a law taxing the notes of all but Maryland-chartered banks.

Speaking for the Bank, James W. McCulloch, secretary of the Baltimore branch of the Bank of the United States, refused to pay Maryland's tax on its operations. The state sued him as the Bank's responsible official, and won in the lower federal courts. The case was appealed to the Supreme Court.

Chief Justice Marshall's very important decision held that no state had the power to tax the national government or any of its agencies. "The power to tax involves the power to destroy," he said, and the supremacy of the national government prevented any state from taxing its activities. The decision thus held the Maryland taxing law unconstitutional.

Marshall also answered the question: "Could the national government pass laws which dealt with activities not specifically listed in the Constitution?" He held that it could, provided such laws were "necessary and proper" in carrying out any of its enumerated powers. This decision did much to strengthen the "elastic clause" in the Constitution, and to strengthen the role of the Supreme Court as the final voice in cases involving the Constitution. Excerpts of this decision are given here.

. . . The first question made in this cause is, has Congress power to incorporate a bank? . . .

In discussing this question, the counsel for the State of Maryland have deemed it of some importance, in the construction of the constitution, to consider that instrument not as emanating from the people, but as the act of sovereign and independent States. . . .

It would be difficult to sustain this proposition. The convention which framed the constitution was indeed elected by the state legislatures. But the instrument, when it came from their hands, was a mere proposal, without obligation, or pretensions to it. It was reported to the then existing Congress of the United States, with a request that it might "be submitted to a convention of delegates, chosen in each state, by the people thereof, under the recommendation of its legislature, for their assent and ratification." This mode of proceeding was adopted; and by the Convention, by Congress, and by the state legislatures, the instrument was submitted to the people. They acted upon it, in the only manner in which they can act safely, effectively, and wisely on such a subject, by assembling in convention. It is true, they assembled in their several states; and where else should they have assembled? No political dreamer was ever wild enough to think of breaking down the lines which separate the states, and of compounding the American people into one common mass. Of consequence, when they act, they act in their states. But the measures they adopt do not, on that account cease to be the measures of the people themselves, or become the measures of the state governments.

The government of the Union, then is emphatically and truly a government of the people. In form and in substance it emanates from them, its powers are granted by them, and are to be exercised directly on them, and for their benefit.

This government is acknowledged by all to be one of enumerated powers. But the question respecting the extent of the powers actually granted is perpetually arising, and will probably continue to arise, as long as our system shall exist.

If any one proposition could command the universal assent of mankind, we might expect it would be this—that the government of the Union, though limited in its powers, is supreme within its sphere of action. This would seem to result necessarily from its nature. It is the government of all; its powers are delegated by all; it represents all, and acts for all. Though any one state may be willing to control its operations, no state is willing to allow others to control them. The nation, on those subjects on which it can act, must necessarily bind its component parts. But this question is not left to mere reason; the people have, in express terms, decided it, by saying, "this constitution, and the laws of the United States, which shall be made in pursuance thereof," "shall be the supreme law of the land," and by requiring that the members of the state legislatures, and the officers of the executive and judicial departments of the states shall take the oath of fidelity to it.

The government of the United States, then, though limited in its powers, is supreme; and its laws, when made in pursuance of the constitution, form the supreme law of the land, "anything in the constitution or laws of any state, to the contrary, notwithstanding."

Among the enumerated powers, we do not find that of establishing a bank or creating a corporation. But there is no phrase in the instrument which, like the articles of confederation, excludes incidental or implied powers; and which requires that everything granted shall be expressly and minutely described. Even the 10th amendment, which was framed for the purpose of quieting the excessive jealousies which had been excited, omits the word "expressly," and declares only that the powers "not delegated to the United States, nor prohibited to the States, are reserved to the States or to the people;" thus leaving the question whether the particular power, which may become the subject of contest, has been delegated to the one government, or prohibited to the other, to depend on a fair construction of the whole instrument. The men who drew and adopted this amendment, had experienced the embarrassments resulting from the insertion of this word in the articles of confederation, and probably omitted it to avoid those embarrassments. A constitution, to contain an accurate detail of all the subdivisions of which its great powers will admit, and of all the means by which they may be carried into execution, would partake of the prolixity of a legal code, and could scarcely be embraced by the human mind. It would probably never be understood by the public. Its nature, therefore, requires that only its great outlines should be marked, its important objects designated, and the minor ingredients which compose those objects be deduced from the nature of the objects themselves. That this idea was entertained by the framers of the American constitution, is not only to be inferred from the nature of the instrument, but from the language. Why else were some of the limitations, found in the ninth section of the 1st article, introduced? Considering this question, then, we must never forget, that it is a constitution we are expounding.

Although, among the enumerated powers of government, we do not find the word "bank," or "incorporation," we find the great powers to lay and collect taxes; to borrow money; to regulate commerce; to declare and conduct a war; and to raise and support armies and navies. The sword and the purse, all the external relations, and no inconsiderable portion of the industry of the nation, are intrusted to its government. . . . It may, with great reason, be contended that a government, intrusted with such ample powers . . . must also be intrusted with ample means for their execution. The power being given, it is the interest of the nation to facilitate its execution. It can never be their interest, and cannot be presumed to have been their intention, to clog and embarrass its execution by withholding the most appropriate means. Throughout this vast republic, from the St. Croix to the Gulf of Mexico, from the Atlantic to the Pacific, revenue is to be collected and expended, armies are to be marched and supported. Is that construction of the constitution to be preferred which would render these operations difficult, hazardous, and expensive? Can we adopt that construction (unless the words imperiously require it) which would impute to the framers of that instrument, when granting these powers for the public good, the intention of impeding their exercise by withholding a choice of means?

It is not denied that the powers given to the government imply the ordinary means of execution. That, for example, of raising revenue and applying it to national purposes, is admitted to imply the power of conveying money from place to place, as the exigencies of the nation may require, and of employing the usual means of conveyance. But it is denied that the government has its choice of means, or that it may employ the most convenient means; if, to employ them, it be necessary to erect a corporation.

The government which has a right to do an act, and has imposed on it the duty of performing that act, must, according to the dictates of reason, be allowed to select the means; and those who contend that it may not select any appropriate means, that one particular mode of effecting the object is excepted, take upon themselves the burden of establishing that exception.

. . . In America, the powers of sovereignty are divided between the government of the Union, and those of the States. They are each sovereign, with respect to the objects committed to it, and neither sovereign with respect to the objects committed to the other. The power of creating a corporation, though appertaining to sovereignty, is not, like the power of making war, or levying taxes, or of regulating commerce, a great substantive and independent power, which cannot be implied as incidental to other powers, or used as a means of executing them. It is never the end for which other powers are exercised, but a means by which other objects are accomplished. . . . The power of creating a corporation is never used for its own sake, but for the purpose of effecting something else. No sufficient reason is therefore, perceived, why it may not pass as incidental to those powers which are expressly given, if it be a direct mode of executing them.

But the constitution of the United States has not left the right of Congress to employ the necessary means for the execution of the powers conferred on the government, to general reasoning. To its enumeration of powers is added that of making "all laws which shall be necessary and proper, for carrying into execution the foregoing powers, and all other powers vested by this constitution, in the government of the United States, or in any department thereof." . . . To employ the means necessary to an end, is generally understood as employing any means calculated to produce the end, and not as being confined to those single means, without which the end would be entirely unattainable. Such is the character of human language, that no word conveys to the mind, in all situations, one single definite idea; and nothing is more common than to use words in a figurative sense. Almost all compositions contain words, which, taken in their rigorous sense, would convey a meaning different from that which is obviously intended. It is essential to just construction, that many words which import something excessive, should be understood in a more mitigated sense—in that sense which common usage justifies. The word "necessary" is of this description. It has not a fixed character peculiar to itself. It admits of all degrees of comparison; and is often connected with other words, which increase or diminish the impression the mind receives of the urgency it imports. A thing may be necessary, very necessary, absolutely or indispensably necessary. This word, then, like others, is used in various senses; and, in its construction, the subject, the context, the intention of the person using them, are all to be taken into view.

Let this be done in the case under consideration. The subject is the execution of those great powers on which the welfare of a nation essentially depends. It must have been the intention of those who gave these powers, to insure, as far as human prudence could insure, their beneficial execution. This could not be done by confiding the choice of means to such narrow limits as not to leave it in the power of Congress to adopt any which might be appropriate, and which were conducive to the end. This provision is made in a constitution intended to endure for ages to come, and, consequently, to be adapted to the various crises of human affairs. To have prescribed the means by which government should, in all future time, execute its powers, would have been to change, entirely, the character of the instrument, and give it the properties of a legal code. It would have been an unwise attempt to provide, by immutable rules, for exigencies which, if foreseen at all, must have been seen dimly, and which can be best provided for as they occur. To have declared that the best means shall not be used, but those alone without which the power given would be nugatory, would have been to deprive the legislature of the capacity to avail itself of experience, to exercise its reason, and to accommodate its legislation to circumstances. . . .

But the argument which most conclusively demonstrates the error of the construction contended for by the counsel for the state of Maryland, is founded on the intention of the convention, as manifested in the whole clause. To waste time and argument in proving that, without it, Congress might carry its powers into execution, would be not much less idle than to hold a lighted taper to the sun. . . .

The clause is placed among the powers of Congress, not among the limitations on those powers.

Its terms purport to enlarge, not to diminish the powers vested in the government. It purports to be an additional power, not a restriction on those already granted. No reason has been or can be assigned, for thus concealing an intention to narrow the discretion of the national legislature, under words which purport to enlarge it. The framers of the constitution wished its adoption, and well knew that it would be endangered by its strength, not by its weakness. Had they been capable of using language which would convey to the eye one idea, and, after deep reflection, impress on the mind another, they would rather have disguised the grant of power, than its limitation. If, then, their intention had been, by this clause, to restrain the free use of means which might otherwise have been implied, that intention would have been inserted in another place, and would have been expressed in terms resembling these: "In carrying into execution the foregoing powers, and all others," etc., "no laws shall be passed but such as are necessary and proper." Had the intention been to make this clause restrictive, it would unquestionably have been so in form as well as in effect.

We admit, as all must admit, that the powers of the government are limited, and that its limits are not to be transcended. But we think the sound construction of the constitution must allow to the national legislature that discretion, with respect to the means by which the powers it confers are to be carried into execution, which will enable that body to perform the high duties assigned to it, in the manner most beneficial to the people. Let the end be legitimate, let it be within the scope of the constitution, and all means which are appropriate, which are plainly adapted to that end, which are not prohibited, but consist with the letter and spirit of the constitution, are constitutional. . . .

After the most deliberate consideration, it is the unanimous and decided opinion of this court, that the act to incorporate the bank of the United States is a law made in pursuance of the constitution, and is a part of the supreme law of the land. . . .

It being the opinion of the Court, that the act incorporating the bank is constitutional, and that the power of establishing a branch in the state of Maryland might be properly exercised by the bank itself, we proceed to inquire:

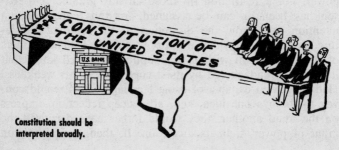

Constitution should be interpreted broadly.

2. Whether the state of Maryland may, without violating the constitution, tax that branch?

That the power of taxation is one of vital importance; that it is retained by the states; that it is not abridged by the grant of a similar power to the government of the Union; that it is to be concurrently exercised by the two governments, are truths which have never been denied. But, such is the paramount character of the constitution, that its capacity to withdraw any subject from the action of even this power, is admitted. The states are expressly forbidden to lay any duties on imports or exports, except what may be absolutely necessary for executing their inspection laws. If the obligation of this prohibition must be conceded—if it may restrain a state from the exercise of its taxing power on imports and exports—the same paramount character would seem to restrain, as it certainly may restrain, a state from such other exercise of this power, as is in its nature incompatible with, and repugnant to, the constitutional laws of the Union. A law, absolutely repugnant to another, as entirely repeals that other as if express terms of repeal were used.

On this ground the counsel for the bank place its claim to be exempted from the power of a state to tax its operations. There is no express provision for the case, but the claim has been sustained on a principle which so entirely pervades the constitution, is so intermixed with the materials which compose it, so interwoven with its web, so blended with its texture, as to be incapable of being separated from it without rending it into shreds.

This great principle is, that the constitution and the laws made in pursuance thereof are supreme; that they control the constitution and laws of the respective states, and cannot be controlled by them. From this . . . 1st. That a power to create implies a power to preserve. 2d. That a power to destroy, if wielded by a different hand, is hostile to, and incompatible with, these powers to create and preserve. 3d. That where this repugnancy exists, that authority which is supreme must control, not yield to that over which it is supreme. . . .

. . . That the power to tax involves the power to destroy; that the power to destroy may defeat and render useless the power to create; that there is a plain repugnance, in conferring on one government a power to control the constitutional measures of another, which other, with respect to those very measures, is declared to be supreme over that which exerts the control, are propositions not to be denied. . . .

. . . Would the people of any one state trust those of another with a power to control the most insignificant operations of their state government? We know they would not. Why, then, should we suppose that the people of any one state should be willing to trust those of another with a power to control the operations of a government to which they have confided their most important and most valuable interests? . . .

If the states may tax one instrument, employed by the government in the execution of its powers, they may tax any and every other instrument. They may tax the mail; they may tax the mint; they may tax patent-rights; they may tax the papers of the custom-house; they may tax judicial process; they may tax all the means employed by the government, to an excess which would defeat all the ends of government. This was not intended by the American people. They did not design to make their government dependent on the states.

. . . The people of all the states have created the general government, and have conferred upon it the general power of taxation. The people of all the states, and the states themselves, are represented in Congress, and, by their representatives, exercise this power. When they tax the chartered institutions of the states, they tax their constituents; and these taxes must be uniform. But when a state taxes the operations of the government of the United States, it acts upon institutions created, not by their own constituents, but by people over whom they claim no control. It acts upon the measures of a government created by others as well as themselves, for the benefit of others in common with themselves. The difference is that which always exists, and always must exist, between the action of the whole on a part, and the action of a part on the whole—between the laws of a government declared to be supreme, and those of a government which, when in opposition to those laws, is not supreme. . . .

The court has bestowed on this subject its most deliberate consideration. The result is a conviction that the states have no power, by taxation or otherwise, to retard, impede, burden, or in any manner control, the operations of the consitional laws enacted by Congress to carry into execution the powers vested in the general government. This is, we think, the unavoidable consequence of that supremacy which the constitution has declared.

We are unanimously of opinion that the law passed by the legislature of Maryland, imposing a tax on the Bank of the United States, is unconstitutional and void.

Judgment Reversed.

TRUE OR FALSE?

Write T *if the statement is correct; Write* F *if it is false.*

_____1. Maryland held that a state could tax any corporation that did business in that state.

_____2. The Constitution gives Congress the specific power to establish a bank.

_____3. Marshall held that the elastic clause gave Congress the power to create a national bank.

_____4. The state and national governments may tax imports but not exports.

_____5. Marshall held that the Supreme Court has the power to decide when a state law is constitutional.

_____6. The federal government may tax a corporation chartered by a state.

_____7. The power to create a corporation is a concurrent power.

_____8. Marshall held that though states can tax other states, they cannot tax the federal government.

_____9. Marshall proved that there are no limits to the laws Congress may pass.

_____10. Marshall believed that Congress could pass any law intended to carry out one of its enumerated powers.

THOUGHT QUESTIONS

1. How did John Marshall's decision in *McCulloch versus Maryland* strengthen the federal government?
2. How did Marshall's approval of the use of the "elastic clause" serve to make the Supreme Court more important?

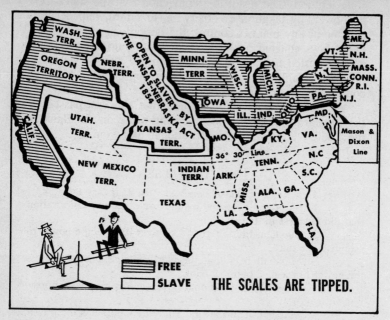

THE SCALES ARE TIPPED.

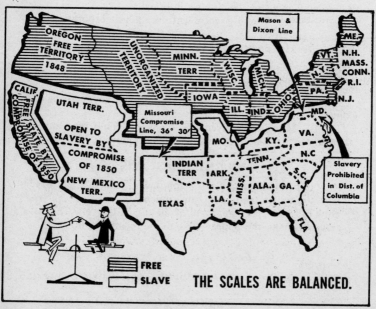

THE SCALES ARE BALANCED.

The Missouri Compromise 1819

* * * * **When the Territory of Missouri** (carved out of the Louisiana Territory) applied for statehood in 1818, the balance of free and slave states in the United States Congress became an important issue. Missouri was slave territory.

Representative James Tallmadge of New York proposed an amendment to the Missouri enabling bill providing for the eventual freeing of slaves in the new state. This bill passed the House, but was rejected by the Senate.

Henry Clay, Speaker of the House of Representatives, proposed a compromise which he hoped would remove the slavery issue from the halls of Congress. One slave state and one free state would be admitted to the Union at the same time. No other slave states would be formed from the territory of the Louisiana Purchase north of 36° 30' north latitude. Tallmadge's amendment was dropped.

The Missouri Compromise enabled the new state of Maine to be admitted as a free state at the same time as Missouri, a slave state. The Compromise succeeded in "burying" the slavery question as a national political issue for some thirty years. But men like John Quincy Adams saw what was to come — "a great, tragic volume" of troubles.

Tallmadge's Amendment
(February 13, 1819)

And provided, That the further introduction of slavery or involuntary servitude be prohibited, except for the punishment of crimes, whereof the party shall have been fully [duly] convicted; and that all children born within the said State, after the admission thereof into the Union, shall be free at the age of twenty-five years.

Missouri Enabling Act — (March 6, 1820)

An Act to Authorize the People of the Missouri Territory to Form a Constitution and State Government, and for the Admission of Such State into the Union on an Equal Footing with the Original States, and to Prohibit Slavery in Certain Territories.

Be it enacted . . . , That the inhabitants of that portion of the Missouri territory included within the boundaries hereinafter designated, be, and they are hereby authorized to form for themselves a constitution and state government, and to assume such name as they shall deem proper; and the said state, when formed, shall be admitted into the Union, upon an equal footing with the original states, in all respects whatsoever.

Section 2. And be it further enacted, That the said state shall consist of all the territory included within the following boundaries, to wit: Beginning in the middle of the Mississippi river, on the parallel of thirty-six degrees of north latitude; thence west, along that parallel of latitude, to the St. Francois river; thence up, and following the course of that river, in the middle of the main channel thereof, to the parallel of latitude of thirty-six degrees and thirty minutes; thence west, along the same, to a point where the said parallel is intersected by a meridian line passing through the middle of the mouth of the Kansas river, where the same empties into the Missouri river, thence, from the point aforesaid north, along the said meridian line, to the intersection of the parallel of latitude which passes through the rapids of the river Des Moines making the said line to correspond with the Indian boundary line; thence east, from the point of intersection last aforesaid, along the said parallel of latitude, to the middle of the channel of the main fork of the said Des Moines; thence down and along the middle of the main channel of the said river Des Moines, to the mouth of the same, where it empties into the Mississippi river; thence, due east, to the middle of the main channel of the Mississippi river; thence down, and following the course of the Mississippi river, in the middle of the main channel thereof, to the place of beginning.

.   .   .   .

Section 8.   And be it further enacted, That in all that territory ceded by France to the United States, under the name of Louisiana, which lies north of thirty-six degrees and thirty minutes north latitude, not included within the limits of the state, contemplated by this act, slavery and involuntary servitude, otherwise than in the punishment of crimes, whereof the parties shall have been duly convicted, shall be, and is hereby, forever prohibited. *Provided always,* That any person escaping into the same, from whom labor or service is lawfully claimed, in any state or territory of the United States, such fugitive may be lawfully reclaimed and conveyed to the person claiming his or her labor or service as aforesaid.

Excerpt from the Constitution of Missouri (July 19, 1820)

[*Article III.*] *Sec. 26.* The general assembly shall not have power to pass laws —

1. For the emancipation of slaves without the consent of their owners; or without paying them, before such emancipation, a full equivalent for such slaves so emancipated;

2. To prevent *bona-fide* immigrants to this State, or actual settlers therein, from bringing from any of the United States, or from any of their Territories, such persons as may there be deemed to be slaves, so long as any persons of the same description are allowed to be held as slaves by the laws of this State.

They shall have power to pass laws—

1. To prohibit the introduction into this State of any

slaves who may have committed any high crime in any other State or Territory;

2. To prohibit the introduction of any slave for the purpose of speculation, or as an article of trade or merchandise;

3. To prohibit the introduction of any slave, or the offspring of any slave, who heretofore may have been, or who hereafter may be, imported from any foreign country into the United States, or any Territory thereof, in contravention of any existing statute of the United States; and,

4. To permit the owners of slaves to emancipate them, saving the right of creditors, where the person so emancipating will give security that the slave so emancipated shall not become a public charge.

It shall be their duty, as soon as may be, to pass such laws, as may be necessary—

1. To prevent free negroes and mulattoes from coming to and settling in this State, under any pretext whatsoever; and,

2. To oblige the owners of slaves to treat them with humanity, and to abstain from all injuries to them extending to life or limb.

Resolution for the Admission of Missouri (March 2, 1821)

Resolution Providing for the Admission of the State of Missouri into the Union, on a Certain Condition.

Resolved, That Missouri shall be admitted into this union on an equal footing with the original states, in all respects whatever, upon the fundamental condition, that the fourth clause of the twenty-sixth section of the third article of the constitution submitted on the part of said state to Congress, shall never be construed to authorize the passage of any law, and that no law shall be passed in conformity thereto, by which any citizen, of either of the states in this Union, shall be excluded from the enjoyment of any of the privileges and immunities to which such citizen is entitled under the constitution of the United States. *Provided,* That the legislature of the said state, by a solemn public act, shall declare the assent of the said state to the said fundamental condition, and shall transmit to the President of the United States, on or before the fourth Monday in November next, an authentic copy of the said act; upon the receipt whereof, the President, by proclamation, shall announce the fact; whereupon, and without any further proceeding on the part of Congress, the admission of the said state into this Union shall be considered as complete.

CHOOSE THE CORRECT ANSWER

Write the letter that best completes the statement or answers the question.

1. Under the Tallmadge Amendment, slave children would have been (*a*) sent out of Missouri, (*b*) freed at age twenty-five, (*c*) sold to the government, (*d*) given free land.   1._____

2. 36° 30′ was the boundary of Missouri to the (*a*) north, (*b*) south, (*c*) east, (*d*) west.   2._____

3. A slave who escaped into the free lands of the Louisiana Territory would be (*a*) returned to his master, (*b*) free, (*c*) able to buy his freedom, (*d*) sent to a federal jail.   3._____

4. Any freed slave who went into Missouri would be (*a*) made a slave again, (*b*) sent out of the state, (*c*) allowed to remain, (*d*) forced to pay a special tax.   4._____

5. Missouri promised not to free its slaves (*a*) without the consent of their owners, (*b*) for twenty years, (*c*) until Congress freed all the slaves in the country, (*d*) at any time. 5._____

6. Importing slaves for sale in Missouri was to be (*a*) allowed, (*b*) limited to those with special licenses, (*c*) under the control of the state legislature, (*d*) prohibited.   6._____

7. The man chiefly responsible for the Missouri Compromise was (*a*) James Tallmadge, (*b*) President Monroe, (*c*) Henry Clay, (*d*) John Marshall.   7._____

8. A slaveowner moving to Missouri was (*a*) not allowed to take his slaves with him, (*b*) allowed to take his slaves with him, (*c*) forced to free the children of his slaves, (*d*) required to get special permission to take his slaves with him. 8._____

THOUGHT QUESTIONS

1. Describe the immediate problem and the long-range problem settled by the Missouri Compromise.

2. Discuss the effect of the Missouri Compromise on each of the following:
    (*a*) the question of slavery in the territories;
    (*b*) the balance of power in the Senate;
    (*c*) the political career of Henry Clay.

The Monroe Doctrine 1823

* * * * *A series of revolutions in Latin* America during the 1820's won freedom for Spain's colonies. The United States quickly recognized the independence of these new, free, neighbor states.

In Europe, the Holy Alliance of kings, joined to prevent another French Revolution, or any other European revolution, seemed ready to crush the revolts in South America. Meantime, Russia claimed all the Pacific coast of North America, north of the 51st parallel, and forbade foreigners to trade in the area.

George Canning, Britain's foreign minister, feared that either the United States or France would gain control over South America's foreign trade. Canning asked the United States to join Britain in warning the European kings to keep hands off the new South American nations.

Former Presidents Jefferson and Madison advised President Monroe to accept the British offer. But John Quincy Adams, Monroe's Secretary of State, persuaded him to act without the British, and to make a declaration that America would oppose any future colonization by European nations in the Western Hemisphere. Monroe included this doctrine in his annual message to Congress on December 2, 1823.

It was aimed only partly at Russia and Spain. Adams was alarmed at the hold the British were strengthening over the Pacific Northwest.

Although the Doctine grew to have other meanings in later years, when first stated it proposed two chief ideas: (1) European nations were not to start any new colonies in the Western Hemisphere; (2) European powers were not to interfere in the political life of the Americas. The doctrine also gave Europe two promises: (1) The United States would not interfere with European colonies already made in the Western Hemisphere; (2) The United States would not become involved in Europe's wars.

Fellow-citizens of the Senate and House of Representatives:

At the proposal of the Russian Imperial Government, made through the minister of the Emperor residing here, a full power and instructions have been transmitted to the minister of the United States at St. Petersburg to arrange by amicable negotiation the respective rights and interests of the two nations on the northwest coast of this continent. A similar proposal had been made by His Imperial Majesty to the government of Great Britain, which has likewise been acceded to. The government of the United States has been desirous, by this friendly proceeding, of manifesting the great value which they have invariably attached to the friendship of the Emperor and their solicitude to cultivate the best understanding with his government. In the discussions to which this interest has given rise and in the arrangements by which they may terminate the occasion has been judged proper for asserting, as a principle in which the rights and interests of the United States are involved, that the American continents, by the free and independent condition which they have assumed and maintain, are henceforth not to be considered as subjects for future colonization by any European powers. . . .

It was stated at the commencement of the last session that a great effort was then making in Spain and Portugal to improve the condition of the people of those countries, and that it appeared to be conducted with extraordinary moderation. It need scarcely be remarked that the result has been so far very different from what was then anticipated. Of events in that quarter of the globe, with which we have so much intercourse and from which we derive our origin, we have always been anxious and interested spectators. The citizens of the United States cherish sentiments the most friendly in favor of the liberty and happiness of their fellow men on that side of the Atlantic. In the wars of the European powers in matters relating to themselves we have never taken any part, nor does it comport with our policy so to do. It is only when our rights are invaded or seriously menaced that we resent injuries or make preparation for our defense. With the movements in this hemisphere we are of necessity more immediately connected, and by causes which must be obvious to all enlightened and impartial observers. The political system of the allied powers is essentially different in this respect from that of America. This difference proceeds from that which exists in their respective governments; and to the defense of our own, which has been achieved by the loss of so much blood and treasure, and matured by the wisdom of their most enlightened citizens, and under which we have enjoyed unexampled felicity, this whole nation is devoted. We owe it, therefore, to candor and to the amicable relations existing between the United States and those powers to declare that we should consider any attempt on their part to extend their system to any portion of this hemisphere as dangerous to our peace and safety. With the existing colonies or dependencies of any European power we have not interfered and shall not interfere. But with the governments who have declared their independence and maintained it, and whose independence we have, on great consideration and on just principles, acknowledged, we could not view any interposition for the purpose of oppressing them, or controlling in any other manner their destiny, by any European power in any other light than as the manifestation of an unfriendly disposition toward the United States. In the war between those new governments and Spain we declared our neutrality at the time of their recognition, and to this we have adhered, and shall continue to adhere, provided no change shall occur which, in the judgment of the competent authorities of this government, shall make a corresponding change on the part of the United States indispensable to their security.

. . . Our policy in regard to Europe, which was adopted at an early stage of the wars which have so long agitated that quarter of the globe, nevertheless remains the same, which is, not to interfere in the internal concerns of any of its powers; to consider the government de facto as the legitimate government for us; to cultivate friendly relations with it, and to preserve those relations by a frank, firm, and manly policy, meeting in all instances the just claims of every power, submitting to injuries from none.

But in regard to those continents circumstances are eminently and conspicuously different. It is impossible that the allied powers should extend their political system to any portion of either continent without endangering our peace and happiness; nor can anyone believe that our southern brethren, if left to themselves, would adopt it of their own accord. It is equally impossible, therefore, that we should behold such interposition in any form with indifference. If we look to the comparative strength and resources of Spain and those new governments, and their distance from each other, it must be obvious that she can never subdue them. It is still the true policy of the United States to leave the parties to themselves, in the hope that other powers will pursue the same course. . . .⌐

FILL IN THE ANSWERS

Write the word or phrase which best completes the statement.

1. The person whose ideas Monroe followed in the Monroe Doctrine was _____.
2. The Doctrine was issued in the year _____.
3. The country which wanted to join the United States in issuing the Doctrine was _____.
4. The name of Britain's foreign minister was _____.
5. The country whose South American colonies had revolted was _____.
6. The name of Monroe's Secretary of State was _____.
7. Monroe promised that the United States would not become involved in the wars of _____.
8. Monroe warned Europe not to attempt any new _____ in the Americas.
9. The Monroe Doctrine was aimed at Great Britain, Spain and _____.
10. _____ claimed all the west coast of North America north of the 51st parallel.

THOUGHT QUESTIONS

1. (*a*) For what reasons was the Monroe Doctrine issued?
   (*b*) State the four ideas included in the Monroe Doctrine.
2. Select one of the statements below. Explain in detail why you agree or disagree with it.
   (*a*) The Monroe Doctrine replaced European control of South America with United States control.
   (*b*) The Monroe Doctrine has grown and changed into a great regional self-help and mutual defense alliance.

South Carolina's Ordinance of Nullification 1832

* * * * *The high protective tariff policy of* the United States effectively forced European goods off the American market. The South, an agricultural section, had to buy the manufactured goods it needed from the new Northern manufacturers. More often than not they had to pay higher prices than they had once paid for similar imported English goods.

South Carolina vigorously opposed the tariff of 1828, popularly called the "tariff of abominations." Vice-President John C. Calhoun resigned so that he could return to the Senate to lead his section's fight. The attack on the tariff was based on the grounds that it was sectional legislation and, therefore, unconstitutional. On November 24, a special convention, called by the legislature of South Carolina, voted an Ordinance of Nullification.

The idea of nullification, previously presented in the Kentucky and Virginia Resolutions was that a single state could decide for itself when it would obey a federal law. Calhoun declared that the only way the federal government could make a law binding on a state once it had been nullified, was by an amendment to the Constitution. Furthermore, if that amendment was proved detrimental to the state, the state could secede.

Had South Carolina's ordinance been successful it would have meant the end of federal control over the areas assigned to the national government by the Constitution. The introduction to the next document will show why the ordinance never went into effect.

An Ordinance to Nullify Certain Acts of the Congress of the United States, Purporting to Be Laws Laying Duties and Imposts on the Importation of Foreign Commodities.

Whereas the Congress of the United States, by various acts, purporting to be acts laying duties and imposts on foreign imports, but in reality intended for the protection of domestic manufactures, and the giving of bounties to classes and individuals engaged in particular employments, at the expense and to the injury and oppression of other classes and individuals, and by wholly exempting from taxation certain foreign commodities, such as are not produced or manufactured in the United States, to afford a pretext for imposing higher and excessive duties on articles similar to those intended to be protected, hath exceeded its just powers under the Constitution, which confers on it no authority to afford such protection, and hath violated the true meaning and intent of the Constitution, which provides for equality in imposing the burdens of taxation upon the several States and portions of the confederacy; And whereas the said Congress, exceeding its just power to impose taxes and collect revenue for the purpose of effecting and accomplishing the specific objects and purposes which the Constitution of the United States authorizes it to effect and accomplish, hath raised and collected unnecessary revenue for objects unauthorized by the Constitution.

We, therefore, the people of the State of South Carolina in Convention assembled, do declare and ordain, and it is hereby declared and ordained, that the several acts and parts of acts of the Congress of the United States, purporting to be laws for the imposing of duties and imposts on the importation of foreign commodities, and now having actual operation and effect within the United States and, more especially, . . . [the tariff acts of 1828 and 1832] . . . , are unauthorized by the Constitution of the United States, and violate the true meaning and intent thereof, and are null, void, and no law, nor binding upon this State, its officers or citizens; and all promises, contracts, and obligations, made or entered into, or to be made or entered into, with purpose to secure the duties imposed by the said acts, and all judicial proceedings which shall be hereafter had in affirmance thereof, are and shall be held utterly null and void.

And it is further ordained, that it shall not be lawful for any of the constituted authorities, whether of this State or of the United States, to enforce the payment of duties imposed by the said acts within the limits of this State; but it shall be the duty of the Legislature to adopt such measures and pass such acts as may be necessary to give full effect to this ordinance, and to prevent the enforcement and arrest the operation of the said acts and parts of acts of the Congress of the United States within the limits of this State, from and after the 1st day of February next, and the duty of all other constituted authorities, and of all persons residing or being within the limits of this State, and they are hereby required and enjoined, to obey and give effect to this ordinance, and such acts and measures of the Legislature as may be passed or adopted in obedience thereto.

And it is further ordained, that in no case of law or equity, decided in the courts of this State, wherein shall be drawn in question the authority of this ordinance, or the validity of such act or acts of the Legislature as may be passed for the purpose of giving effect thereto, or the validity of the aforesaid acts of Congress, imposing duties, shall any appeal be taken or allowed to the Supreme Court of the United States, nor shall any copy of the record be permitted or allowed for that purpose; and if any such appeal shall be attempted to be taken, the courts of this State shall proceed to execute and enforce their judgments, according to the laws and usages of the State, without reference to such attempted appeal, and the person or persons attempting to take such appeal may be dealt with as for a contempt of the court.

And it is further ordained, that all persons now holding any office of honor, profit, or trust, civil or military, under this State, (members of the Legislature excepted,) shall, within such time, and in such manner as the Legislature shall prescribe, take an oath well and truly to obey, execute, and enforce, this ordinance, and such act or acts of the Legislature as may be passed in pursuance thereof, according to the true intent and meaning of the same; and on the neglect or omission of any such person or persons so to do, his or their office or offices shall be forthwith vacated, and shall be filled up as if such person or persons were dead or had resigned; and no person hereafter elected to any office of honor, profit, or trust, civil or military, (members of the Legislature excepted,) shall, until the Legislature shall otherwise provide and direct, enter on the execution of his office, or be in any respect competent to discharge the duties thereof, until he shall, in like manner, have taken a similar oath; and no juror shall be empannelled in any of the courts of this State, in any cause in which shall be in question this ordinance, or any act of the Legislature passed in pursuance thereof, unless he shall first, in addition to the usual oath, have taken an oath that he will well and truly obey, execute, and enforce this ordinance, and such act or acts of the Legislature as may be passed to carry the same into operation and effect, according to the true intent and meaning thereof.

And we, the people of South Carolina, to the end that it may be fully understood by the Government of the United States, and the people of the co-States, that we are determined to maintain this, our ordinance and declaration, at every hazard, do further declare that we will not submit to the application of force, on the part of the Federal Government, to reduce this State to obedience; but that we will consider the passage, by Congress, of any act authorizing the employment of a military or naval force against the State of South Carolina, her constituted authorities or citizens; or any act abolishing or closing the ports of this State, or any of them, or otherwise obstructing the free ingress and egress of vessels to and from the said ports, or any other act on the part of the Federal Government to coerce the State, shut up her ports, destroy or harass her commerce, or to enforce the acts hereby declared to be null and void, otherwise than through the civil tribunals of the country, as inconsistent with the longer continuance of South Carolina in the Union; and that the people of this State will thenceforth hold themselves absolved from all further obligation to maintain or preserve their political connection with the people of the other States, and will forthwith proceed to organize a separate Government, and do all other acts and things which sovereign and independent States may of right to do.

TRUE OR FALSE?

Write T *if the statement is correct; Write* F *if it is false.*

_____1. The Ordinance of Nullification was directed against the protective tariff laws.

_____2. The judges of South Carolina were ordered not to enforce the tariff laws.

_____3. Calhoun, who opposed the Ordinance, was forced to resign as Vice-President.

_____4. South Carolina stated that she would not obey any federal orders directed against the Ordinance.

_____5. The Ordinance did not try to control the actions of men who would serve on juries.

_____6. South Carolina admitted it could not leave the Union.

_____7. Public officials of South Carolina were ordered to take an oath to support the Ordinance.

_____8. The Ordinance opposed the tariff laws even though it admitted they were permitted under the Constitution.

_____9. The people of South Carolina were told that only public officials had to obey the Ordinance.

_____10. The Ordinance showed that South Carolina would even resist federal troops.

THOUGHT QUESTIONS

1. For what reasons did the people of South Carolina support the Ordinance of Nullification?

2. Explain why the idea of nullification has never succeeded in United States history.

Jackson's Proclamation to South Carolina 1832

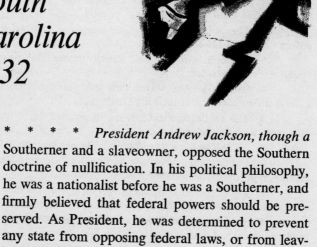

 * * * * *President Andrew Jackson, though a* Southerner and a slaveowner, opposed the Southern doctrine of nullification. In his political philosophy, he was a nationalist before he was a Southerner, and firmly believed that federal powers should be preserved. As President, he was determined to prevent any state from opposing federal laws, or from leaving the Union.

The South Carolina Ordinance of Nullification had expressed that state's refusal to obey the country's tariff laws. It threatened that South Carolina would secede; in fact, state militia groups were arming and training.

Jackson wasted little time. He issued a proclamation to the people of the rebellious state. He warned them that their actions were treasonable and that he would never permit the doctrine of nullification to break up the Union. The federal troops in Charleston were placed on alert. Jackson asked Congress to pass a Force Bill to give him power to take any necessary military action against South Carolina.

Jackson never had to carry out his threats, although it is clear that he would have done so. Congress quickly passed a new tariff law (1833) which lowered the objectionable tariff rates over a ten-year period. South Carolina then withdrew the Ordinance of Nullification. However, the Ordinance was a sign of trouble to come, and the President had shown that attempts at nullification or secession would be met by the power of the federal government. No state again attempted to oppose federal rule until the Civil War.

And whereas, the said ordinance prescribes to the people of South Carolina a course of conduct in direct violation of their duty as citizens of the United States, contrary to the laws of their country, subversive of its Constitution, and having for its object the destruction of the Union.... To preserve this bond of our political existence from destruction, to maintain inviolate this state of national honor and prosperity, and to justify the confidence my fellow citizens have reposed in me, I, Andrew Jackson, *President of the United States,* have thought proper to issue this my PROCLAMATION, stating my views of the Constitution and laws applicable to the measures adopted by the Convention of South Carolina, and to the reasons they have put forth to sustain them, declaring the course which duty will require me to pursue, and, appealing to the understanding and patriotism of the people, warn them of the consequences that must inevitably result from an observance of the dictates of the Convention....

The ordinance is founded, not on the indefeasible right of resisting acts which are plainly unconstitutional, and too oppressive to be endured; but on the strange position that any one State may not only declare an act of Congress void, but prohibit its execution — that they may do this consistently with the Constitution — that the true construction of that instrument permits a State to retain its place in the Union, and yet be bound by no other of its laws than those it may choose to consider as constitutional. It is true, they add, that to justify this abrogation of a law, it must be palpably contrary to the Constitution; but it is evident, that, to give the right of resisting laws of that description, coupled with the uncontrolled right to decide what laws deserve that character, is to give the power of resisting all laws. For, as by the theory, there is no appeal, the reasons alleged by the State, good or bad, must prevail. If it should be said that public opinion is a sufficient check against the abuse of this power, it may be asked why it is not deemed a sufficient guard against the passage of an unconstitutional act by Congress? There is, however, a restraint in this last case, which makes the assumed power of a State more indefensible, and which does not exist in the other. There are two appeals from an unconstitutional act passed by Congress — one to the Judiciary, the other to the people and the States. There is no appeal from the State decision in theory, and the practical illustration shows that the courts are closed against an application to review it, both judges and jurors being sworn to decide in its favor. But reasoning on this subject is superfluous, when our social compact, in express terms, declares that the laws of the United States, its Constitution, and treaties made under it, are the supreme law of the land; and, for greater caution, adds "that the judges in every State shall be bound thereby, anything in the Constitution or laws of any State to the contrary notwithstanding." And it may be asserted without fear of refutation, that no Federative Government could exist without a similar provision. Look for a moment to the consequence. If South Carolina considers the revenue laws unconstitutional, and has a right to prevent their execution in the port of Charleston, there would be a clear constitutional objection to their collection in every other port, and no revenue could be collected anywhere; for all imposts must be equal. It is no answer to repeat, that an unconstitutional law is no law, so long as the question of its legality is to be decided by the State itself; for every law operating injuriously upon any local interest will be perhaps thought, and certainly represented, as unconstitutional, and, as has been shown, there is no appeal. . . .

If the doctrine of a State veto upon the laws of the Union carries with it internal evidence of its impracticable absurdity, our constitutional history will also afford abundant proof that it would have been repudiated with indignation had it been proposed to form a feature in our Government. . . .

I consider, then, the power to annul a law of the United States, assumed by one State, *incompatible with the existence of the Union, contradicted expressly by the letter of the Constitution, unauthorized by its spirit, inconsistent with every principle on which it was founded, and destructive of the great object for which it was formed.*

After this general view of the leading principle, we must examine the particular application of it which is made in the ordinance.

The preamble rests its justification on these grounds: It assumes, as a fact, that the obnoxious laws, although they purport to be laws for raising revenue, were in reality intended for the protection of manufactures, which purpose it asserts to be unconstitutional; that the operation of these laws is unequal; that the amount raised by them is greater than is required by the wants of the Government; and, finally, that the proceeds are to be applied to objects unauthorized by the Constitution. These are the only causes alleged to justify an open opposition to the laws of the country, and a threat of seceding from the Union, if any attempt should be made to enforce them. The first virtually acknowledges that the law in question was passed under a power expressly given by the Constitution to lay and collect imposts; but its constitutionality is drawn in question from the *motives* of those who passed it. However apparent this purpose may be in the present case, nothing can be more dangerous than to admit the position that an unconstitutional purpose, entertained by the members who assent to a law enacted under a constitutional power, shall make that law void: for how is that purpose to be ascertained? Who is to make the scrutiny? How often may bad purposes be falsely imputed — in how many cases are they concealed by false professions — in how many is no declaration of motive made? Admit this doctrine, and you give to the States an uncontrolled right to decide, and every law may be annulled under this pretext. If, therefore, the absurd and dangerous doctrine should be admitted, that a State may annul an unconstitutional law, or one that it deems such, it will not apply to the present case.

The next objection is, that the laws in question operate unequally. This objection may be made with truth, to every law that has been or can be passed. The wisdom of man never yet contrived a system of taxation that would operate with perfect equality. If the unequal operation of a law makes it unconstitutional, and if all laws of that description may be abrogated by any State for that cause, then indeed is the Federal Constitution unworthy of the slightest effort for its preservation. . . .

The two remaining objections made by the ordinance to these laws, are that the sums intended to be raised by them are greater than are required, and that the proceeds will be unconstitutionally employed.

The Constitution has given, expressly, to Congress the right of raising revenue, and of determining the sum the public exigencies will require. The States have no control over the exercise of this right other than that which results from the power of changing the representatives who abuse it, and thus procure redress. Congress may, undoubtedly, abuse this discretionary power, but the same may be said of others with which they are vested. Yet the discretion must exist somewhere. The Constitution has given it to the representatives of all the people, checked by the representatives of the States, and by the Executive Power. The South Carolina construction gives it to the Legislature or the Convention of a single State, where neither the people of the different States, nor the States in their separate capacity, nor the Chief Magistrate elected by the people, have any representation. Which is the most discreet disposition of the power? . . .

The ordinance, with the same knowledge of the future that characterizes a former objection, tells you that the proceeds of the tax will be unconstitutionally applied. If this could be ascertained with certainty, the objection would, with more propriety, be reserved for the law so applying the proceeds, but surely can not be urged against the laws levying the duty. . . .

On such expositions and reasonings, the ordinance grounds not only an assertion of the right to annul the laws of which it complains, but to enforce it by a threat of seceding from the Union if any attempt is made to execute them.

This right to secede is deduced from the nature of the Constitution, which, they say, is a compact between sovereign States, who have preserved their whole sovereignty, and, therefore, are subject to no superior; that, because they made the compact, they can break it when, in their opinion, it has been departed from by the other States. . . .

The people of the United States formed the Constitution, acting through the State Legislatures in making the compact, to meet and discuss its provisions, and acting in separate Conventions when they ratified those provisions; but the terms used in its construction, show it to be a government in which the people of all the States collectively are represented. . . .

The Constitution of the United States then forms a *government,* not a league; and whether it be formed by compact between the States, or in any other manner, its character is the same. It is a government in which all the people are represented, which operates directly on the people individually, not upon the States — they retained all the power they did not grant. But each State having expressly parted with so many powers as to constitute, jointly with the other States, a single nation, cannot, from that period, possess any right to secede, because such secession does not break a league, but destroys the unity of a nation; and any injury to that unity is not only a breach which would result from the contravention of a compact, but it is an offense against the whole Union. To say that any State may at pleasure secede from the Union, is to say that the United States are not a nation, because it would be a solecism to contend that any part of a nation might dissolve its connection with the other parts, to their injury or ruin, without committing any offense. Secession, like any other revolutionary act, may be morally justified by the extremity of oppression; but to call it a constitutional right, is confounding the meaning of terms; and can only be done through gross error, or to deceive those who are willing to assert a right, but would pause before they made a revolution, or incur the penalties consequent on a failure.

Because the Union was formed by compact, it is said the parties to that compact may, when they feel themselves aggrieved, depart from it; but it is precisely because it is a compact that they cannot. A compact is an agreement or binding obligation. It may by its terms have a sanction or penalty for its breach or it may not. If it contains no sanction, it may be broken with no other consequence than moral guilt; if it have a sanction, then the breach insures the designated or implied penalty. A league between independent nations, generally, has no sanction other than a moral one; or if it should contain a penalty, as there is no common superior, it cannot be enforced. A government, on the contrary, always has a sanction, express or implied; and, in our case, it is both necessarily implied and expressly given. An attempt, by force of arms, to destroy a government, is an offense by whatever means the constitutional compact may have been formed, and such government has the right, by the law of self-defense, to pass acts for punishing the offender, unless that right is modified, restrained, or resumed by the constitutional act. In our system, although it is modified in the case of treason, yet authority is expressly given to pass all laws necessary to carry its powers into effect, and, under this grant, provision has been made for punishing acts which obstruct the due administration of the laws.

. . . No one, fellow citizens, has a higher reverence for the reserved rights of the States than the magistrate who now addresses you. No one would make greater personal sacrifices, or official exertions, to defend them from violation; but equal care must be taken to prevent, on their part, an improper interference with, or resumption of, the rights they have vested in the nation. The line has not been so distinctly drawn as to avoid doubts in some cases of the exercise of power. Men of the best intentions and soundest views may differ in their construction of some parts of the Constitution; but there are others on which dispassionate reflection can leave no doubt. Of this nature appears to be the assumed right of secession. . . .

These are the alternatives that are presented by the Convention: a repeal of all the acts for raising revenue, leaving the Government without the means of support, or an acquiescence in the dissolution of our Union by the secession of one of its members. When the first was proposed, it was known that it could not be listened to for a moment. It was known, if force was applied to oppose the execution of the laws that it must be repelled by force; that Congress could not, without involving itself in disgrace and the country in ruin, accede to the proposition; and yet if this is not done in a given day, or if any attempt is made to execute the laws, the State is, by the ordinance, declared to be out of the Union. The majority of a Convention assembled for the purpose, have dictated these terms, or rather this rejection of all terms, in the name of the people of South Carolina. It is true that the Governor of the State speaks of the submission of their grievances to a Convention of all the States, which, he says, they "sincerely and anxiously seek and desire." Yet this obvious and constitutional mode of obtaining the sense of the other States on the construction of the federal compact, and amending it, if necessary, has never been attempted by those who have urged the State on to this destructive measure. The State might have proposed the call for a General Convention to the other States; and Congress, if a sufficient number of them concurred, must have called it. But the first magistrate of South Carolina, when he expressed a hope that, "on a review by Congress and the functionaries of the General Government, of the merits of the controversy," such a Convention will be accorded to them, must have known that neither Congress, nor any functionary of the General Government, has authority to call such a Convention, unless it be demanded by two-thirds of the States. This suggestion, then, is another instance of the reckless inattention to the provisions of the Constitution with which this crisis has been madly hurried on; or of the attempt to persuade the people that a constitutional remedy had been sought and refused. If the Legislature of South Carolina "anxiously desire" a General Convention to consider their complaints, why have they not made application for it in the way the Constitution points out? The assertion that they "earnestly seek it" is completely negatived by the omission.

This, then, is the position in which we stand. A small majority of the citizens of one State in the Union have elected delegates to a State Convention; that Convention has ordained that all the revenue laws of the United States must be repealed, or that they are no longer a member of the Union.

The Governor of that State has recommended to the Legislature the raising of an army to carry the secession into effect, and that he may be empowered to give clearances to vessels in the name of the State. No act of violent opposition to the laws has yet been committed, but such a state of things is hourly apprehended; and it is the intent of this instrument to proclaim, not only that the duty imposed on me by the Constitution "to take care that the laws be faithfully executed," shall be performed to the extent of the powers already vested in me by law, or of such others as the wisdom of Congress shall devise and entrust to me for that purpose, but to warn the citizens of South Carolina who have been deluded into an opposition to the laws, of the danger they will incur by obedience to the illegal and disorganizing ordinance of the Convention; to exhort those who have refused to support it to persevere in their determination to uphold the Constitution and laws of their country; and to point out to all the perilous situation into which the good people of that State have been led, and that the course they are urged to pursue is one of ruin and disgrace to the very State whose rights they affect to support. . . .

CHOOSE THE CORRECT ANSWER

Write the letter that best completes the statement or answers the question.

1. The Ordinance of Nullification was strongly supported by (*a*) Andrew Jackson, (*b*) John C. Calhoun, (*c*) John Quincy Adams, (*d*) Henry Clay.   1._____

2. Jackson felt that nullification would destroy (*a*) the armed forces, (*b*) the country's foreign trade, (*c*) the Union, (*d*) South Carolina.   2._____

3. A proclamation is (*a*) a law, (*b*) a statement of policy, (*c*) an order to the armed forces, (*d*) a request for action by Congress.   3._____

4. Jackson felt that South Carolina, if it felt the high tariff law was unfair, could have taken the matter to (*a*) the Supreme Court, (*b*) the President, (*c*) the tariff commissioners, (*d*) countries with which it wished to trade.   4._____

5. Jackson argued that a state did not have the power to (*a*) ask for a change in a federal law, (*b*) ask its representatives to vote against a proposed federal law, (*c*) pass laws which the

President did not approve, (*d*) refuse to obey a law passed by Congress. 5._____

6. The Constitution requires that all federal laws (*a*) must be acceptable to all the states, (*b*) must be voted for at each session of Congress, (*c*) must be the same all over the Union, (*d*) must raise money. 6._____

7. Jackson held that the United States was (*a*) a permanent government, (*b*) a league of independent states, (*c*) a confederation of equal nations, (*d*) an alliance of friendly states. 7._____

8. Jackson felt that the theory of nullification could (*a*) delay approval of laws, (*b*) weaken the powers of the states, (*c*) require greater care in changing tax laws, (*d*) destroy the Union. 8._____

9. An ordinance is (*a*) a threat, (*b*) a law, (*c*) a court decision, (*d*) a statement of policy. 9._____

10. Jackson thought the Constitution was really made by (*a*) the country's wisest men, (*b*) the state legislatures, (*c*) Congress, (*d*) the people of the United States. 10._____

THOUGHT QUESTIONS

1. Describe Jackson's concept of the supremacy of the federal government as stated in his Proclamation of 1832.

2. For what reasons did South Carolina withdraw the Ordinance of Nullification?

The Constitution of the American Anti-Slavery Society — 1833

* * * * *A number of anti-slavery societies* had been formed throughout the North by the early 1830's. Their leaders called a convention to form a national abolitionist organization.

Sixty delegates from Northern cities and states met in Philadelphia to draw up a constitution and a declaration of beliefs. William Lloyd Garrison, the most prominent abolitionist, was the outstanding personality at the convention. The society's constitution reflects Garrison's point of view. He considered slavery to be a legal crime which should be ended at once by peaceful means.

The Anti-Slavery Society was never very large or very powerful. However, this group, and others like it, spread anti-slavery propaganda for more than 25 years. By 1856, when the Republican Party ran Fremont for President, anti-slavery feeling was so widespread that the new party won a large part of the Northern vote.

Whereas the Most High God "hath made of one blood all nations of men to dwell on all the face of the earth," and hath commanded them to love their neighbors as themselves; and whereas, our National Existence is based upon this principle, as recognized in the Declaration of Independence, "that all mankind are created equal, and that they are endowed by their Creator with certain inalienable rights, among which are life, liberty, and the pursuit of happiness;" and whereas, after the lapse of nearly sixty years, since the faith and honor of the American people were pledged to this avowal, before Almighty God and the World, nearly one-sixth part of the nation are held in bondage by their fellow-citizens; and whereas, Slavery is contrary to the principles of natural justice, of our republican form of government, and of the Christian religion, and is destructive of the prosperity of the country, while it is endangering the peace, union, and liberties of the States; and whereas, we believe it the duty and interest of the masters immediately to emancipate their slaves, and that no scheme of expatriation, either voluntary or by compulsion, can remove this great and increasing evil; and whereas, we believe that it is practicable, by appeals to the consciences, hearts, and interests of the people, to awaken a public sentiment throughout the nation that will be opposed to the continuance of Slavery in any part of the Republic, and by effecting the speedy abolition of Slavery, prevent a general convulsion; and whereas, we believe we owe it to the oppressed, to our fellow-citizens who hold slaves, to our whole country, to posterity, and to God, to do all that is lawfully in our power to bring about the extinction of Slavery, we do hereby agree, with a prayerful reliance on the Divine aid, to form ourselves into a society, to be governed by the following Constitution: —

Article I.—This Society shall be called the American Anti-Slavery Society.

Article II. — The objects of this Society are the entire abolition of Slavery in the United States. While it admits that each State, in which Slavery exists, has, by the Constitution of the United States, the exclusive right to *legislate* in regard to its abolition in said State, it shall aim to convince all our fellow-citizens, by arguments addressed to their understandings and consciences, that Slaveholding is a heinous crime in the sight of God, and that the duty, safety, and best interests of all concerned, require its *immediate abandonment,* without expatriation. The Society will also endeavor, in a constitutional way, to influence Congress to put an end to the domestic Slave trade, and to abolish Slavery in all those portions of our common country which come under its control, especially in the District of Columbia, — and likewise to prevent the extension of it to any State that may be hereafter admitted to the Union.

Article III. — This Society shall aim to elevate the character and condition of the people of color, by encouraging their intellectual, moral, and religious improvement, and by removing public prejudice, that thus they may, according to their intellectual and moral worth, share an equality with the whites, of civil and religious privileges; but this Society will never, in any way, countenance the oppressed in vindicating their rights by resorting to physical force.

Article IV. — Any person who consents to the principles of this Constitution, who contributes to the funds of this Society, and is not a Slaveholder, may be a member of this Society, and shall be entitled to vote at the meetings. . . .

FILL IN THE ANSWERS

Write the word or phrase which best completes the statement.

1. The members of the Anti-Slavery Society were also called _____.

2. The Society said that one person out of each _____ in the nation was a slave.

3. The Society held that slavery could be ended without the use of _____.

4. The only people who were barred from membership in the Society were _____.

5. The Society wanted Congress to end the slave trade in the _____.

6. The leader of the convention which drew up the constitution of the society was _____.

7. The section of the country in which the Society was most successful was the _____.

8. The Anti-Slavery Society recognized the right of individual _____ to legislate against slavery.

9. The Society demanded that slavery be abolished immediately without voluntary or compulsory _____.

10. Nearly _____ of the American population was held in slavery in 1836.

THOUGHT QUESTIONS

1. Show how the abolitionist movement failed in its immediate goal, but proved successful in a long-range sense.

2. In what ways did the American Anti-Slavery Society hope to end slavery and improve the condition of the Negro?

Commonwealth vs Hunt 1842

* * * * *There had been organized labor* unions from the very beginning of the United States, the most successful including such craftsmen as printers and carpenters. As trade societies they provided their members with various welfare services. They were most numerous in large Northern cities. In some cities different labor groups joined to become city-wide federations.

The unions were hampered by the "conspiracy" laws which were then common in Europe and in many American states. These laws were interpreted by state courts to mean that any action which prevented a business from operating, as a strike would, was a criminal conspiracy. The leaders of the union involved would then be charged with criminal conspiracy. If found guilty, they could be fined or sentenced to jail.

A group of shoemakers, organized as the Boston Journeymen Bootmakers' Society, had set up a strong union in Boston. They required union membership before any worker could be hired by the shoemaking shops with which they made agreements. When the union forced the dismissal of one shoemaker, its leaders were charged with conspiracy and taken to the Massachusetts court.

The decision in the case, handed down by Chief Justice Lemuel Shaw, upheld the right of workers to organize unions, to try to raise their wages, and to strike for a closed shop.

This decision was the first of many to follow which placed unions in their present protected position as legal organizations.

SHAW, C. J. . . . The general rule of the common law is that it is a criminal and indictable offense for two or more to confederate and combine together, by concerted means, to do that which is unlawful or criminal, to the injury of the public, or portions or classes of the community, or even to the rights of an individual. This rule of law may be equally in force as a rule of the common law in England and in this commonwealth; and yet it must depend upon the local laws of each country to determine whether the purpose to be accomplished by the combination, or the concerted means of accomplishing it, be unlawful or criminal in the respective countries. . . .

. . . the defendants and others formed themselves into a society, and agreed not to work for any person who should employ any journeyman or other person not a member of such society, after notice given him to discharge such workman.

The manifest intent of the association is to induce all those engaged in the same occupation to become members of it. Such a purpose is not unlawful. It would give them a power which might be exerted for useful and honorable purposes, or for dangerous and pernicious ones. If the latter were the real and actual object, and susceptible of proof, it should have been specially charged. Such an association might be used to afford each other assistance in times of poverty, sickness and distress; or to raise their intellectual, moral and social condition; or to make improvement in their art; or for other proper purposes. Or the association might be designed for purposes of oppression and injustice. But in order to charge all those who become members of an association with the guilt of a criminal conspiracy, it must be averred and proved that the actual, if not the avowed object of the association, was criminal. An association may be formed, the declared objects of which are innocent and laudable, and yet they may have secret articles, or an agreement communicated only to the members, by which they are banded together for purposes injurious to the peace of society or the rights of its members. Such would undoubtedly be a criminal conspiracy, on proof of the fact, however meritorious and praiseworthy the declared objects might be. The law is not to be hoodwinked by colorable pretenses. It looks at truth and reality, through whatever disguise it may assume. But to make such an association, ostensibly innocent, the subject of prosecution as a criminal conspiracy, the secret agreement, which makes it so, is to be averred and proved as the gist of the offense. But when an association is formed for purposes actually innocent, and afterwards its powers are abused by those who have the control and management of it, to purposes of oppression and injustice, it will be criminal in those who thus misuse it or give consent thereto, but not in the other members of the association. In this case, no such secret agreement varying the objects of the association from those avowed is set forth in this count of the indictment.

Nor can we perceive that the objects of this association, whatever they may have been, were to be attained by criminal means. The means which they proposed to employ, as averred in this count, and which, as we are now to presume, were established by the proof, were that they would not work for a person who, after due notice, should employ a journeyman not a member of their society. Supposing the object of the association to be laudable and lawful, or at least not unlawful, are these means criminal? The case supposes that these persons are not bound by contract, but free to work for whom they please, or not to work, if they so prefer. In this state of things, we cannot perceive that it is criminal for men to agree together to exercise their own acknowledged rights in such a manner as best to subserve their own interests. One way to test this is to consider the effect of such an agreement where the object of the association is acknowledged on all hands to be a laudable one. Suppose a class of workmen, impressed with the manifold evils of intemperance, should agree with each other not to work in a shop in which ardent spirit was furnished, or not to work in a shop with any one who used it, or not to work for an employer who should, after notice, employ a journeyman who habitually used it. The consequences might be the same. A workman who should still persist in the use of ardent spirit, would find it more difficult to get employment; a master employing such an one might, at times, experience inconvenience in his work in losing the services of a skillful but intemperate workman. Still it seems to us that as the object would be lawful, and the means not unlawful, such an agreement could not be pronounced a criminal conspiracy.

From this count in the ·indictment, we do not understand that the agreement was, that the defendants would refuse to work for an employer, to whom they were bound by contract for a certain time, in violation of that contract; nor that they would insist that an employer should discharge a workman engaged by contract for a certain time, in violation of such contract. It is perfectly consistent with every thing stated in this count, that the effect of the agreement was that when they were free to act, they would not engage with an employer, or continue in his employment, if such employer, when free to act, should engage with a workman, or continue a workman in his employment, not a member of the association. If a large number of men, engaged for a certain time, should combine together to violate their contract, and quit their employment together, it would present a very different question. Suppose a farmer, employing a large number of men, engaged for the year at fair monthly wages, and suppose that just at the moment that his crops were ready to harvest, they should all combine to quit his service unless he would advance their wages at a time when other laborers could not be obtained. It would surely be a conspiracy to do an unlawful act, though of such a character that, if done by an individual, it would lay the foundation of a civil action only, and not of a criminal prosecution. It would be a case very different from that stated in this count.

The second count, omitting the recital of unlawful intent and evil disposition, and omitting the direct averment of an unlawful club or society, alleges that the defendants, with others unknown, did assemble, conspire, confederate and agree together, not to work for any master or person who should employ any workman not being a member of a certain club, society or combination, called the Boston Journeymen Bootmaker's Society, or who should break any of their by-laws, unless such workmen should pay to said club, such sum as should be agreed upon as a penalty for the breach of such unlawful rules, &c; and that by means of said conspiracy they did compel one Isaac B. Wait, a master cordwainer, to turn out of his employ one Jeremiah Horne, a journeyman boot-maker, &c. in evil example, &c. So far as the averment of a conspiracy is concerned, all the remarks made in reference to the first count are equally applicable to this. It is simply an averment of an agreement amongst themselves not to work for a person who should employ any person not a member of a certain association. It sets forth no illegal or criminal purpose to be accomplished, nor any illegal or criminal means to be adopted for the accomplishment of any purpose. It was an agreement as to the manner in which they would exercise an acknowledged right to contract with others for their labor. It does not aver a conspiracy or even an intention to raise their wages, and it appears by the bill of exceptions that the case was not put upon the footing of a conspiracy to raise their wages. . . .

We think, therefore, that associations may be entered into, the object of which is to adopt measures that may have a tendency to impoverish another, that is, to diminish his gains and profits, and yet so far from being criminal or unlawful, the object may be highly meritorious and public spirited. The legality of such an association will therefore depend upon the means to be used for its accomplishment. If it is to be carried into effect by fair or honorable and lawful means, it is, to say the least, innocent; if by falsehood or force, it may be stamped with the character of conspiracy. It follows as a necessary consequence that if criminal and indictable, it is so by reason of the criminal means intended to be employed for its accomplishment; and as a further legal consequence, that as the criminality will depend on the means, those means must be stated in the indictment. . . .

It appears by the bill of exceptions, that it was contended on the part of the defendants, that this indictment did not set forth any agreement to do a criminal act, or to do any lawful act by criminal means, and that the agreement therein set forth did not constitute a conspiracy indictable by the law of this State, and that the court was requested so to instruct the jury. This the court declined doing, but instructed the jury that the indictment did describe a confederacy among the defendants to do an unlawful act, and to effect the same by unlawful means—that the society, organized and associated for the purposes described in the indictment, was an unlawful conspiracy against the laws of this State, and that if the jury believed, from the evidence, that the defendants or any of them had engaged in such confederacy, they were bound to find such of them guilty.

In this opinion of the learned judge, this court, for the reason stated, cannot concur. Whatever illegal purpose can be found in the constitution of the Bootmakers' Society, it not being clearly set forth in the indictment, cannot be relied upon to support this conviction. So if any facts were disclosed at the trial, which, if properly averred, would have given a different character to the indictment, they do not appear in the bill of exceptions, nor could they, after verdict, aid the indictment. But looking solely at the indictment, disregarding the qualifying epithets, recitals and immaterial allegations, and confining ourselves to facts so averred as to be capable of being traversed and put in issue, we cannot perceive that it charges a criminal conspiracy punishable by law. The exceptions must, therefore, be sustained, and the judgment arrested. . . .

TRUE OR FALSE?

Write T *if the statement is correct; Write* F *if it is false.*

_____1. A conspiracy is a confederation of unions.

_____2. "Commonwealth" meant the state of Massachusetts.

_____3. Justice Shaw said only criminal actions would make a union a conspiracy.

_____4. The members of the union forced the Hunt Company to close down.

_____5. The union was charged with trying to raise the wages of its members.

_____6. Justice Shaw overthrew the conviction of the men charged with conspiracy.

_____7. It was charged that the constitution of the Bootmakers' Society showed it was organized for illegal purposes.

_____8. The court agreed that the Bootmakers' Society had a right to try to get all bootmakers to join it.

_____9. The lower court had insisted that the union was an unlawful conspiracy.

_____10. The decision ordered the union members to work for all companies, whether or not these companies employed non-union workers.

THOUGHT QUESTIONS

1. Describe the treatment state legislatures and state courts gave labor unions in the early years of the 19th Century.
2. Make specific references to the decision in *Commonwealth versus Hunt* to show why Chief Justice Shaw felt that unions were proper and legal associations.

The Compromise of 1850

* * * * *In 1849 the people of California* adopted a state constitution which included a provision that prohibited slavery. California then applied for statehood as a free state. For the next six months Congress was torn by discord, as its Southern members refused to admit another free state. Henry Clay returned to the Senate to make his last great effort to keep peace between the sections.

Clay developed a series of bills which are collectively known as the Compromise of 1850. California was admitted as a free state. The slave trade was ended in the District of Columbia. A new and stricter Fugitive Slave Law was added to please the South. The new idea of "popular sovereignty" was to be applied to the territories of Utah and New Mexico, whose people would later decide the question of slavery for themselves. Texas was made smaller, and was paid for the land it lost.

Clay, Webster, and the others who had worked to gain the approval of the Compromise, felt that they had settled the slavery question. They were wrong, for the events of the next ten years were to end in a bitter civil war.

Clay's Resolutions (January 29, 1850)

It being desirable, for the peace, concord, and harmony of the Union of these States, to settle and adjust amicably all existing questions of controversy between them arising out of the institution of slavery upon a fair, equitable and just basis: therefore,

1. *Resolved,* That California, with suitable boundaries, ought, upon her application to be admitted as one of the States of this Union, without the imposition by Congress of any restriction in respect to the exclusion or introduction of slavery within those boundaries.

2. *Resolved,* That as slavery does not exist by law, and is not likely to be introduced into any of the territory acquired by the United States from the republic of Mexico, it is inexpedient for Congress to provide by law either for its introduction into, or exclusion from, any part of the said territory; and that appropriate territorial governments ought to be established by Congress in all of the said territory, not assigned as the boundaries of the proposed State of California, without the adoption of any restriction or condition on the subject of slavery.

3. *Resolved,* That the western boundary of the State of Texas ought to be fixed on the Rio del Norte, commencing one marine league from its mouth, and running up that river to the southern line of New Mexico; thence with that line eastwardly, and so continuing in the same direction to the line as established between the United States and Spain, excluding any portion of New Mexico, whether lying on the east or west of that river.

4. *Resolved,* That it be proposed to the State of Texas, that the United States will provide for the payment of all

that portion of the legitimate and bona fide public debt of that State contracted prior to its annexation to the United States, and for which the duties on foreign imports were pledged by the said State to its creditors, not exceeding the sum of —— dollars, in consideration of the said duties so pledged having been no longer applicable to that object after the said annexation, but having thenceforward become payable to the United States; and upon the condition, also, that the said State of Texas shall, by some solemn and authentic act of her legislature or of a convention, relinquish to the United States any claim which it has to any part of New Mexico.

5. *Resolved,* That it is inexpedient to abolish slavery in the District of Columbia whilst that institution continues to exist in the State of Maryland, without the consent of that State, without the consent of the people of the District, and without just compensation to the owners of slaves within the District.

6. *But, resolved,* That it is expedient to prohibit, within the District, the slave trade in slaves brought into it from States or places beyond the limits of the District, either to be sold therein as merchandise, or to be transported to other markets without the District of Columbia.

7. *Resolved,* That more effectual provision ought to be made by law, according to the requirement of the constitution, for the restitution and delivery of persons bound to service or labor in any State, who may escape into any other State or Territory in the Union. And,

8. *Resolved,* That Congress has no power to prohibit or obstruct the trade in slaves between the slaveholding States; but that the admission or exclusion of slaves brought from one into another of them, depends exclusively upon their own particular laws.

Extract from the Utah Act
(September 9, 1850)

An Act to Establish a Territorial Government for Utah.

Be it enacted . . . , That all that part of the territory of the United States included within the following limits, to wit: bounded on the west by the State of California, on the north by the Territory of Oregon, and on the east by the summit of the Rocky Mountains, and on the south by the thirty-seventh parallel of north latitude, be, and the same is hereby, created into a temporary government, by the name of the Territory of Utah; and, when admitted as a State, the said Territory, or any portion of the same, shall be received into the Union, with or without slavery, as their constitution may prescribe at the time of their admission: *Provided,* That nothing in this act contained shall be construed to inhibit the government of the United States from dividing said Territory into two or more Territories, in such manner and at such times as Congress shall deem convenient and proper, or from attaching any portion of said Territory to any other State or Territory of the United States. . . .

Extract from the Texas and New Mexico Act (September 9, 1850)

Section 2. And be it further enacted, That all that portion of the Territory of the United States bounded as follows: Beginning at a point in the Colorado River where the boundary line with the republic of Mexico crosses the same; thence eastwardly with the said boundary line to the Rio Grande; thence following the main channel of said river to the parallel of the thirty-second degree of north latitude; thence east with said degree to its intersection with the one hundred and third degree of longitude west of Greenwich; thence north with said degree of longitude to the parallel of thirty-eighth degree of north latitude; thence west with said parallel to the summit of the Sierra Madre; thence south with the crest of said mountains to the thirty-seventh parallel of north latitude; thence west with said parallel to its intersection with the boundary line of the State of California; thence with said boundary line to the place of beginning — be, and the same is hereby, erected into a temporary government, by the name of the Territory of New Mexico: *Provided,* That nothing in this act contained shall be construed to inhibit the government of the United States from dividing said Territory into two or more Territories, in such manner and at such times as Congress shall deem convenient and proper, or from attaching any portion thereof to any other Territory or State: *And provided, further,* That, when admitted as a State, the said Territory, or any portion of the same, shall be received into the Union, with or without slavery, as their constitution may prescribe at the time of their admission.

Extracts from the Fugitive Slave Act (September 18, 1850)

Section 5. And be it further enacted, That it shall be the duty of all marshals and deputy marshals to obey and execute all warrants and precepts issued under the provisions of this act, when to them directed; . . . and after arrest of such fugitive, by such marshal or his deputy, or whilst at any time in his custody under the provisions of this act, should such fugitive escape, whether with or without the assent of such marshal or his deputy, such marshal shall be liable, on his official bond, to be prosecuted for the benefit of such claimant, for the full value of the service or labor of said fugitive in the State, Territory, or District whence he escaped. . . .

Section 6. And be it further enacted, That when a person held to service or labor in any State or Territory of the United States, has heretofore or shall hereafter escape into another State or Territory of the United States, the person or persons to whom such service or labor may be due, or his, her, or their agent or attorney, duly authorized, by power of attorney, in writing, . . . may pursue and reclaim such fugitive person, . . . and upon satisfactory proof being made, by deposition or affidavit, in writing, . . . and with proof, also by affidavit, of the identity of the person whose service or labor is claimed to be due as aforesaid, that the person so arrested does in fact owe service or labor to the person or persons claiming him or her, in the State or Territory from which such fugitive may have escaped as aforesaid, and that said person escaped, to make out and deliver to such claimant, his or her agent or attorney, a certificate setting forth the substantial facts as to the service or labor due from such fugitive to the claimant, and of his or her escape from the State or Territory in which he or she was arrested, with authority to such claimant, or his or her agent or attorney, to use such reasonable force and restraint as may be necessary, under the circumstances of the case, to take and remove such fugitive person back to the State or Territory whence he or she may have escaped as aforesaid. In no trial or hearing under this act shall the testimony of such alleged fugitive be admitted in evidence; and the certificates in this and the first [fourth] section mentioned, shall be conclusive of the right of the person or persons in whose favor granted, to remove such fugitive to the State or Territory from which he escaped, and shall prevent all molestation of such person or persons by any process issued by any court, judge, magistrate, or other person whomsoever.

Section 7. And be it further enacted, That any person who shall knowingly and willingly obstruct, hinder, or prevent such claimant, his agent or attorney, or any person or persons lawfully assisting him, her, or them, from arresting such a fugitive from service or labor, either with or without process as aforesaid, or shall rescue, or attempt to rescue, such fugitive from service or labor, from the custody of such claimant, his or her agent or attorney, or other person or persons lawfully assisting as aforesaid, when so arrested, pursuant to the authority herein given and declared; or shall aid, abet, or assist such person so owing service or labor as aforesaid, directly or indirectly, to escape from such claimant, his agent or attorney, or other person or persons legally authorized as aforesaid; or shall harbor or conceal such fugitive, so as to prevent the discovery and arrest of such person, after notice or knowledge of the fact that such person was a fugitive from service or labor as aforesaid, shall, for either of said offenses, be subject to a fine not exceeding one thousand dollars, and imprisonment not exceeding six months . . . ; and shall moreover forfeit and pay, by way of civil damages to the party injured by such illegal conduct, the sum of one thousand dollars, for each fugitive so lost as aforesaid. . . .

Section 9. And be it further enacted, That, upon affidavit made by the claimant of such fugitive, his agent or attorney, after such certificate has been issued, that he has reason to apprehend that such fugitive will be rescued by force from his or their possession before he can be taken beyond the limits of the State in which the arrest is made, it shall be the duty of the officer making the arrest to retain such fugitive in his custody, and to remove him to the State whence he fled, and there to deliver him to said claimant, his agent, or attorney. And to this end, the officer aforesaid is hereby authorized and required to employ so many persons as he may deem necessary to overcome such force, and to retain them in his service so long as circumstances may require. . . .

Section 10. And be it further enacted, That when any person held to service or labor in any State or Territory, or in the District of Columbia, shall escape therefrom, the party to whom such service or labor shall be due, his, her, or their agent or attorney, may apply to any court of record therein, or judge thereof in vacation, and make satisfactory proof to such court, or judge in vacation, of the escape aforesaid, and that the person escaping owed service or labor to such party. Whereupon the court shall cause a record to be made of the matters so proved, and also a general description of the person so escaping, with such convenient certainty as may be; and a transcript of such record, authenticated by the attestation of the clerk and of the seal of the said court, being produced in any other State, Territory, or district in which the person so escaping may be found, and being exhibited to any judge, commissioner, or the officer authorized by the law of the United States to cause persons escaping from service or labor to be delivered up, shall be held and taken to be full and conclusive evidence of the fact of escape, and that the service or labor of the person escaping is due to the party in such record mentioned. And upon the production by the said party of other and further evidence if necessary, either oral or by affidavit, in addition to what is contained in the said record of the identity of the person escaping, he or she shall be delivered up to the claimant. And the said court, commissioner, judge, or other person authorized by this act to grant certificates to claimants of fugitives, shall, upon the production of the record and other evidences aforesaid, grant to such claimant a certificate of his right to take any such person identified and proved to be owing service or labor as aforesaid, which certificate shall authorize such claimant to seize or arrest and transport such person to the State or Territory from which he escaped . . .

Act Abolishing the Slave Trade in the District of Columbia (September 20, 1850)

Be it enacted . . . , That from and after . . . [January 1, 1851], . . . it shall not be lawful to bring into the District of Columbia any slave whatever, for the purpose of being sold, or for the purpose of being placed in depot, to be subsequently transferred to any other State or place to be sold as merchandise. And if any slave shall be brought into the said District by its owner, or by the authority or consent of its owner, contrary to the provisions of this act, such slave shall thereupon become liberated and free.

Section 2. And be it further enacted, That it shall and may be lawful for each of the corporations of the cities of Washington and Georgetown, from time to time, and as often as may be necessary, to abate, break up, and abolish any depot or place of confinement of slaves brought into the said District as merchandise, contrary to the provisions of this act, by such appropriate means as may appear to either of the said corporations expedient and proper. And the same power is hereby vested in the Levy Court of Washington county, if any attempt shall be made, within its jurisdictional limits, to establish a depot or place of confinement for slaves brought into the said District as merchandise for sale contrary to this act.

CHOOSE THE CORRECT ANSWER

Write the letter that best completes the statement or answers the question.

1. Henry Clay felt that the question of slavery in the territories (*a*) would never be decided, (*b*) should not be decided by Congress, (*c*) had to be decided at once, (*d*) must never be discussed in public.   1._____

2. The state which was made smaller was (*a*) Texas, (*b*) Utah, (*c*) New Mexico, (*d*) California.   2._____

3. Clay felt that the slave trade (*a*) could never be ended, (*b*) should be regulated by Congress, (*c*) should be controlled by the states, (*d*) should be ended in all states at once.   3._____

4. The question of slavery in Utah was to be decided by (a) the state legislature, (b) the state's governor, (c) a special state convention, (d) the state's constitution.   4._____

5. The territory which might be divided into two or more territories by Congress was (a) California, (b) Maryland, (c) New Mexico, (d) Texas.   5._____

6. A fugitive is one who has (a) committed a crime, (b) run away illegally, (c) refused to obey a public official, (d) been in jail.   6._____

7. Suppose a marshal had caught and then lost a runaway slave. The marshal would then (a) lose his job, (b) have to pay the value of the slave, (c) be jailed as a criminal, (d) be made a slave.   7._____

8. A slave brought into the District of Columbia to be sold or traded would (a) be freed, (b) be sent back to his home state, (c) become the property of the United States government, (d) be placed in a special depot.   8._____

9. "Popular sovereignty" refers to the decision of the people of a territory regarding (a) becoming a state, (b) choosing their legislature, (c) secession, (d) slavery.   9._____

10. A person who helped a slave escape (a) could be made a slave as punishment, (b) could be forced to leave the United States, (c) could be jailed and fined, (d) could not be punished.   10._____

THOUGHT QUESTIONS

1. In what ways did the Compromise of 1850 satisfy the North? The South?

2. Explain the statement: The Compromise of 1850 seemed to settle everything, but only postponed the final settlement.

The Dred Scott Decision 1857

* * * * *Dred Scott was a Negro slave who* belonged to Dr. John Emerson, an army doctor. In 1834, Dr. Emerson took Scott from Missouri — slave territory — to his new posts in Illinois and Wisconsin — free territory. In 1838, Emerson returned to Missouri, taking Scott with him. After Emerson's death in 1847, Dred Scott sued for his freedom in a Missouri state court. He argued that he had become free by living in free territory. He was freed by the court, but the Missouri Supreme Court overturned the decision on the grounds that Scott had returned to Missouri voluntarily and resumed his slavery.

During the long suit, Scott and his family became the property of John Sandford of New York. Sandford, who was anti-slavery, decided to reopen the case so that the United States Supreme Court would have to decide it. Scott sued Sandford for his freedom in a federal court, for he was from Missouri and Sandford from New York.

The Supreme Court, under Chief Justice Taney,

included seven Democrats, five of them Southerners. Taney read the majority decision in the case, supported by the six other Democrats. The decision held that Scott was not a citizen of Missouri, and that a slave did not become free when he lived in free territory. It also held that Congress could not limit or prohibit slavery in any territories belonging to the United States. This meant that the Missouri Compromise of 1820, which had been repealed in 1854, was unconstitutional.

The Dred Scott decision, excerpts of which are given here, was viewed as a great Southern victory. Slavery could be extended to the West, and protected all over the country. Northern reaction was bitter. Abolitionist sentiment increased, and the new Republican Party won ever greater popular support.

Taney's distinction between state and United States citizenship was overturned by the 14th Amendment to the Constitution.

Taney's Opinion

The plaintiff in error, who was also the plaintiff in the court below, was, with his wife and children, held as slaves by the defendant, in the State of Missouri, and he brought this action in the Circuit Court of the United States for that district, to assert the title of himself and his family to freedom.

The declaration is in the form usually adopted in that State to try questions of this description, and contains the averment necessary to give the court jurisdiction; that he and the defendant are citizens of different States; that is, that he is a citizen of Missouri, and the defendant a citizen of New York.

The defendant pleaded in abatement to the jurisdiction of the court, that the plaintiff was not a citizen of the State of Missouri, as alleged in his declaration, being a Negro of

African descent, whose ancestors were of pure African blood, and who were brought into this country and sold as slaves.

The question is simply this: can a Negro, whose ancestors were imported into this country and sold as slaves, become a member of the political community formed and brought into existence by the Constitution of the United States, and as such become entitled to all the rights, and privileges, and immunities, guarantied by that instrument to the citizen? One of these rights is the privilege of suing in a court of the United States in the cases specified in the Constitution. . . . The court must be understood as speaking in this opinion . . . of those persons [only] who are the descendants of Africans who were imported into this country and sold as slaves. . . .

The words "people of the United States" and "citizens" are synonymous terms, and mean the same thing. They both describe the political body who, according to our republican institutions, form the sovereignty, and who hold the power and conduct the government through their representatives. They are what we familiarly call the "sovereign people," and every citizen is one of this people, and a constituent member of this sovereignty. The question before us is, whether the class of persons described in the plea in abatement compose a portion of this people, and are constituent members of this sovereignty? We think they are not, and that they are not included, and were not intended to be included, under the word "citizens" in the Constitution, and can, therefore, claim none of the rights and privileges which that instrument provides for and secures to citizens of the United States. On the contrary, they were at that time considered as a subordinate and inferior class of beings, who had been subjugated by the dominant race, and whether emancipated or not, yet remained subject to their authority, and had no rights or privileges but such as those who held the power and the government might choose to grant them. . . .

In discussing this question, we must not confound the rights of citizenship which a state may confer within its own limits, and the rights of citizenship as a member of the Union. It does not by any means follow, because he has all the rights and privileges of a citizen of a State, that he must be a citizen of the United States. He may have all of the rights and privileges of the citizen of a State, and yet not be entitled to the rights and privileges of a citizen in any other State. For, previous to the adoption of the Constitution of the United States, every State had the undoubted right to confer on whomsoever it pleased the character of a citizen, and to endow him with all its rights. But this character, of course, was confined to the boundaries of the State, and gave him no rights or privileges in other States beyond those secured to him by the laws of nations and the comity of States. Nor have the several States surrendered the power of conferring these rights and privileges by adopting the Constitution of the United States. Each State may still confer them upon an alien, or any one it thinks proper, or upon any class or description of persons; yet he would not be a citizen in the sense in which that word is used in the Constitution of the United States, nor entitled to sue as such in one of its courts, nor to the privileges and immunities of a citizen in the other States. The rights which he would acquire would be restricted to the state which gave them. . . .

It is very clear, therefore, that no State can, by any Act or law of its own, passed since the adoption of the Constitution, introduce a new member into the political community created by the Constitution of the United States. It cannot make him a member of this community by making him a member of its own. And for the same reason it cannot introduce any person, or description of persons, who were not intended to be embraced in this new political family, which the Constitution brought into existence, but were intended to be excluded from it.

The question then arises, whether the provisions of the Constitution, in relation to the personal rights and privileges to which the citizen of a State should be entitled, embraced the Negro African race, at that time in this country, or who might afterwards be imported, who had then or should afterwards be made free in any State; and to put it in the power of a single State to make him a citizen of the United States, and endue him with the full rights of citizenship in every other State without their consent. Does the Constitution of the United States act upon him whenever he shall be made free under the laws of a State, and raised there to the rank of a citizen, and immediately clothe him with all the privileges of a citizen in every other State, and in its own courts?

The court think the affirmative of these propositions cannot be maintained. And if it cannot, the plaintiff in error could not be a citizen of the State of Missouri, within the meaning of the Constitution of the United States, and, consequently, was not entitled to sue in its courts.

It becomes necessary, therefore, to determine who were citizens of the several States when the Constitution was adopted. And in order to do this, we must recur to the governments and institutions of the thirteen Colonies, when they separated from Great Britain and formed new sovereignties. . . . We must inquire who, at that time, were recognized as the people or citizens of a State. . . .

In the opinion of the court, the legislation and histories of the times, and the language used in the Declaration of Independence, show, that neither the class of persons who had been imported as slaves, nor their descendants, whether they had become free or not, were then acknowledged as a part of the people, nor intended to be included in the general words used in that memorable instrument. . . .

The legislation of the States therefore shows, in a manner not to be mistaken, the inferior and subject condition of that race at the time the Constitution was adopted, and long afterwards, throughout the thirteen States by which that instrument was framed. . . .

But it is said that a person may be a citizen, and entitled to that character, although he does not possess all the rights which may belong to other citizens; as, for example, the right to vote, or to hold particular offices; and that yet, when he goes into another State, he is entitled to be recognized there as a citizen, although the State may measure his rights by the rights which it allows to persons of a like character or class, resident in the State, and refuse to him the full rights of citizenship. . . .

Undoubtedly, a person may be a citizen, that is, a member of the community who form the sovereignty, although he exercises no share of the political power, and is incapacitated from holding particular offices. . . .

So, too, a person may be entitled to vote by the law of the State, who is not a citizen even of the State itself. And in some of the States of the Union foreigners not naturalized are allowed to vote. And the State may give the right to free Negroes and mulattoes, but that does not make them citizens of the State, and still less of the United States. And the provision in the Constitution giving privileges and immunities in other States, does not apply to them.

Neither does it apply to a person who, being the citizen of a State, migrates to another State. For then he becomes subject to the laws of the State in which he lives, and he is no longer a citizen of the State from which he removed. And the State in which he resides may then, unquestionably, determine his *status* or condition, and place him among the class of persons who are not recognized as citizens, but belong to an inferior and subject race; and may deny him the privileges and immunities enjoyed by its citizens.

. . . But if he ranks as a citizen of the State to which he belongs, within the meaning of the Constitution of the United States, then, whenever he goes into another State, the Constitution clothes him, as to the rights of person, with all the privileges and immunities which belong to citizens of the State. And if persons of the African race are citizens of a state, and of the United States, they would be entitled to all of these privileges and immunities in every State, and the State could not restrict them. . . .

And upon a full and careful consideration of the subject, the court is of opinion that, upon the facts stated in the plea in abatement, Dred Scott was not a citizen of Missouri within the meaning of the Constitution of the United States, and not entitled as such to sue in its courts; and, consequently, that the Circuit Court had no jurisdiction of the case, and that the judgment on the plea in abatement is erroneous. . . .

We proceed, therefore, to inquire whether the facts relied on by the plaintiff entitled him to his freedom. . . .

In considering this part of the controversy, two questions arise: 1st, Was he, together with his family, free in Missouri by reason of the stay in the territory of the United States hereinbefore mentioned? And 2d, If they were not, is Scott himself free by reason of his removal to Rock Island, in the State of Illinois, as stated in the above admissions?

We proceed to examine the first question.

The Act of Congress, upon which the plaintiff relies, declares that slavery and involuntary servitude, except as a punishment for crime, shall be forever prohibited in all that part of the territory ceded by France, under the name of Louisiana, which lies north of thirty-six degrees thirty minutes north latitude, and not included within the limits of Missouri. And the difficulty which meets us at the threshold of this part of the inquiry is, whether Congress was authorized to pass this law under any of the powers granted to it by the Constitution; for if the authority is not given by that instrument, it is the duty of this court to declare it void and inoperative, and incapable of conferring freedom upon any one who is held as a slave under the laws of any one of the States.

Now . . . the right of property in a slave is distinctly and expressly affirmed in the Constitution. The right to traffic in it, like an ordinary article of merchandise and property, was guaranteed to the citizens of the United States, in every State that might desire it, for twenty years. And the government in express terms is pledged to protect it in all future time, if the slave escapes from his owner. . . . And no word can be found in the Constitution which gives Congress a greater power over slave property, or which entitles property of that kind to less protection than property of any other description. The only power conferred is the power coupled with the duty of guarding and protecting the owner in his rights.

Upon these considerations, it is the opinion of the court that the Act of Congress which prohibited a citizen from holding and owning property of this kind in the territory of the United States north of the line therein mentioned, is not warranted by the Constitution, and is therefore void; and that neither Dred Scott himself, nor any of his family, were made free by being carried into this territory; even if they had been carried there by the owner, with the intention of becoming a permanent resident. . . .

But there is another point in the case which depends on state power and state law. And it is contended, on the part of the plaintiff, that he is made free by being taken to Rock Island, in the State of Illinois, independently of his residence in the territory of the United States; and being so made free, he was not again reduced to a state of slavery by being brought back to Missouri.

. . . as Scott was a slave when taken into the State of Illinois by his owner, and was there held as such, and brought back in that character, his *status,* as free or slave, depended on the laws of Missouri, and not of Illinois.

It has, however, been urged in the argument, that by the laws of Missouri he was free on his return . . . But . . . we are satisfied, upon a careful examination of all the cases decided in the State courts of Missouri referred to, that it is now firmly settled by the decisions of the highest court in the State, that Scott and his family upon their return were not free, but were, by the laws of Missouri, the property of the defendant; and that the Circuit Court of the United States had no jurisdiction, when, by the laws of the State, the plaintiff was a slave, and not a citizen. . . .

Upon the whole, therefore, it is the judgment of this court, that it appears by the record before us that the plaintiff in error is not a citizen of Missouri, in the sense in which that word is used in the Constitution; and that the Circuit Court of the United States, for that reason, had no jurisdiction in the case, and could give no judgment in it.

Its judgment for the defendant must, consequently, be reversed, and a mandate issued directing the suit to be dismissed for want of jurisdiction.

Justice Curtis's Dissenting Opinion

. . . the question is, whether any person of African descent, whose ancestors were sold as slaves in the United States, can be a citizen of the United States. If any such person can be a citizen, this plaintiff has the right to the judgment of the court that he is so; for no cause is shown by the plea why he is not so, except his descent and the slavery of his ancestors.

The 1st Section of the 2nd Article of the Constitution uses the language, "a citizen of the United States at the time of the adoption of the Constitution." One mode of approaching this question is to inquire who were citizens of the United States at the time of the adoption of the Constitution.

Citizens of the United States at the time of the adoption of the Constitution can have been no other than the citizens of the United States under the Confederation. . . .

To determine whether any free persons, descended from Africans held in slavery, were citizens of the United States under the Confederation, and consequently at the time of the adoption of the Constitution of the United States, it is only necessary to know whether any such persons were citizens of either of the States under the Confederation at the time of the adoption of the Constitution.

Of this there can be no doubt. At the time of the ratification of the Articles of Confederation, all free native-born inhabitants of the States of New Hampshire, Massachusetts, New York, New Jersey and North Carolina, though descended from African slaves, were not only citizens of those States, but such of them as had the other necessary qualifications possessed the franchise of electors, on equal terms with other citizens. . . .

I can find nothing in the Constitution which . . . deprives of their citizenship any class of persons who were citizens of the United States at the time of its adoption, or who should be native-born citizens of any State after its adoption; nor any power enabling Congress to disfranchise persons born on the soil of any State, and entitled to citizenship of such State by its constitution and laws. And my opinion is, that, under the Constitution of the United States, every free person born on the soil of a State, who is a citizen of that State by force of its Constitution or laws, is also a citizen of the United States. . . .

The Constitution having recognized the rule that persons born within the several States are citizens of the United States, one of four things must be true:

First. That the Constitution itself has described what native-born persons shall or shall not be citizens of the United States; or,

Second. That it has empowered Congress to do so; or,

Third. That all free persons, born within the several States, are citizens of the United States; or,

Fourth. That it is left to each State to determine what free persons, born within its limits, shall be citizens of such State, and thereby be citizens of the United States. . . .

The conclusions at which I have arrived on this part of the case are:

First. That the free native-born citizens of each State are citizens of the United States.

Second. That as free colored persons born within some of the States are citizens of those States, such persons are also citizens of the United States.

Third. That every such citizen, residing in any State, has

the right to sue and is liable to be sued in the federal courts, as a citizen of that State in which he resides.

Fourth. That as the plea to the jurisdiction in this case shows no facts, except that the plaintiff was of African descent, and his ancestors were sold as slaves, and as these facts are not inconsistent with his citizenship of the United States, and his residence in the State of Missouri, the plea to the jurisdiction was bad, and the judgment of the Circuit Court overruling it, was correct.

I dissent, therefore, from the part of the opinion of the majority of the court, in which it is held that a person of African descent cannot be a citizen of the United States; and I regret I must go further, and dissent both from what I deem their assumption of authority to examine the constitutionality of the Act of Congress commonly called the Missouri Compromise Act, and the grounds and conclusions announced in their opinion. . . .

But as, in my opinion, the Circuit Court had jurisdiction, I am obliged to consider the question whether its judgment on the merits of the case should stand or be reversed.

The residence of the plaintiff in the State of Illinois, and the residence of himself and his wife in the Territory acquired from France lying north of latitude thirty-six degrees thirty minutes, and north of the State of Missouri, are each relied on by the plaintiff in error. As the residence in the Territory affects the plaintiff's wife and children as well as himself, I must inquire what was its effect.

The general question may be stated to be, whether the plaintiff's *status,* as a slave, was so changed by his residence within that Territory, that he was not a slave in the State of Missouri, at the time this action was brought.

In such cases, two inquiries arise, which may be confounded, but should be kept distinct.

The first is, what was the law of the Territory into which the master and slave went, respecting the relation between them?

The second is, whether the State of Missouri recognizes and allows the effect of that law of the Territory, on the *status* of the slave, on his return within its jurisdiction. . . .

To avoid misapprehension on this important and difficult subject, I will state, distinctly, the conclusions at which I have arrived. They are:

First. The rules of international law respecting the emancipation of slaves, by the rightful operation of the laws of another State or country upon the *status* of the slave, while resident in such foreign State or country, are part of the common law of Missouri, and have not been abrogated by any statute law of that State.

Second. The laws of the United States, constitutionally enacted which operated directly on and changed the *status* of a slave coming into the Territory of Wisconsin with his master, who went thither to reside for an indefinite length of time, in the performance of his duties as an officer of the United States, had a rightful operation on the *status* of the slave, and it is in conformity with the rules of international law that this change of *status* should be recognized everywhere.

Third. The laws of the United States, in operation in the Territory of Wisconsin at the time of the plaintiff's residence there, did act directly on the *status* of the plaintiff, and change his *status* to that of a free man. . . .

Fifth. That the consent of the master that his slave, residing in a country which does not tolerate slavery, may enter into a lawful contract of marriage, attended with the civil rights and duties which belong to that condition, is an effectual act of emancipation. . . .

I have thus far assumed, merely for the purpose of the argument, that the laws of the United States, respecting slavery in this Territory, were Constitutionally enacted by Congress. It remains to inquire whether they are constitutional and binding laws. . . .

But it is insisted, that whatever other power Congress may have respecting the Territory of the United States, the subject of Negro slavery forms an exception. . . .

. . . it would, in my opinion, violate every sound rule of interpretation to force that exception into the Constitution upon the strength of abstract political reasoning, which we are bound to believe the people of the United States thought insufficient to induce them to limit the power of Congress, because what they have said contains no such limitation. . . .

But it is further insisted that the Treaty of 1803, between the United States and France, by which this Territory was acquired, has so restrained the constitutional powers of Congress, that it cannot, by law, prohibit the introduction of slavery into that part of this Territory north and west of Missouri, and north of thirty-six degrees thirty minutes north latitude.

By a treaty with a foreign nation, the United States may rightfully stipulate that the Congress will or will not exercise its legislative power in some particular manner, on some particular subject. . . . But that a treaty with a foreign nation can deprive the Congress of any part of the legislative power conferred by the people, so that it no longer can legislate as it was empowered by the Constitution to do, I more than doubt. . . .

But, in my judgment, this Treaty contains no stipulation in any manner affecting the action of the United States respecting the Territory in question. . . . In my opinion, this Treaty has no bearing on the present question.

For these reasons, I am of opinion that so much of the several Acts of Congress as prohibited slavery and involuntary servitude within that part of the Territory of Wisconsin lying north of thirty-six degrees thirty minutes north latitude, and west of the River Mississippi, were constitutional and valid laws. . . .

In my opinion, the judgment of the Circuit Court should be reversed, and the case remanded for a new trial.

FILL IN THE ANSWERS

Write the word or phrase which best completes the statement.

1. Dred Scott claimed his freedom because he had moved from _____ to _____ territory.

2. Justice Taney held that Negroes were not _____ and therefore couldn't _____ in court.

3. Taney believed that Negroes could not be _____ of the United States.

4. Justice Taney upheld the laws of the state of _____ in his decision.

5. Justice Curtis argued that a free Negro could be a _____ of the United States.

6. The law held unconstitutional by the majority of the Supreme Court was the _____.

7. Slavery had been prohibited since 1787 in Wisconsin Territory by the law called _____.

8. The growth of Northern abolitionist sentiment following the Dred Scott Decision strengthened the _____ Party.

9. Chief Justice Taney questioned whether a freed slave granted citizenship in any one state, became automatically a citizen of the _____.

10. Justice Curtis argued that the treaty with France could not deprive the American _____ of its power to legislate under the Constitution.

THOUGHT QUESTIONS

1. What part did the Dred Scott Decision play in the growing national controversy over slavery?

2. Compare the arguments of Justices Taney and Curtis with reference to the meaning of citizenship, the rights of Negroes, and Congress's power to legislate regarding slavery.

Lincoln Documents 1858-1865

* * * * *In 1858, Abraham Lincoln, a comparatively* unknown political figure, was nominated by the Illinois Republican Party to run for the Senate against Stephen A. Douglas, one of the best-known men in the nation. Douglas had appealed to pro-slavery groups by his support of the Dred Scott decision. He appealed also to anti-slavery groups in presenting the theory of "squatter sovereignty." This theory was based on the argument that the people of any territory could decide the question of slavery for themselves.

Lincoln's speech to the Republican convention presented his strong reaction to the Dred Scott decision, and to Douglas' support of it.

The "House Divided" Speech
(June 16, 1858)

. . . We are now far into the fifth year since a policy was initiated with the avowed object and confident promise of putting an end to slavery agitation. Under the operation of that policy, that agitation has not only not ceased, but has constantly augmented. In my opinion, it will not cease until a crisis shall have been reached and passed. A house divided against itself ˎcannot stand. I believe this government cannot endure permanently half slave and half free. I do not expect the Union to be dissolved; I do not expect the house to fall; but I do expect it will cease to be divided. It will become all one thing, or all the other. Either the opponents of slavery will arrest the further spread of it, and place it where the public mind shall rest in the belief that it is in the course of ultimate extinction, or its advocates will push it forward till it shall become alike lawful in all the States, old as well as new, North as well as South.

. . . .

While the Nebraska Bill was passing through Congress, a *law case,* involving the question of a Negro's freedom, by reason of his owner having voluntarily taken him first into a free State, and then into a territory covered by the Congressional prohibition, and held him as a slave for a long time in each, was passing through the United States Circuit Court for the District of Missouri; and both Nebraska Bill and lawsuit were brought to a decision in the same month of May, 1854. The Negro's name was "Dred Scott," which name now designates the decision finally made in the case. Before the then next Presidential election, the law case came to, and was argued in, the Supreme Court of the United States; but the decision of it was deferred until after the election. Still, before the election, Senator Trumbull, on the floor of the Senate, requested the leading advocate of the Nebraska Bill to state *his opinion* whether the people of a Territory can constitutionally exclude slavery from their limits; and the latter answers: "That is a question for the Supreme Court."

The election came. Mr. Buchanan was elected, and the indorsement, such as it was, secured. That was the second point gained. . . . The Presidential inauguration came, and still no decision of the court; but the incoming President, in his inaugural address, fervently exhorted the people to abide by the forthcoming decision, whatever it might be. Then, in a few days, came the decision.

The reputed author of the Nebraska Bill finds an early occasion to make a speech at this capital indorsing the Dred Scott decision, and vehemently denouncing all opposition to it. The new President, too, seizes the early occasion of the Silliman letter to indorse and strongly construe that decision, and to express his astonishment that any different view had ever been entertained!

. . . .

The several points of the Dred Scott decision, in connection with Senator Douglas's "care not" policy, constitute the piece of machinery, in its present state of advancement. . . . The working points of that machinery are:

Firstly, That no Negro slave, imported as such from Africa, and no descendant of such slave, can ever be a citizen of any State, in the sense of that term as used in the Constitution of the United States. This point is made in order to deprive the Negro, in every possible event, of the benefit of that provision of the United States Constitution which declares that "The citizens of each State shall be entitled to all privileges and immunities of citizens in the several States."

Secondly, That, "subject to the Constitution of the United States," neither Congress nor a Territorial Legislature can exclude slavery from any United States Territory. This point is made in order that individual men may fill up the Territories with slaves, without danger of losing them as property, and thus to enhance the chances of permanency to the institution through all the future.

Thirdly, That whether the holding a Negro in actual slavery in a free State makes him free, as against the holder, the United States courts will not decide, but will leave to be decided by the courts of any slave State the Negro may be forced into by the master. . . .

. . . .

. . . Two years ago the Republicans of the nation mustered over thirteen hundred thousand strong. We did this under the single impulse of resistance to a common danger, with every external circumstance against us. Of strange, discordant, and even hostile elements we gathered from the four winds, and formed and fought the battle through, under the constant hot fire of a disciplined, proud, and pampered enemy. Did we brave all then to falter now,— now, when that same enemy is wavering, dissevered, and belligerent? The result is not doubtful. We shall not fail; if we stand firm, we *shall not fail*. Wise counsels may accelerate, or mistakes delay it, but sooner or later, the victory is sure to come.

Lincoln - Douglas Debate
(October 15, 1858)

* * * * *This was the last of the seven debates* between the two senatorial candidates. Lincoln's anti-slavery stand and his repeated critical questions had greatly weakened Douglas' reputation and his voter support. Douglas, unable to advocate slavery in the territories, continued to argue that

the people of any territory made the final decision regarding slavery by the laws they passed or failed to pass to regulate it.

In this last speech of the series, Lincoln again spoke strongly against slavery as a "moral, social, and political wrong." To Lincoln, Douglas' positions regarding slavery were both monstrous and disreputable. Speeches such as this one made Lincoln nationally known, synonymous with Republican anti-slavery sentiment, and the natural, strong presidential candidate for 1860.

. . . At Galesburgh, the other day, I said, in answer to Judge Douglas, that three years ago there never had been a man, so far as I knew or believed, in the whole world, who had said that the Declaration of Independence did not include Negroes in the term "all men." I reassert it today. . . . I believe the first man who ever said it was Chief Justice Taney in the Dred Scott case, and the next to him was our friend Stephen A. Douglas. And now it has become the catchword of the entire party. I would like to call upon his friends everywhere to consider how they have come in so short a time to view this matter in a way so entirely different from their former belief; to ask whether they are not being borne along by an irresistible current,—whither, they know not. . . .

. . . I have said, and I repeat, my wish is that the further spread of [slavery] may be arrested, and that it may be placed where the public mind shall rest in the belief that it is in course of ultimate extinction. . . . I entertain the opinion, upon evidence sufficient to my mind, that the fathers of this government placed that institution where the public mind *did* rest in the belief that it was in the course of ultimate extinction. Let me ask why they made provision that the source of slavery—the African slave-trade—should be cut off at the end of twenty years? Why did they make provision that in all the new territory we owned at that time slavery should be forever inhibited? . . .

Again: the institution of slavery is only mentioned in the Constitution of the United States two or three times, and in neither of these cases does the world "slavery" or "Negro race" occur; . . .

. . . Language is used not suggesting that slavery existed or that the black race were among us. And I understand the contemporaneous history of those times to be that covert language was used with a purpose, and that purpose was that in our Constitution, which it was hoped and is still hoped will endure forever,—when it should be read by intelligent and patriotic men, after the institution of slavery had passed from among us,—there should be nothing on the face of the great charter of liberty suggesting that such a thing as Negro slavery had ever existed among us. . . . It is not true that our fathers, as Judge Douglas assumes, made this government part slave and part free. . . . The exact truth is, that they found the institution existing among us, and they left it as they found it. But in making the government they left this institution with many clear marks of disapprobation upon it. . . .

. . . .

. . . We have no power as citizens of the free States, or in our Federal capacity as members of the Federal Union through the General Government, to disturb slavery in the States where it exists. . . . What I insist upon is, that the new Territories shall be kept free from it while in the Territorial condition. . . .

Now, irrespective of the moral aspect of this question as to whether there is a right or wrong in enslaving a Negro, I am still in favor of our new Territories being in such a condition that white men may find a home,—may find some spot where they . . . can settle upon new soil and better their condition in life. I am in favor of this, not merely (I must say it here as I have elsewhere) for our own people who are born amongst us, but as an outlet for *free white people everywhere*—the world over—in which Hans, and Baptiste, and Patrick, and all other men from all the world, may find new homes and better their condition in life.

. . . The real issue in this controversy—the one pressing upon every mind—is the sentiment on the part of one class that looks upon the institution of slavery *as a wrong,* and of another class that *does not* look upon it as a wrong. The sentiment that contemplates the institution of slavery in this country as a wrong is the sentiment of the Republican party. It is the sentiment around which all their actions, all their arguments circle, from which all their propositions radiate. They look upon it as being a moral, social, and political wrong; and while they contemplate it as such, they nevertheless have due regard for its actual existence among us, and the difficulties of getting rid of it in any satisfactory way, and to all the constitutional obligations thrown about it. Yet, having a due regard for these, they desire a policy in regard to it that looks to its not creating any more danger. They insist that it should, as far as may be, be *treated* as a wrong; and one of the methods of treating it a wrong is to *make provision that it shall grow no larger*. They also desire a policy that looks to a peaceful end of slavery at some time, . . . I have said, and I repeat it here, that if there be a man amongst us who does not think that the institution of slavery is wrong in any one of the aspects of which I have spoken, he is misplaced, and ought not to be with us. And if there be a man amongst us who is so impatient of it as a wrong as to disregard its actual presence among us and the difficulty of getting rid of it suddenly in a satisfactory way, and to disregard the constitutional obligations thrown about it, that man is misplaced if he is on our platform. We disclaim sympathy with him in practical action. He is not placed properly with us.

On this subject of treating it as a wrong, and limiting its spread, let me say a word. Has anything ever threatened the existence of this Union save and except this very institution of slavery? What is it that we hold most dear amongst us? Our own liberty and prosperity. What has ever threatened our liberty and prosperity, save and except this institution of slavery? If this is true, how do you propose to improve the condition of things by enlarging slavery,—by spreading it out and making it bigger? You may have a wen or cancer upon your person, and not be able to cut it out, lest you bleed to death; but surely it is no way to cure it, to engraft it and spread it over your whole body. That is no proper way of treating what you regard a wrong. You see this peaceful way of dealing with it as a wrong,—restricting the spread of it, and not allowing it to go into new countries where it has not already existed. That is the peaceful way, the old-fashioned way, the way in which the fathers themselves set us the example.

. . . .

I understand I have ten minutes yet. I will employ it in saying something about this argument Judge Douglas uses, while he sustains the Dred Scott decision, that the people of the Territories can still somehow exclude slavery. The first thing I ask attention to is the fact that Judge Douglas constantly said, before the decision, that whether they could or not, *was a question for the Supreme Court.* But after the court had made the decision he virtually says it is *not* a question for the Supreme Court, but for the people. And how is it he tells us they can exclude it? He says it needs "police regulations," and that admits of "unfriendly legislation." Although it is a right established by the Constitution of the United States to take a slave into a Territory of the United States and hold him as property, yet unless the Territorial Legislature will give friendly legislation, and more especially if they adopt unfriendly legislation, they can practically exclude him. Now, without meeting this proposition as a matter of fact, I pass to consider the real constitutional obligation. Let me take the gentleman who looks me in the face before me, and let us suppose that he is a member of the Territorial Legislature. The first thing he will do will be to swear that he will support the Constitution of the United States. His neighbor by his side in the Territory has slaves and needs Territorial legislation to enable him to enjoy that constitutional right. Can he withhold the legislation which his neighbor needs for the enjoyment of a right which is fixed in his favor in the Constitution of the United States which he has sworn to support? Can he withhold it without violating his oath? And, more especially, can he pass unfriendly legislation to violate his oath? Why, this is a *monstrous* sort of talk about the Constitution of the United States. *There has never been as outlandish or lawless a doctrine from the mouth of any respectable man on earth.* I do not believe it is a constitutional right to hold slaves in a Territory of the United States. I believe the decision was improperly made and I go for reversing it. Judge Douglas is furious against those who go for reversing a decision. But he is for legislating it out of all force while the law itself stands. I repeat that there has never been so monstrous a doctrine uttered from the mouth of a respectable man.

First Inaugural Address
(March 4, 1861)

* * * * *By March 4, 1861, seven Southern* states had seceded from the Union. President Buchanan had stated in his annual message to Congress that the federal government did not have the power to use force to prevent secession.

The Confederate States of America were being formed. The attack on Fort Sumter had begun. Jefferson Davis had issued his call for a Southern army; it was being organized, and in many places, it was arming itself with equipment taken from federal stores and garrisons.

Lincoln, in his first inaugural address uttered a stern warning to those who were breaking up the Union.

Fellow-Citizens of the United States:

In compliance with a custom as old as the Government itself, I appear before you to address you briefly, and to take in your presence the oath prescribed by the Constitution of the United States to be taken by the President "before he enters on the execution of his office." . . .

Apprehension seems to exist among the people of the Southern States that by the accession of a Republican Administration their property and their peace and personal security are to be endangered. There has never been any reasonable cause for such apprehension. Indeed, the most ample evidence to the contrary . . . is found in nearly all the published speeches of him who now addresses you. I do but quote from one of those speeches when I declare that—

I have no purpose, directly or indirectly, to interfere with the institution of slavery in the States where · it exists. I believe I have no lawful right to do so, and I have no inclination to do so. . . .

I now reiterate these sentiments, and, in doing so, I only press upon the public attention the most conclusive evidence of which the case is susceptible, that the property, peace, and security of no section are to be in any wise endangered by the now incoming Administration. I add, too, that all the protection which, consistently with the Constitution and the laws, can be given will be cheerfully given to all the States when lawfully demanded, for whatever cause—as cheerfully to one section as to another. . . .

I take the official oath to-day with no mental reservations, and with no purpose to construe the Constitution or laws by any hypercritical rules; and, while I do not choose now to specify particular acts of Congress as proper to be enforced, I do suggest that it will be much safer for all, both in official and private stations, to conform to and abide by all those acts which stand unrepealed than to violate any of them, trusting to find impunity in having them held to be unconstitutional.

. . . A disruption of the Federal Union, heretofore only menaced, is now formidably attempted.

. . . .

I therefore consider that, in view of the Constitution and the laws the Union is unbroken and to the extent of my ability I shall take care, as the Constitution itself expressly enjoins upon me, that the laws of the Union be faithfully executed in all the States. Doing this I deem to be only a simple duty on my part, and I shall perform it so far as practicable unless my rightful masters, the American people, shall withhold the requisite means, or in some authoritative manner direct the contrary. I trust this will not be regarded as a menace, but only as the declared purpose of the Union that it *will* constitutionally defend and maintain itself.

In doing this there needs to be no bloodshed or violence, and there shall be none unless it be forced upon the national authority. The power confided to me will be used to hold, occupy, and possess the property and places belonging to the Government and to collect the duties and imposts; but beyond what may be necessary for these objects, there will be no invasion, no using of force against or among the people anywhere. Where hostility to the United States, in any interior locality, shall be so great and universal as to prevent competent resident citizens from holding the Federal offices, there will be no attempt to force obnoxious strangers among the people for that object. While the strict legal right may exist in the government to enforce the exercise of these offices, the attempt to do so would be so irritating, and so nearly impracticable withal, that I deem it better to forego for the time the uses of such offices. . . .

. . . .

Plainly the central idea of secession is the essence of anarchy. A majority held in restraint by constitutional checks and limitations, and always changing easily with deliberate changes of popular opinions and sentiments, is the only true sovereign of a free people. Whoever rejects it does, of necessity, fly to anarchy or to despotism. Unanimity is impossible. The rule of a minority, as a permanent arrangement, is wholly inadmissible; so that, rejecting the majority principle, anarchy or despotism in some form is all that is left. . . .

. . . .

One section of our country believes slavery is *right* and ought to be extended, while the other believes it is *wrong* and ought not to be extended. This is the only substantial dispute. The fugitive-slave clause of the Constitution and the law for the suppression of the foreign slave trade are each as well enforced, perhaps, as any law can ever be in a community where the moral sense of the people imperfectly supports the law itself. The great body of the people abide by the dry legal obligation in both cases, and a few break over in each. This, I think, can not be perfectly cured, and it would be worse in both cases *after* the separation of the sections than before. The foreign slave trade, now imperfectly suppressed, would be ultimately revived without restriction in one section, while fugitive slaves, now only partially surrendered, would not be surrendered at all by the other.

Physically speaking, we cannot separate. We cannot remove our respective sections from each other nor build an impassable wall between them. A husband and wife may be divorced and go out of the presence and beyond the reach of each other, but the different parts of our country can not do this. They can not but remain face to face, and intercourse either amicable or hostile must continue between them. Is it possible, then, to make that intercourse more advantageous or more satisfactory *after* separation than *before?* Can aliens make treaties easier than friends can make laws? Can treaties be more faithfully enforced between aliens than laws can among friends? Suppose you go to war, you can not fight always; and when, after much loss on both sides and no gain on either, you cease fighting, the identical old questions, as to terms of intercourse, are again upon you.

. . . .

My countrymen, one and all, think calmly and *well* upon this whole subject. Nothing valuable can be lost by taking time. If there be an object to *hurry* any of you in hot haste to a step which you would never take *deliberately,* that object will be frustrated by taking time; but no good object can be frustrated by it. Such of you as are now dissatisfied still have the old Constitution unimpaired, and, on the sensitive point, the laws of your own framing under it; while the new Administration will have no immediate power, if it would, to change either. If it were admitted that you who are dissatisfied hold the right side in the dispute, there still is no single good reason for precipitate action. Intelligence, patriotism, Christianity, and a firm reliance on Him who has never yet forsaken this favored land, are still competent to adjust in the best way all our present difficulty.

In *your* hands, my dissatisfied fellow-countrymen, and not in *mine,* is the momentous issue of civil war. The government will not assail *you.* You can have no conflict without being yourselves the aggressors. *You* have no oath registered in heaven to destroy the government, while *I* shall have the most solemn one to "preserve, protect, and defend it."

I am loath to close. We are not enemies, but friends. We must not be enemies. Though passion may have strained it must not break our bonds of affection. The mystic chords of memory, stretching from every battlefield and patriot grave to every living heart and hearthstone all over this broad land, will yet swell the chorus of the Union when again touched, as surely they will be, by the better angels of our nature.

Emancipation Proclamation
(January 1, 1863)

* * * * *Lincoln had repeatedly assured the* South that he would not interfere with slavery where it already existed. As the war to preserve the Union continued, there were periods when Southern successes or Northern failures weakened public support in the North.

Many of the leaders of Lincoln's Republican Party wanted the ending of slavery to be made the chief issue and aim of the war. Lincoln finally gave in, but for two other reasons. He hoped the announced ending of slavery in the seceded states would weaken the war effort of the South. He also knew that his proclamation would have a strong effect in Europe, whose people would then oppose any efforts by their governments to aid the Confederacy.

Whereas, On the twenty-second day of September, in the year of our Lord one thousand eight hundred and sixty-two, a proclamation was issued by the President of the United States, containing, among other things, the following, to wit:

"That on the first day of January, in the year of our Lord one thousand eight hundred and sixty-three, all persons held as slaves within any state or designated part of a state, the people whereof shall then be in rebellion against the United States, shall be then, thenceforward, and forever free; and the executive government of the United States, including the military and naval authority thereof, will recognize and maintain the freedom of such persons, and will do no act or acts to repress such persons, or any of them, in any efforts they may make for their actual freedom.

"That the Executive will, on the first day of January afore-said, by proclamation, designate the states and parts of states, if any, in which the people thereof, respectively, shall then be in rebellion against the United States; and the fact that any state, or the people thereof, shall on that day be, in good faith, represented in the Congress of the United States by members chosen thereto at elections wherein a majority of the qualified voters of such state shall have participated, shall, in the absence of strong countervailing testimony, be deemed conclusive evidence that such state, and the people thereof, are not then in rebellion against the United States."

Now, therefore I, Abraham Lincoln, President of the United States, by virtue of the power in me vested as Com-mander-in-Chief of the Army and Navy of the United States in time of actual armed rebellion against authority and gov-ernment of the United States, and as a fit and necessary war measure for suppressing said rebellion, do, on this first day of January, in the year of our Lord one thousand eight hun-dred and sixty-three, and in accordance with my purpose so to do publicly proclaimed for the full period of one hundred days, from the day first above mentioned, order and desig-nate as the states and parts of states wherein the people thereof respectively, are this day in rebellion against the United States, the following, to wit:

Arkansas, Texas, Louisiana (except the parishes of St. Bernard, Plaquemines, Jefferson, St. Johns, St. Charles, St. James, Ascension, Assumption, Terrebonne, Lafourche, St. Mary, St. Martin, and Orleans, including the City of New Orleans), Mississippi, Alabama, Florida, Georgia, South Carolina, North Carolina, and Virginia, (except the forty-eight counties designated as West Virginia, and also the counties of Berkeley, Accomac, Northampton, Elizabeth City, York, Princess Ann, and Norfolk, including the cities of Norfolk and Portsmouth); and which excepted parts are, for the present, left precisely as if this proclamation were not issued.

And by virtue of the power, and for the purpose afore-said, I do order and declare that all persons held as slaves within said designated states, and parts of states, are, and henceforward shall be free; and that the executive govern-ment of the United States, including the military and naval authorities thereof, will recognize and maintain the freedom of said persons.

And I hereby enjoin upon the people so declared to be free to abstain from all violence, unless in necessary self-defense; and I recommend to them that, in all cases when allowed, they labor faithfully for reasonable wages.

And I further declare and make known, that such persons of suitable condition, will be received into the armed service of the United States to garrison forts, positions, stations, and other places, and to man vessels of all sorts in said service.

And upon this act, sincerely believed to be an act of justice, warranted by the Constitution, upon military necessity, I invoke the considerate judgment of mankind, and the gracious favor of Almighty God.

The Gettysburg Address
(November 19, 1863)

* * * * *The Battle of Gettysburg at the* beginning of July, 1863, was a turning point of the Civil War. It was then clear that, whatever the cost, the Union's greater military strength and industrial power would bring victory. Casualties had been very heavy.

On November 19, 1863, a national cemetery was dedicated at the Gettysburg battlefield. A long speech by Edward Everett, one of the nation's most celebrated orators, preceded President Lincoln's address. Lincoln's words were few, his sentiments deep, and his speech one of the great documents of the world's history.

Fourscore and seven years ago our fathers brought forth on this continent a new nation, conceived in liberty, and dedicated to the proposition that all men are created equal.

Now we are engaged in a great civil war, testing whether that nation, or any nation so conceived and so dedicated, can long endure. We are met on a great battlefield of that war. We have come to dedicate a portion of that field, as a final resting-place for those who here gave their lives that that nation might live. It is altogether fitting and proper that we should do this.

But, in a larger sense, we cannot dedicate—we cannot consecrate—we cannot hallow—this ground. The brave men, living and dead, who struggled here, have consecrated it, far above our poor power to add or detract. The world will little note, nor long remember what we say here, but it can never forget what they did here. It is for us the living, rather, to be dedicated here to the unfinished work which they who fought here have thus far so nobly advanced. It is rather for us to be here dedicated to the great task remaining before us—that from these honored dead we take increased devotion to that cause for which they gave the last full measure of devotion—that we here highly resolve that these dead shall not have died in vain—that this nation, under God, shall have a new birth of freedom—and that government of the people, by the people, for the people, shall not perish from the earth.

Second Inaugural Address
(March 4, 1865)

* * * * *By March 4, 1865, victory for the* Union was only weeks away. The President's second inauguration address could have been a victory speech. Instead, it was a calm review of the issues over which the war had been fought. It ended with his prayerful hopes for a nation again united in the common cause of peace and brotherhood.

Fellow-countrymen:

At this second appearing to take the oath of the presidential office, there is less occasion for an extended address than there was at the first. Then a statement, somewhat in detail, of a course to be pursued, seemed fitting and proper. Now, at the expiration of four years, during which public declarations have been constantly called forth on every point and phase of the great contest which still absorbs the attention, and engrosses the energies of the nation, little that is new could be presented. The progress of our arms, upon which all else chiefly depends, is as well known to the public as to myself; and it is, I trust, reasonably satisfactory and encouraging to all. With high hope for the future, no prediction in regard to it is ventured.

On the occasion corresponding to this four years ago, all thoughts were anxiously directed to an impending civil war. All dreaded it—all sought to avert it. While the inaugural address was being delivered from this place, devoted altogether to saving the Union without war, insurgent agents were in the city seeking to destroy it without war—seeking to dissolve the Union, and divide effects, by negotiation. Both parties deprecated war; but one of them would make war rather than let the nation survive; and the other would accept war rather than let it perish. And the war came.

One-eighth of the whole population were colored slaves, not distributed generally over the Union, but localized in the southern part of it. These slaves constituted a peculiar and powerful interest. All knew that this interest was, somehow, the cause of the war. To strengthen, perpetuate, and extend this interest was the object for which the insurgents would rend the Union, even by war; while the government claimed no right to do more than to restrict the territorial enlargement of it. Neither party expected for the war, the magnitude, or the duration, which it has already attained. Neither anticipated that the cause of the conflict might cease without, or even before, the conflict itself should cease. Each looked for an easier triumph, and a result less fundamental and astounding.

Both read the same Bible, and pray to the same God; and each invokes His aid against the other. It may seem strange that any men should dare to ask a just God's assistance in wringing their bread from the sweat of other men's faces; but let us judge not that we be not judged. The prayers of both could not be answered; that of neither has been answered fully.

The Almighty has His own purposes. "Woe unto the world because of offenses! for it must needs be that offenses come; but woe to that man by whom the offense cometh!" If we shall suppose that American slavery is one of those offenses which, in the providence of God, must needs come, but which, having continued through His appointed time, He now wills to remove, and that He gives to both North and South, this terrible war, as the woe due to those by whom the offense came, shall we discern therein any departure from those divine attributes which the believers in a living God always ascribe to Him? Fondly do we hope—fervently do we pray—that this mighty scourge of war may speedily pass away. Yet, if God wills that it continue, until all the wealth piled by the bondman's two hundred and fifty years of unrequited toil shall be sunk, and until every drop of blood drawn with the lash, shall be paid by another drawn with the sword, as was said three thousand years ago, so still it must be said "the judgments of the Lord are true and righteous altogether."

With malice toward none; with charity for all; with firmness in the right, as God gives us to see the right, let us strive on to finish the work we are in; to bind up the nation's wounds; to care for him who shall have borne the battle, and for his widow, and his orphan—to do all which may achieve and cherish a just, and a lasting peace, among ourselves, and with all nations.

TRUE OR FALSE?

Write T *if the statement is correct; Write* F *if it is false.*

_____1. Lincoln knew the Union would break up as early as 1858.

_____2. Lincoln's Emancipation Proclamation was in part a war measure.

_____3. Douglas and Lincoln agreed that the Dred Scott decision, as a Supreme Court decision, was corrrect and should be supported.

_____4. Lincoln respected Douglas as a sincere and honest man.

_____5. In his first inaugural address, Lincoln warned the South that he would not permit the breakup of the Union.

_____6. Lincoln had expected victory in the war to come quickly.

_____7. The Emancipation Proclamation had been promised in the Gettysburg Address.

_____8. The Emancipation Proclamation did not free all slaves in the United States.

_____9. The Emancipation Proclamation was supported by the leaders of Congress.

_____10. Lincoln's second inaugural address included the announcement of Lee's surrender and the end of the war.

_____11. Lincoln's Second Inaugural Address was a denunciation of the South.

_____12. Lincoln hoped that the Emancipation Proclamation would discourage European support of the Confederacy.

_____13. In Lincoln's First Inaugural Address he argued against secession on the grounds that it would help the slave trade.

_____14. The Battle of Gettysburg marked the turning point of the war.

_____15. In his Second Inaugural Address Lincoln estimated that one half of the population of the South was slave.

THOUGHT QUESTIONS

1. Select three of the following Lincoln statements. For each explain his meaning and relate the statement to the problem to which it referred.
   a. A house divided against itself cannot stand.
   b. They insist that it should . . . be treated as a wrong; and one of the methods of treating it as a wrong is to make provision that it shall grow no larger.
   c. . . . there needs be no bloodshed or violence, and there shall be none unless it be forced upon the national authority.
   d. . . . I do order and declare that all persons held as slaves . . . henceforward shall be free.
   e. But in a larger sense, we cannot dedicate — we cannot consecrate — we cannot hallow — this ground.
   f. Both read the same Bible; and pray to the same God . . .

2. Explain, by reference to two or more of the Lincoln documents, how he was able to pinpoint the real issues facing his country and how he was able to propose clear solutions to them.

The Freedmen's Bureau Act 1865

* * * * *Large numbers of slaves, freed as* Union armies passed victoriously through the South in the last year of the Civil War, wandered in the wake of the Northern forces. As the war drew to a close, it became necessary to establish a federal relief program to provide former slaves with the essentials of independent life. This relief was furnished by a law passed in March, 1865, which set up the Freedmen's Bureau.

This was the first federal large-scale relief program in American history. The men who operated it did wonderful work. They provided food and clothing to hundreds of thousands of Negroes. They distributed large amounts of medical supplies, in many cases setting up clinics and hospitals. In areas which had been devastated by the war, the Bureau extended its operations to needy white families. An important achievement was the establishment of large numbers of small independent farms for Negroes. Thousands of classrooms were opened in which Negro children for the first time could receive instruction.

The Bureau was regarded by many in Congress as a "bureau of emancipation." It functioned until 1868, and its three years of major activity did much, at great cost, to bring order out of the chaos which followed sudden emancipation. Its significant side effect, of course, was the Negro vote won by the Republican Party during Reconstruction.

An Act to Establish a Bureau for the Relief of Freedmen and Refugees.

Be it enacted . . . , That there is hereby established in the War Department, to continue during the present war of rebellion, and for one year thereafter, a bureau of refugees, freedmen, and abandoned lands, to which shall be committed, as hereinafter provided, the supervision and management of all abandoned lands, and the control of all subjects relating to refugees and freedmen from rebel states, or from any district or county within the territory embraced in the operations of the army, under such rules and regulations as may be prescribed by the head of the bureau and approved by the President. The said bureau shall be under the management and control of a commissioner to be appointed by the President, by and with the advice and consent of the Senate. . . .

THE SOUTH AT THE END OF THE WAR

Cities, railroads and farms were devastated.

The freeing of the slaves wiped out the planters' major asset.

Planters were forced to break up huge plantations.

Cotton production fell far below the pre-war level.

Carpetbaggers and scalawags took political control from planters.

Confederate currency and bonds became worthless.

Section 2. And be it further enacted, That the Secretary of War may direct such issues of provisions, clothing, and fuel, as he may deem needful for the immediate and temporary shelter and supply of destitute and suffering refugees and freedmen and their wives and children, under such rules and regulations as he may direct.

Section 3. And be it further enacted, That the President may, by and with the advice and consent of the Senate, appoint an assistant commissioner for each of the states declared to be in insurrection, not exceeding ten in number, who shall, under the direction of the commissioner, aid in the execution of the provisions of this act; . . . And any military officer may be detailed and assigned to duty under this act without increase of pay or allowances. . . .

Section 4. And be it further enacted, That the commissioner, under the direction of the President, shall have authority to set apart, for the use of loyal refugees and freedmen, such tracts of land within the insurrectionary states as shall have been abandoned, or to which the United States shall have acquired title by confiscation or sale, or otherwise, and to every male citizen, whether refugee or freedman, as aforesaid, there shall be assigned not more than forty acres of such land, and the person to whom it was assigned shall be protected in the use and enjoyment of the land for the term of three years at an annual rent not exceeding six per centum upon the value of such land, as it was appraised by the state authorities in the year eighteen hundred and sixty, for the purpose of taxation, and in case no such appraisal can be found, then the rental shall be based upon the estimated value of the land in said year, to be ascertained in such manner as the commissioner may by regulation prescribe. At the end of said term, or at any time during said term, the occupants of any parcels so assigned may purchase the land and receive such title thereto as the United States can convey, upon paying therefor the value of the land, as ascertained and fixed for the purpose of determining the annual rent aforesaid.

* * * * * * * * * * * * * * *

CHOOSE THE CORRECT ANSWER

Write the letter that best completes the statement or answers the question.

1. The Freedmen's Bureau was (*a*) part of the Department of Welfare, (*b*) part of the War Department, (*c*) an independent agency, (*d*) part of the Department of Interior.   1._____

2. The Bureau operated for (*a*) 1 year, (*b*) 2 years, (*c*) 3 years, (*d*) 4 years.   2._____

3. The assistance provided by the Act was intended for Negroes (*a*) in any part of the United States, (*b*) in the states of the Confederacy, (*c*) only in areas where battles had been fought, (*d*) only in areas where slavery still existed.   3._____

4. The Bureau did much to improve (*a*) transportation, (*b*) communcation, (*c*) legislation, (*d*) education.   4._____

5. The Bureau provided many Negroes with (*a*) land for farms, (*b*) guns for hunting, (*c*) courts where they could receive fair trials, (*d*) medical training.   5._____

6. Most Bureau offices were managed by (*a*) Southern whites, (*b*) literate Negroes, (*c*) army officers, (*d*) Northern doctors.   6._____

7. The Freedmen's Bureau should be considered part of (*a*) the attack on the Southern armies, (*b*) Reconstruction, (*c*) Democratic Party planning, (*d*) Lincoln's plan to punish the Southern whites.   7._____

8. Land (farms) for Negroes was (*a*) rented only, (*b*) sold to them at once, (*c*) given away to them, (*d*) first rented to them and then sold to them.   8._____

9. Another group which benefitted from the work of the Bureau was (*a*) the Republican Party, (*b*) the Democratic Party, (*c*) Western settlers, (*d*) Southern businessmen.   9._____

10. The commissioner who ran the Bureau was appointed by (*a*) the Secretary of War, (*b*) the House of Representatives, (*c*) the President, (*d*) the Cabinet.   10._____

THOUGHT QUESTIONS

1. State three problems faced by the emancipated Negroes, and show how the Freedmen's Bureau tried to solve each.

2. In what ways was the Freedmen's Bureau both a humanitarian act and a wise political move?

Ex Parte Milligan
1866

* * * * *In March, 1863, Congress gave* President Lincoln power to suspend the writ of *habeas corpus* as part of his war powers. This was intended to permit military officers to take emergency action against spies and Confederate sympathizers who might impede the war effort. In September, 1863, President Lincoln issued orders which suspended *habeas corpus* in cases where military officers held persons who had acted against the operations of the army or navy.

Milligan was a citizen of Indiana who appears to have been a Confederate sympathizer. He was arrested and charged with stirring up rebellion. Milligan was tried by a military court, found guilty and sentenced to be hanged. He sued for a writ of *habeas corpus* in a federal court. Such a writ would have required that he be charged with the violation of a specific law in a regular court, permitted counsel, witnesses, and all the rights of a person under trial in any civil court.

The Supreme Court held that military courts could not be permitted in any district where civil courts were able to function. To this day military courts have not tried civilians in the United States.

The controlling question in this case is this: Upon the *facts* stated in Milligan's petition, and the exhibits filed, had the military commission mentioned in it jurisdiction, *legally,* to try and sentence him? Milligan, not a resident of one of the rebellious states, or a prisoner of war, but a citizen of Indiana for twenty years past, and never in the military or naval service, is, while at his home, arrested by the military power of the United States, imprisoned, and, on certain criminal charges preferred against him, tried, convicted, and sentenced to be hanged by a military commission, organized under the direction of the military commander of the military district of Indiana. Had this tribunal the legal power and authority to try and punish this man?

No graver question was ever considered by this court, nor one which more nearly concerns the rights of the whole people; for it is the birthright of every American citizen when charged with crime, to be tried and punished according to law. The power of punishment is alone through the means which the laws have provided for that purpose, and if they are ineffectual, there is an immunity from punishment no matter how great an offender the individual may be, or how great his crimes may have shocked the sense of justice of the country, or endangered its safety. *By the protection of the law human rights are secured;* withdraw that protection, and they are at the mercy of wicked rulers, or the clamor of an excited people. If there was law to justify this military trial, it is not our province to interfere; if there was not, *it is our duty to declare the nullity of the whole proceedings.*

. . . The Constitution of the United States is a law for rulers and people, equally in war and in peace, and covers with the shield of its protection all classes of men, at all times, and under all circumstances. No doctrine involving more pernicious consequences was ever invented by the wit of man than that any of its provisions can be suspended during any of the great exigencies of government.

. . . This court has judicial knowledge that in Indiana the federal authority was always unopposed, and its courts always open to hear criminal accusations and redress grievances; and no usage of war could sanction a military trial there for any offense whatever of a *citizen* in civil life, in nowise connected with the military service. Congress could grant no such power; and to the honor of our national legislature let it be said, it has never been provoked by the state of the country even to attempt its exercise. One of the plainest constitutional provisions was, therefore, infringed when Milligan was tried by a court not ordained and established by Congress, and not composed of judges appointed during good behavior.

. . . It is claimed that martial law covers with its broad mantle the proceedings of this military commission. The proposition is this: that in a time of war the commander of an armed force (if, in his opinion, the exigencies of the country demand it, and of which he is to judge) has the power, within the lines of his military district, to *suspend* all civil rights and their remedies, and subject citizens as well as soldiers to *the rule of his will;* and in the exercise of his lawful authority cannot be restrained, except by his superior officer or the President of the United States.

. . . The statement of this proposition shows its importance; for, if true, republican government is a failure, and there is an end of liberty regulated by law. Martial law, established on such a basis, destroys every guarantee of the Constitution, and effectually renders the military independent of, and superior to, the civil power, — the attempt to do which by the king of Great Britain was deemed by our fathers such an offense, that they assigned it to the world as one of the causes which impelled them to declare their independence. *Civil liberty and this kind of martial law cannot endure together. . . .*

. . . It is difficult to see how the *safety* of the country required martial law in Indiana. If any of her citizens were plotting treason, the power of arrest could secure them, until the government was prepared for their trial, when the courts were open and ready to try them. It was as easy to protect witnesses before a civil as a military tribunal; and as there could be no wish to convict, except on sufficient legal evidence, surely an ordained and established court was better able to judge of this than a military tribunal composed of gentlemen not trained to the profession of the law.

. . . *Martial rule can never exist where the courts are open,* and in the proper and unobstructed exercise of their jurisdiction. It is also confined to the locality of actual war. Because, during the late rebellion it could have been enforced in Virginia, where the national authority was overturned and the courts driven out, it does not follow that it should obtain in Indiana, where that authority was never disputed, and justice was always administered. . . .

TRUE OR FALSE?

Write T *if the statement is correct; Write* F *if it is false.*

_____1. Milligan was a soldier who was tried for refusing to obey orders.

_____2. As a government employee, Milligan was under military law.

_____3. The courts of Indiana operated during the Civil War.

_____4. The trial of Milligan was proper, but the Supreme Court held that the sentence of death was too severe.

_____5. The Court held that the writ of *habeas corpus* cannot be suspended at any time or in any place.

_____6. The Court held that martial law can exist only in a locality where war is being fought.

_____7. The authority of the federal government was never opposed in Indiana.

_____8. Under our Constitution, military officers must obey the orders of a federal court.

_____9. The military court which tried Milligan was not established by Congress.

_____10. Martial law had been declared in Indiana because the state was in danger of immediate invasion by Southern armies.

THOUGHT QUESTIONS

1. Under what conditions can martial law be imposed in our country?
2. In what ways did the decision in Ex Parte Milligan strengthen the civil rights of all Americans?

First Civil Rights Act 1866

* * * * *The Thirteenth Amendment prohib-iting "slavery or involuntary servitude" did not give the freed Negroes the rights of citizens. The citizens of slave states found various ways to continue to treat ex-slaves as they had always been treated.*

The First Civil Rights Act was specifically intended to prevent Southern white efforts to control Negroes by harsh state legislation. It expressly prohibited state legislation which discriminated on the basis of race or color.

President Johnson feared that laws limiting the powers of Southern state legislatures were both unwise and unconstitutional. He vetoed the bill, but it was passed over his veto.

These guarantees of equal protection under the law were later made permanent by the Fourteenth Amendment. This Amendment states that "all persons born or naturalized in the United States are citizens of the United States and of the state in which they reside."

An Act to Protect All Persons in the United States in Their Civil Rights, and Furnish the Means of Their Vindication

Be it enacted . . . , That all persons born in the United States and not subject to any foreign power, excluding Indians not taxed, are hereby declared to be citizens of the United States; and such citizens, of every race and color, without regard to any previous condition of slavery or involuntary servitude, except as a punishment for crime whereof the party shall have been duly convicted, shall have the same right, in every State and Territory in the United States, to make and enforce contracts, to sue, be parties, and give evidence, to inherit, purchase, lease, sell, hold, and convey real and personal property, and to full and equal benefit of all laws and proceedings for the security of person and property, as is enjoyed by white citizens, and shall be subject to like punishment, pains, and penalties, and to none other, any law, statute, ordinance, regulation, or custom, to the contrary notwithstanding.

Section 2. And be it further enacted, That any person who, under color of any law, statute, ordinance, regulation, or custom, shall subject, or cause to be subjected, any inhabitant of any State or Territory to the deprivation of any right secured or protected by this act, or to different punishment, pains, or penalties on account of such person having at any time been held in a condition of slavery or involuntary servitude, except as a punishment for crime whereof the party shall have been duly convicted, or by reason of his color or race, than is prescribed for the punishment of white persons, shall be deemed guilty of a misdemeanor, and, on conviction, shall be punished by fine not exceeding one thousand dollars, or imprisonment not exceeding one year, or both, in the discretion of the court.

Section 3. And be it further enacted, That the district courts of the United States, within their respective districts, shall have, exclusively of the courts of the several States, cognizance of all crimes of offenses committed against the provisions of this act, and also, concurrently with the circuit courts of the United States, of all causes, civil and criminal, affecting persons who are denied or cannot enforce in the courts or judicial tribunals of the State or locality where they may be any of the rights secured to them by the first section of this act. . . .

Section 4. And be it further enacted, That the district attorneys, marshals, and deputy marshals of the United States, the commissioners appointed by the circuit and territorial courts of the United States, with powers of arresting, imprisoning, or bailing offenders against the laws of the United States, the officers and agents of the Freedmen's Bureau, and every other officer who may be specially empowered by the President of the United States, shall be, and they are hereby, specially authorized and required, at the expense of the United States, to institute proceedings against all and every person who shall violate the provisions of this act, and cause him or them to be arrested and imprisoned, or bailed, as the case may be, for trial before such court of the United States or territorial courts as by this act has cognizance of the offense. And with a view to affording reasonable protection to all persons in their constitutional rights of equality before the law, without distinction of race or color, or previous condition of slavery or involuntary servitude, except as a punishment for crime, whereof the party shall have been duly convicted, and to the prompt discharge of the duties of this act, it shall be the duty of the circuit courts of the United States, from time to time, to increase the number of commissioners, so as to afford a speedy and convenient means for the arrest and examination of persons charged with a violation of this act. . . .

. . . .

Section 9. And be it further enacted, That it shall be lawful for the President of the United States, or such person as he may empower for that purpose, to employ such part of the land or naval forces of the United States, or of the militia, as shall be necessary to prevent the violation and enforce the due execution of this act.

Section 10. And be it further enacted, That upon all questions of law arising in any cause under the provisions of this act a final appeal may be taken to the Supreme Court of the United States.

FILL IN THE ANSWERS

Write the word or phrase which best completes the statement.

1. The Civil Rights Act of 1866 was vetoed by President _____.

2. The Act was intended to give full civil rights to Southern _____.

3. A person who violated the Act could be imprisoned for a term of as long as _____.

4. All cases under the Act would be tried in _____ courts.

5. Final appeals in cases arising under the Civil Rights Act could be taken to the _____ Court.

6. The purpose of the Act was added to the Constitution by the _____ Amendment.

7. The persons born in the United States who were not made citizens by the Act were the _____.

8. The President was authorized to use the _____ of the United States to enforce the Civil Rights Act.

9. Officers and agents of the _____ were required to institute proceedings against violators of the Act.

10. The Civil Rights Act was intended to prevent harsh treatment of _____ in Southern states.

THOUGHT QUESTIONS

1. For what reasons did Congress pass a Civil Rights Act in 1866?
2. In what ways did the Civil Rights Act protect the Negro?

Comparison of
NORTH and SOUTH in 1860

COMPARISON OF RESOURCES IN PERCENT

POPULATION

NORTH 71%

SOUTH 29%

WEALTH PRODUCED

NORTH 75%

SOUTH 25%

FARM ACREAGE

NORTH 65%

SOUTH 35%

VALUE OF CROPS

NORTH 70%

SOUTH 30%

RAILROAD MILEAGE

NORTH 72%

SOUTH 28%

FACTORIES

NORTH 85%

SOUTH 15%

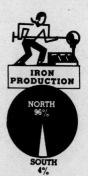

IRON PRODUCTION

NORTH 96%

SOUTH 4%

BANK DEPOSITS

NORTH 81%

SOUTH 19%

First Reconstruction Act 1867

* * * * *The Republican leaders of Congress* were determined that no Southern state should be readmitted to the Union unless it first approved the Fourteenth Amendment. All the Southern states except Tennessee refused to do so. Thus, Tennessee was readmitted. Congress then decided upon military occupation of the other ten states until they had accepted the amendment and given guarantees of fair treatment for their Negro citizens. President Johnson vetoed this Military Reconstruction Act. He felt it was too harsh and an unconstitutional infringement of the rights of the Southern states; however, it was passed over his veto.

The Reconstruction Act divided the South into five military districts, each under the command of an army general. These officers had the power to put their districts under martial law, and to replace local courts and officials as they saw fit.

The Reconstruction Act, together with the Freedmen's Bureau and the civil rights laws, was intended to remake the South in lasting democratic form. However, many abuses developed as military governors permitted friends and old army associates from the North to enter Southern politics. The conduct of Southern governments by these so-called *carpetbaggers* was corrupt, extravagant and inefficient.

New legislatures, dominated by these carpetbaggers, eventually ratified the Fourteenth Amendment, and the Southern states were restored to full membership in the Union by 1870.

An Act to Provide for the More Efficient Government of the Rebel States.

Whereas no legal State governments or adequate protection for life or property now exists in the rebel States of Virginia, North Carolina, South Carolina, Georgia, Mississippi, Alabama, Louisiana, Florida, Texas, and Arkansas; and whereas it is necessary that peace and good order should be enforced in said States until loyal and republican State governments can be legally established: Therefore,

Be it enacted . . . , That said rebel States shall be divided into military districts and made subject to the military authority of the United States as hereinafter prescribed, and for that purpose Virginia shall constitute the first district; North Carolina and South Carolina the second district; Georgia, Alabama, and Florida the third district; Mississippi and Arkansas the fourth district; and Louisiana and Texas the fifth district.

Section 2. And be it further enacted, That it shall be the duty of the President to assign to the command of each of said districts an officer of the army, not below the rank of brigadier-general, and to detail a sufficient military force to enable such officer to perform his duties and enforce his authority within the district to which he is assigned.

Section 3. And be it further enacted, That it shall be the duty of each officer assigned as aforesaid, to protect all persons in their rights of person and property, to suppress insurrection, disorder, and violence, and to punish, or cause to be punished, all disturbers of the public peace and criminals; and to this end he may allow local civil tribunals to take jurisdiction of and to try offenders, or, when in his judgment it may be necessary for the trial of offenders, he shall have power to organize military commissions or tribunals for that purpose, and all interference under color of State authority with the exercise of military authority under this act, shall be null and void.

Section 4. And be it further enacted, That all persons put under military arrest by virtue of this act shall be tried without unnecessary delay, and no cruel or unusual punishment shall be inflicted, and no sentence of any military commission or tribunal hereby authorized, affecting the life or liberty of any person, shall be executed until it is approved by the officer in command of the district, and the laws and regulations for the government of the army shall not be affected by this act, except in so far as they conflict with its provisions: *Provided,* That no sentence of death under the provisions of this act shall be carried into effect without the approval of the President.

Section 5. And be it further enacted, That when the people of any one of said rebel States shall have formed a constitution of government in conformity with the Constitution of the United States in all respects, framed by a convention of delegates elected by the male citizens of said State, twenty-one years old and upward, of whatever race, color, or previous condition, who have been resident in said State for one year previous to the day of such election, except such as may be disfranchised for participation in the rebellion or for felony at common law, and when such consititution shall provide that the elective franchise shall be enjoyed by all such persons as have the qualifications herein stated for electors of delegates, and when such constitution shall be ratified by a majority of the persons voting on the question of ratification who are qualified as electors for delegates, and when such constitution shall have been submitted to Congress for examination and approval, and Congress shall have approved the same, and when said State, by a vote of its legislature elected under said constitution, shall have adopted the amendment to the Constitution of the United States, proposed by the Thirty-ninth Congress, and known as article fourteen, and when said article shall have become a part of the Constitution of the United States said State shall be declared entitled to representation in Congress, and senators and representatives shall be admitted therefrom on their taking the oath prescribed by law, and then and thereafter the preceding sections of this act shall be inoperative in said State: *Provided,* That no person excluded from the privilege of holding office by said proposed amendment to the Constitution of the United States, shall be eligible to election as a member of the convention to frame a constitution for any of said rebel States, nor shall any such person vote for members of such convention.

Section 6. And be it further enacted, That, until the people of said rebel States shall be by law admitted to representation in the Congress of the United States, any civil governments which may exist therein shall be deemed provisional only, and in all respects subject to the paramount authority of the United States at any time to abolish, modify, control or supersede the same; and in all elections to any office under such provisional governments all persons shall be entitled to vote, and none others, who are entitled to vote, under the provisions of the fifth section of this act; and no persons shall be eligible to any office under any such provisional governments who would be disqualified from holding office under the provisions of the third *article* of said constitutional amendment.

CHOOSE THE CORRECT ANSWER

Write the letter that best completes the statement or answers the question.

1. Reconstruction means (a) repairing, (b) refining, (c) rebuilding, (d) recognizing.   1._____

2. The military commanders of the districts were appointed by (a) Congress, (b) the President, (c) the Secretary of War, (d) the Supreme Court.   2._____

3. When the Bill was first passed, President Johnson (a) signed it, (b) vetoed it, (c) used the pocket veto, (d) referred it to the Supreme Court.   3._____

4. The military commander of a district could (a) set up courts, (b) make laws, (c) execute any person who opposed him, (d) decide who could live in his district.   4._____

5. The Southern state not affected by the Reconstruction Act was (a) Virginia, (b) Arkansas, (c) Florida, (d) Tennessee.
   5._____

6. Southern states would remain under the Act until they accepted a change in (a) their tax laws, (b) their right to enslave Negroes, (c) their schools, (d) the United States Constitution.
   6._____

7. The Act stated that it was needed because (a) the slaves had been freed, (b) the rebel states had no legal governments,

(c) national transportation had broken down, (d) the war was
over.   7._____

8. A military court (a) always convicts, (b) holds no trials, (c)
   follows rules different from a civil court, (d) allows no appeals.   8._____

9. Under the Act Southern state courts (a) were closed, (b) could
   sometimes continue to operate, (c) could not try criminals,
   (d) had to accept officers as judges.   9._____

10. Reconstruction (a) helped rebuild the South, (b) destroyed
    all Southern courts; (c) prevented the Freedmen's Bureau
    from operating, (d) did not give civil rights to former slaves.
                                                                  10._____

THOUGHT QUESTIONS

1. What were the purposes of the Reconstruction Acts?
2. Describe in detail the problems of inefficiency and dishonesty
   which characterized some Reconstruction state and local governments.

The Pendleton Act 1883

* * * * *Under the spoils system of Andrew* Jackson's administration, government positions (postmasterships, diplomatic posts, customs collectorships, etc.) were given to "deserving" politicians as rewards for helping the party to victory. The need for civil service reform became obvious during the local, state and national scandals that followed the Civil War. Then, in 1881, President Garfield was assassinated by a disappointed office-seeker. The public demand for a federal civil service law based on the merit system roused Congress to pass a law that would protect federal employees from political pressure.

Senator George Pendleton of Ohio headed the committee which drew up the Civil Service Act. President Arthur received the power to appoint a bipartisan civil service commission to hold competitive examinations for federal jobs. Holders of these jobs were protected in their positions, and free from political party demands for funds.

By the end of Arthur's administration, about one-seventh of all federal employees were under civil service regulations and protection. The merit system has been extended regularly since then. Today only a few federal jobs are appointive positions.

Be it enacted . . . ,That the President is authorized to appoint, by and with the advice and consent of the Senate, three persons, not more than two of whom shall be adherents of the same party, as Civil Service Commissioners, . . .

That it shall be the duty of said commissioners:

First. To aid the President, as he may request, in preparing suitable rules for carrying this act into effect, . . .

Second. And, among other things, said rules shall provide and declare, as nearly as the conditions of good administration will warrant, as follows:

First, for open, competitive examinations for testing the fitness of applicants for the public service now classified or to be classified hereunder. Such examinations shall be practical in their character, and so far as may be shall relate to those matters which will fairly test the relative capacity and fitness of the persons examined to discharge the duties of the service into which they seek to be appointed.

Second, that all the offices, places, and employments so arranged or to be arranged in classes shall be filled by selections according to grade from among those graded highest as the results of such competitive examinations.

Third, appointments to the public service aforesaid in the departments at Washington shall be apportioned among the several States and Territories and the District of Columbia

upon the basis of population as ascertained at the last preceding census. . . .

Fourth, that there shall be a period of probation before any absolute appointment or employment aforesaid.

Fifth, that no person in the public service is for that reason under any obligations to contribute to any political fund, or to render any political service, and that he will not be removed or otherwise prejudiced for refusing to do so.

Sixth, that no person in said service has any right to use his official authority or influence to coerce the political action of any person or body. . . .

Seventh, there shall be non-competitive examinations in all proper cases before the commission, when competent persons do not compete, after notice has been given of the existence of the vacancy, under such rules as may be prescribed by the commissioners as to the manner of giving notice.

TRUE OR FALSE?

Write T *if the statement is correct; Write* F *if it is false.*

_____1. Most federal jobs today are given to members of the President's party who have worked for his election.

_____2. The President appoints only members of his own party as civil service commissioners.

_____3. Our first federal civil service act was named for the Senator who wrote it.

_____4. A federal civil service employee can never be discharged.

_____5. A federal civil service employee cannot be forced to contribute to a political fund.

_____6. A federal civil service employee may be active in a political party.

_____7. Residents of the District of Columbia may not receive federal employment.

_____8. Probation is the period of time during which a civil service employee works without pay.

_____9. The Senate must approve persons appointed as civil service commissioners.

_____10. Andrew Jackson would probably have vetoed any *merit system* law passed by Congress during his administration.

THOUGHT QUESTIONS

1. In what ways is the *merit system* superior to the *spoils system?*
2. Discuss the operation of the merit system in the city or state you know best.

Interstate Commerce Act 1887

* * * * *It was clear to the nation and to* Congress that the demands of state legislatures for the regulation of railroads could no longer be denied. The Wabash Case had made clear that only Congress could regulate the railroads, and this Congress proceeded to do. It concerned itself with unreasonable rates, the short haul abuse, pooling, and rebates. Each of these railroad practices had aroused the public which was paying the high cost of building railroad fortunes.

The Interstate Commerce Act of 1887 attacked each of these abuses. An Interstate Commerce Commission was set up to supervise the activities of the railroads. All rates were to be published, and changes in them could be made only after proper advance notice. The railroads were required to keep accurate records, and to make annual financial reports to the Commission. Failure to obey the provisions of the law brought fines of up to $5,000 for each violation.

Although the Commission could not itself fix railroad rates, and was required to go to court to enforce its rulings, it was an important beginning. It demonstrated the federal government's power to control any business which affected the life of the nation and which carried on its activities across state lines. The Interstate Commerce Commission set a pattern for other regulatory agencies created by Congress.

An Act to Regulate Commerce

Be it enacted . . . , That the provisions of this act shall apply to any common carrier or carriers engaged in the transportation of passengers or property wholly by railroad, or partly by railroad and partly by water when both are used, under a common control, management, or arrangement, for a continuous carriage or shipment, from one State or Territory of the United States, or the District of Columbia, to any other State or Territory of the United States, or the District of Columbia, or from any place in the United States to an adjacent foreign country, or from any place in the United States through a foreign country to any other place in the United States, and also to the transportation in like manner of property shipped from any place in the United States to a foreign country and carried from such place to a port of transshipment, or shipped from a foreign country to any place in the United States and carried to such place from a port of entry either in the United States or an adjacent foreign country: *Provided, however,* That the provisions of this act shall not apply to the transportation of passengers or property, or to the receiving, delivering, storage, or handling of property, wholly within one State, and not shipped to or from a foreign country from or to any State or Territory as aforesaid.

.   .   .   .

. . . All charges made for any service rendered or to be rendered in the transportation of passengers or property as aforesaid, or in connection therewith, or for the receiving, delivering, storage, or handling of such property, shall be reasonable and just; and every unjust and unreasonable charge for such service is prohibited and declared to be unlawful.

Section 2. That if any common carrier subject to the provisions of this act shall, directly or indirectly, by any special rate, rebate, drawback, or other device, charge, demand, collect, or receive from any person or persons a greater or less compensation for any service rendered, or to be rendered, in the transportation of passengers or property, subject to the provisions of this act, than it charges, demands, collects, or receives from any other person or persons for doing for him or them a like and contemporaneous service in the transportation of a like kind of traffic under substantially similar circumstances and conditions, such common carrier shall be deemed guilty of unjust discrimination, which is hereby prohibited and declared to be unlawful.

Section 3. That it shall be unlawful for any common carrier subject to the provisions of this act to make or give any undue or unreasonable preference or advantage to any particular person, company, firm, corporation, or locality, or any particular description of traffic, in any respect whatsoever, or to subject any particular person, company, firm, corporation, or locality, or any particular description of traffic, to any undue or unreasonable prejudice or disadvantage in any respect whatsoever.

Every common carrier subject to the provisions of this act shall, according to their respective powers, afford all reasonable, proper, and equal facilities for the interchange of traffic between their respective lines, and for the receiving, forwarding, and delivering of passengers and property to and from their several lines and those connecting therewith, and shall not discriminate in their rates and charges between such connecting lines; . . .

Section 4. That it shall be unlawful for any common carrier subject to the provisions of this act to charge or receive any greater compensation in the aggregate for the transportation of passengers or of like kind of property, under substantially similar circumstances and conditions, for a shorter than for a longer distance over the same line, in the same direction, the shorter being included within the longer distance; but this shall not be construed as authorizing any common carrier within the terms of this act to charge and receive as great compensation for a shorter as for a longer distance: *Provided, however,* That upon application to the Commission appointed under the provisions of this act, such common carrier may, in special cases, after investigation by the Commission, be authorized to charge less for longer than for shorter distances for the transportation of passengers or property; and the Commission may from time to time prescribe the extent to which such designated common carrier may be relieved from the operation of this section of this act.

Section 5. That it shall be unlawful for any common carrier subject to the provisions of this act to enter into any contract, agreement, or combination with any other common carrier or carriers for the pooling of freights of different and competing railroads, or to divide between them the aggregate or net proceeds of the earnings of such railroads, or any portion thereof; and in any case of an agreement for the pooling of freights as aforesaid, each day of its continuance shall be deemed a separate offense.

Section 6. That every common carrier subject to the provisions of this act shall print and keep for public inspection schedules showing the rates and fares and charges for the transportation of passengers and property which any such common carrier has established and which are in force at the time upon its railroad. . . . Such schedules shall be plainly printed in large type, . . . and copies for the use of the public shall be kept in every depot or station upon any such railroad, in such places and in such form that they can be conveniently inspected.

. . . .

No advance shall be made in the rates, fares, and charges which have been established and published as aforesaid by any common carrier in compliance with the requirements of this section, except after ten days' public notice, which shall plainly state the charges proposed to be made in the schedule then in force, and the time when the increased rates, fares, or charges will go into effect. . . . Reductions in such published rates, fares, or charges may be made without previous public notice; but whenever any such reduction is made, notice of the same shall immediately be publicly posted. . . .

Every common carrier subject to the provisions of this act shall file with the Commission hereinafter provided for copies of its schedules of rates, fares, and charges which have been established and published in compliance with the requirements of this section, and shall promptly notify said Commission of all changes made in the same. Every such common carrier shall also file with said Commission copies of all contracts, agreements, or arrangements with other common carriers in relation to any traffic affected by the provisions of this act to which it may be a party. . . .

Section 7. That it shall be unlawful for any common carrier subject to the provisions of this act to enter into any combination, contract, or agreement, expressed or implied, to prevent, by change of time schedule, carriage in different cars, or by other means or devices, the carriage of freights from being continuous from the place of shipment to the place of destination; . . .

Section 8. That in case any common carrier subject to the provisions of this act shall do, cause to be done, or permit to be done any act, matter, or thing in this act prohibited or declared to be unlawful, or shall omit to do any act, matter, or thing in this act required to be done, such common carrier shall be liable to the person or persons injured thereby for the full amount of damages sustained in consequence of any such violation of the provisions of this act, together with a reasonable counsel or attorney's fee, to be fixed by the court in every case of recovery, which attorney's fee shall be taxed and collected as part of the costs in the case.

Section 9. That any person or persons claiming to be damaged by any common carrier subject to the provisions of this act may either make complaint to the Commission as hereinafter provided for, or may bring suit in his or their own behalf for the recovery of the damages for which such common carrier may be liable under the provisions of this act, in any district or circuit court of the United States of competent jurisdiction . . .

Section 10. That any common carrier subject to the provisions of this act, or, whenever such common carrier is a corporation, any director or officer thereof, or any receiver, trustee, lessee, agent, or person acting for or employed by such corporation, who, . . . shall be guilty of any infraction of this act, or shall aid or abet therein, shall be deemed guilty of a misdemeanor, and shall, upon conviction thereof in any district court of the United States within the jurisdiction of which such offense was committed, be subject to a fine of not to exceed five thousand dollars for each offense.

Section 11. That a Commission is hereby created and established to be known as the Inter-State Commerce Commission, which shall be composed of five Commissioners, who shall be appointed by the President, by and with the advice and consent of the Senate. . . . Any Commissioner may be removed by the President for inefficiency, neglect of duty, or malfeasance in office. Not more than three of the Commissioners shall be appointed from the same political party. . . . Said Commissioners shall not engage in any other business, vocation, or employment. No vacancy in the Commission shall impair the right of the remaining Commissioners to exercise all the powers of the Commission.

Section 12. That the Commission hereby created shall have authority to inquire into the management of the business of all common carriers subject to the provisions of this act, and shall keep itself informed as to the manner and method in which the same is conducted, and shall have the right to obtain from such common carriers full and complete information necessary to enable the Commission to perform the duties and carry out the objects for which it was created;

. . . .

Section 13. That any person, firm, corporation, or association, or any mercantile, agricultural, or manufacturing society, or any body politic or municipal organization complaining of anything done or omitted to be done by any common carrier subject to the provisions of this act in contravention of the provisions thereof, may apply to said Commission by petition, which shall briefly state the facts;. . . If such carrier shall not satisfy the complaint within the time specified, or there shall appear to be any reasonable ground for investigating said complaint, it shall be the duty of the Commission to investigate the matters complained of in such manner and by such means as it shall deem proper.

Section 15. That if in any case in which an investigation shall be made by said Commission it shall be made to appear to the satisfaction of the Commission, either by the testimony of witnesses or other evidence, that anything has been done or omitted to be done in violation of the provisions of this act, or of any law cognizable by said Commission, by any common carrier, or that any injury, or damage has been sustained by the party or parties complaining, or by other parties aggrieved in consequence of any such violation, it shall be the duty of the Commission to forthwith cause a copy of its report in respect thereto to be delivered to such common carrier, together with a notice to said common carrier to cease and desist from such violation, or to make reparation for the injury so found to have been done, or both, within a reasonable time, to be specified by the Commission; . . .

Section 16. That whenever any common carrier, shall violate or refuse or neglect to obey any lawful order or requirement of the Commission in this act named, it shall be the duty of the Commission, and lawful for any company or person interested in such order or requirement, to apply, in a summary way, by petition, to the circuit court of the United States sitting in equity in the judicial district in which the common carrier complained of has its principal office, or in which the violation or disobedience of such order or requirement shall happen, alleging such violation or disobedience, as the case may be; and the said court shall have power to hear and determine the matter, on such short notice to the common carrier complained of as the court shall deem reasonable . . . When the subject in dispute shall be of the value of two thousand dollars or more, either party to such proceeding before said court may appeal to the Supreme Court of the United States. . . .

- - - - - - - - - - - - - - - - -

Section 20. That the Commission is hereby authorized to require annual reports from all common carriers subject to the provisions of this act, to fix the time and prescribe the manner in which such reports shall be made, and to require from such carriers specific answers to all questions upon which the Commission may need information. . . .

. . . .

Section 22. That nothing in this act shall apply to the carriage, storage, or handling of property free or at reduced rates for the United States, State, or municipal governments, or for charitable purposes, or to or from fairs and expositions for exhibition thereat, or the issuance of mileage, excursion, or commutation passenger tickets: nothing in this act shall be construed to prohibit any common carrier from giving reduced rates to ministers of religion; nothing in this act shall be construed to prevent railroads from giving free carriage to their own officers and employees, or to prevent the principal officers of any railroad company or companies from exchanging passes or tickets with other railroad companies for their officers and employees; and nothing in this act contained shall in any way abridge or alter the remedies now existing at common law or by statute, but the provisions of this act are in addition to such remedies: *Provided,* That no pending litigation shall in any way be affected by this act.

. . . .

CHOOSE THE CORRECT ANSWER

Write the letter that best completes the statement or answers the question.

1. One cause of the Interstate Commerce Act was (*a*) the high rates paid railroads by the United States government, (*b*) the Wabash Case, (*c*) the failure of state legislatures to pass needed laws, (*d*) the number of huge railroad fortunes.   1._____

2. The Interstate Commerce Commission was composed of (*a*) 3 men, (*b*) 5 men, (*c*) 7 men, (*d*) 9 men.   2._____

3. Railroads were required to (*a*) publish their rates, (*b*) lower their rates, (*c*) charge less for short trips, (*d*) lend their engines to one another.   3._____

4. The returning of part of a charge to a favored customer is called (*a*) pooling, (b) a short haul, (*c*) scheduling, (*d*) a rebate.   4._____

5. The Commission enforced its rules by (*a*) closing down railroads, (*b*) suing the railroads, (*c*) using the Army, (*d*) refusing railroad permits.   5._____

6. The Commission was not able to (*a*) end pooling agreements, (*b*) require continuous shipment of freight, (*c*) require financial reports, (*d*) fix rates. 6._____

7. The Interstate Commerce Commission was the first (*a*) Federal law regarding railroads, (*b*) federal commission, (*c*) federal regulatory agency, (*d*) bi-partisan federal group.
7._____

8. The Act required that the rates charged by a railroad be (*a*) no more than other railroads charged, (*b*) publicly posted, (*c*) set for a year at a time, (*d*) enough to give the railroad a profit. . 8._____

9. The Act was intended to control (*a*) businesses in which the federal government had a financial interest, (*b*) transportation from one part of a state to another part of the same state, (*c*) the construction of new railroads, (*d*) transportation of property from one state to another. 9._____

10. Railroads were specifically prohibited from all of the following practices *except* (*a*) charging one customer less than another for similar services, (*b*) discriminating against any particular locality, (*c*) charging more for a short trip than for a long one, (*d*) reducing rates and fares without previous public notice. 10._____

THOUGHT QUESTIONS

1. For what reasons was it necessary for Congress to pass the Interstate Commerce Act?

2. In what ways did the Interstate Commerce Act change the relationship between the United States government and American business?

The Sherman Anti-Trust Act 1890

* * * * *The second half of the nineteenth* century was a period of fantastic business growth. Some businesses grew so large and powerful that they controlled many industries. The most glaring example was Standard Oil, whose effective monopoly of the oil industry was steered by John D. Rockefeller. In other industries, territory was divided among major firms to prevent competition, and to assure the advantages of monopoly in given areas. Pressures applied against smaller producers forced them to follow pricing policies set by major producers. Such practices built many great fortunes at the expense of helpless consumers.

The demand for the elimination of monopolies or trusts came from every part of the nation. Both political parties promised to act. After the election of 1888, a law was passed which prohibited monopolies, set fines and imprisonment for violations, and gave triple damages to a person or company hurt by a monopoly.

Unfortunately, the courts did not use the Act to end the country's growing number of monopolies. It did, however, warn business that the nation insisted on changes in monopolistic business practices. Twenty-five years were to pass before more effective anti-trust legislation ended the biggest monopolies.

Be it enacted . . . ,

Section 1. Every contract, combination in the form of trust or otherwise, or conspiracy, in restraint of trade or commerce among the several States, or with foreign nations, is hereby declared to be illegal. Every person who shall make any such contract or engage in any such combination or conspiracy, shall be deemed guilty of a misdemeanor, and, on conviction thereof, shall be punished by fine not exceeding five thousand dollars, or by imprisonment not exceeding one year, or by both said punishments, in the discretion of the court.

Section 2. Every person who shall monopolize, or attempt to monopolize, or combine or conspire with any other person or persons, to monopolize any part of the trade or commerce among the several States, or with foreign nations, shall be deemed guilty of a misdemeanor, and, on conviction therefor, shall be punished by fine not exceeding five thousand dollars, or by imprisonment not exceeding one year, or by both said punishments, in the discretion of the court.

Section 3. Every contract, combination in form of trust or otherwise, or conspiracy, in restraint of trade or commerce in any Territory of the United States or of the District of Columbia, or in restraint of trade or commerce between any such Territory and another, or between any such Territory or Territories and any State or States or the District of Columbia, or with foreign nations, or between the District of Columbia and any State or State or foreign nations, is hereby declared illegal. Every person who shall make any such contract or engage in any such combination or conspiracy, shall be deemed guilty of a misdemeanor, and, on conviction thereof, shall be punished by fine not exceeding five thousand dollars, or by imprisonment not exceeding one year, or by both said punishments, in the discretion of the court.

Section 4. The several circuit courts of the United States are hereby invested with jurisdiction to prevent and restrain violations of this act; and it shall be the duty of the several district attorneys of the United States, in their respective districts, under the direction of the Attorney-General to institute proceedings in equity to prevent and restrain such violations. . . .

Section 6. Any property owned under any contract or by any combination, or pursuant to any conspiracy (and being the subject thereof) mentioned in section one of this act, and being in the course of transportation from one State to another, or to a foreign country, shall be forfeited to the United States, and may be seized and condemned by like proceedings as those provided by law for the forfeiture, seizure, and condemnation of property imported into the United States contrary to law.

Section 7. Any person who shall be injured in his business or property by any other person or corporation by reason of anything forbidden or declared to be unlawful by this act, may sue therefor in any circuit court of the United States in the district in which the defendant resides or is found, without respect to the amount in controversy, and shall recover three fold the damages by him sustained, and the costs of suit, including a reasonable attorney's fee.

Section 8. That the word "person," or "persons," wherever used in this act shall be deemed to include corporations and associations existing under or authorized by the laws of either the United States, the laws of any of the Territories, the laws of any State, or the laws of any foreign country.

FILL IN THE ANSWERS

Write the word or phrase which best completes the statement.

1. The act forbade combinations in a restraint of _____.
2. A person found guilty of monopolistic practices could be fined as much as _____, and jailed for as long as _____.
3. A person damaged by a monopoly could collect _____ damages.
4. The best known monopoly in 1890 was _____.
5. The enforcement of the law was left to the federal officials called _____.

THOUGHT QUESTIONS

1. For what reasons has it become public policy in the United States to prevent the existence of monopolies?
2. State the way in which the Sherman Act tried to end monopolies, and explain why the act failed to accomplish its purpose.

The Populist Party Platform 1892

*   *   *   * *The Populist Party, formed in 1892, was composed mainly of Southern and Western farmers. Since the Civil War these farmers had received very little help from the government. Many of them were in debt, and were suffering from the price-fixing of the railroads. In spite of previous legislation, the government was letting the railroad monopolies continue practically unchecked.*

The farmers' main demands were for (1) an expanded money supply which would serve as an inflationary measure and raise farm prices, and (2) increased government control over the railroads.

On July 4, 1862, Populist groups from all over the country met in Omaha to start a national organization and adopt a platform.

The conditions which surround us best justify our co-operation; we meet in the midst of a nation brought to the verge of moral, political, and material ruin. Corruption dominates the ballot-box, the legislatures, the Congress, and touches even the ermine of the bench. The people are demoralized; most of the states have been compelled to isolate the voters at the polling places to prevent universal intimidation and bribery. The newspapers are largely subsidized or muzzled, public opinion silenced, business prostrated, homes covered with mortgages, labor impoverished, and the land concentrating in the hands of capitalists. The urban workmen are denied the right to organize for self-protection; imported, pauperized labor beats down their wages; a hireling standing army, unrecognized by our laws, is established to shoot them down, and they are rapidly degenerating into European conditions. The fruits of the toil of millions are boldly stolen to build up colossal fortunes for a few, unprecedented in the history of mankind; and the possessors of those, in turn, despise the Republic and endanger Liberty. From the same prolific womb of governmental injustice we breed two great classes—tramps and millionaires.

The national power to create money is appropriated to enrich bondholders; a vast public debt payable in legal tender currency has been funded into gold-bearing bonds, thereby adding millions to the burden of the people.

Silver, which has been accepted as coin since the dawn of history, has been demonetized to add to all the purchasing power of gold by decreasing the value of all forms of property as well as human labor, and the supply of currency is purposely abridged to fatten usurers, bankrupt enterprise, and enslave industry. A vast conspiracy against mankind has been organized on two continents, and it is rapidly taking possession of the world. If not met and overthrown at once it forbodes terrible social convulsions, the destruction of civilization, or the establishment of an absolute despotism.

We have witnessed for more than a quarter of a century the struggles of the two great political parties for power and plunder, while grievous wrongs have been inflicted upon the suffering people. We charge that the controlling influences dominating both the parties have permitted the existing dreadful conditions to develop without serious effort to prevent or restrain them. Neither do they now promise us any substantial reform. They have agreed together to ignore, in the coming campaign, every issue but one. They propose to drown the outcries of a plundered people with the uproar of a sham battle over the tariff, so that capitalists, corporations, national banks, rings, trusts, watered stock, the demonetization of silver and the oppressions of the usurers may all be lost sight of. They propose to sacrifice our homes, lives, children on the altar of mammon; to destroy the multitude in order to secure corruption funds from the millionaires. . . .

Our country finds itself confronted by conditions for which there is no precedent in the history of the world; our annual agricultural productions amount to billions of dollars in value, which must, within a few weeks or months, be exchanged for billions of dollars' worth of commodities consumed in their production; the existing currency supply is wholly inadequate to make this exchange; the results are falling prices, the formation of combines or rings, the impoverishment of the producing class. We pledge ourselves that if given the power we will labor to correct these evils by wise and reasonable legislation, in accordance with the terms of our platform. . . .

We declare, therefore:

First. — That the union of the labor forces of the United States this day consummated shall be permanent and perpetual; may its spirit enter into all hearts for the salvation of the Republic and the uplifting of mankind.

Second. — Wealth belongs to him who creates it, and every dollar taken from industry without an equivalent is robbery. "If any will not work, neither shall he eat." The interests of rural and civic labor are the same; their enemies are identical.

Third. — We believe that the time has come when the railroad corporations will either own the people or the people must own the railroads, and should the government enter upon the work of owning and managing all railroads, we should favor an amendment to the Constitution by which all persons engaged in the Government service shall be placed under a civil service regulation of the most rigid character, so as to prevent the increase of the power of the national administration by the use of such additional Government employees.

Finance. — We demand a national currency, safe, sound, and flexible, issued by the general Government only, a full legal tender for all debts, public and private, and that without the use of banking corporations, a just, equitable, and efficient means of distribution direct to the people, at a tax not to exceed 2 per cent per annum, to be provided as set forth in the sub-treasury plan of the Farmers' Alliance, or a better system; also by payments in discharge of its obligations for public improvements.

1. We demand free and unlimited coinage of silver and gold at the present legal ratio of 16 to 1.

2. We demand that the amount of circulating medium be speedily increased to not less than $50 per capita.

3. We demand a graduated income tax.

4. We believe that the money of the country should be kept as much as possible in the hands of the people, and hence we demand that all State and national revenues shall be limited to the necessary expenses of the Government, economically and honestly administered.

5. We demand that postal savings banks be established by the government for the safe deposit of the earnings of the people and to facilitate exchange.

Transportation. — Transportation being a means of exchange and a public necessity, the Government should own and operate the railroads in the interests of the people. The telegraph, telephone, like the post-office system, being a necessity for the transmission of news, should be owned and operated by the Government in the interests of the people.

Land. — The land, including all the natural resources of wealth, is the heritage of the people, and should not be monopolized for speculative purposes, and alien ownership of land should be prohibited. All land now held by railroads and other corporations in excess of their actual needs, and all lands now owned by aliens should be reclaimed by the Government and held for actual settlers only.

TRUE OR FALSE?

Write T *if the statement is correct, write* F *if it is false.*

_____1. The farmers believed that the more money there was in circulation, the higher prices would be, and the more money they would make.

_____2. One plank in the Populist Party platform was to get the government to buy up all the silver that was being mined to use as backing for government-printed paper money.

_____3. The Populist Party advocated the free and unlimited coinage of silver, in a ratio of 16 to 1 with gold.

_____4. The Populists were opposed to any form of income tax.

_____5. The Populists favored unlimited sale of land to aliens.

THOUGHT QUESTIONS

1. Many of the Populists' demands sounded radical in 1892. Which of their reforms have since been accepted as part of our political and economic system?

2. The Populist Party is considered the most influential third party in American history. Explain.

Bryan's "Cross of Gold" Speech 1896

* * * * *In the Presidential election of 1892,* the Populist Party polled more than a million popular votes and won 22 votes in the electoral college.

In 1896, the Republicans nominated Governor William McKinley for President, and declared themselves strongly opposed to the Populist platform. The Democrats came out in favor of many of the reforms demanded by the Populists. William Jennings Bryan's stirring "Cross of Gold" speech helped win the Democratic party to the cause of silver, and it also helped Bryan win the Democratic Presidential nomination. Later, the Populist Party also nominated Bryan for President. After a bitter campaign, McKinley defeated Bryan.

I would be presumptuous, indeed, to present myself against the distinguished gentlemen to whom you have listened if this were a mere measuring of abilities; but this is not a contest between persons. The humblest citizen in all the land, when clad in the armor of a righteous cause, is stronger than all the hosts of error. I come to speak to you in defense of a cause as holy as the cause of liberty — the cause of humanity.

When this debate is concluded, a motion will be made to lay upon the table the resolution offered in commendation of the administration, and also the resolution offered in condemnation of the administration. We object to bringing this question down to the level of persons. The individual is but an atom; he is born, he acts, he dies; but principles are eternal; and this has been a contest over a principle.

Never before in the history of this country has there been witnessed such a contest as that through which we have just passed. Never before in the history of American politics has a great issue been fought out as this issue has been, by the voters of a great party. . .

Ah, my friends, we say not one word against those who live upon the Atlantic coast, but the hardy pioneers who have braved all the dangers of the wilderness, who have made the desert to bloom as the rose — the pioneers away out there (pointing to the West), who rear their children near to Nature's heart, where they can mingle their voices with the voices of the birds — out there where they have erected schoolhouses for the education of their young, churches where they praise their Creator, and cemeteries where rest the ashes of their dead — these people, we say, are as deserving of the consideration of our party as any people in this country. It is for these that we speak. We do not come as aggressors. Our war is not a war of conquest; we are fighting in the defense of our homes, our families and posterity. We have petitioned, and our petitions have been scorned; we have entreated, and our entreaties have been disregarded; we have begged, and they have mocked when our calamity came. We beg no longer; we entreat no more; we petition no more. We defy them. . . .

They tell us that this platform was made to catch votes. We reply to them that changing conditions make new issues; that the principles upon which Democracy rests are as everlasting as the hills, but that they must be applied to new conditions as they arise. Conditions have arisen, and we are here to meet these conditions. They tell us that the income tax ought not to be brought in here; that it is a new idea. They criticize us for our criticism of the Supreme Court of the United States. My friends, we have not criticized; we have simply called attention to what you already know. If you want criticisms, read the dissenting opinions of the court. There you will find criticisms. They say that we passed an unconstitutional law; we deny it. The income tax law was not unconstitutional when it was passed; it was not unconstitutional when it went before the Supreme Court for the first time; it did not become unconstitutional until one of the judges changed his mind, and we cannot be expected to know when a judge will change his mind. The income tax is just. It simply intends to put the burdens of government justly on the backs of the people. I am in favor of an income tax. When I find a man who is not willing to bear his share of the burdens of the government which protects him, I find a man who is unworthy to enjoy the blessings of a government like ours. . . .

And now, my friends, let me come to the paramount issue. If they ask us why it is that we say more on the money question than we say upon the tariff question, I reply that, if protection has slain its thousands, the gold standard has slain its tens of thousands. If they ask us why we do not embody in our platform all the things that we believe in, we reply that when we have restored the money of the Constitution all other necessary reforms will be possible; but that until this is done there is no other reform that can be accomplished. . . .

We go forth confident that we shall win. Why? Because upon the paramount issue of this campaign there is not a spot of ground upon which the enemy will dare to challenge battle. If they tell us that the gold standard is a good thing, we shall point to their platform and tell them that their platform pledges the party to get rid of the gold standard and substitute bimetalism. If the gold standard is a good thing, why try to get rid of it? I call your attention to the fact that some of the very people who are in this convention today and who tell us that we ought to declare in favor of international bimetalism — thereby declaring that the gold standard is wrong and that the principle of bimetalism is better — these very people four months ago were open and avowed advocates of the gold standard, and were then telling us that we could not legislate two metals together, even with the aid of all the world. If the gold standard is a good thing, we ought to declare in favor of its retention and not in favor of abandoning it; and if the gold standard is a bad thing why should we wait until other nations are willing to help us let it go? Here is the line of battle, and we care not upon which issue they force the fight; we are prepared to meet them on either issue or on both. If they tell us that the gold standard is the standard of civilization, we reply to them that this, the most enlightened of all the nations of the earth, has never declared for a gold standard and that both the great parties this year are declaring against it. If the gold standard is the standard of civilization, why, my friends, should we not have it? If they come to meet us on that issue we can present the history of our nation. More than that; we can tell them that they will search the pages of history in vain to find a single instance where the common people of any land have ever declared themselves in favor of the gold standard. They can find where the holders of fixed investments have declared for a gold standard, but not where the masses have . . .

. . . The sympathies of the Democratic party, as shown by the platform, are on the side of the struggling masses who have ever been the foundation of the Democratic party. There are two ideas of government. There are those who believe that, if you will only legislate to make the well-to-do prosperous, their prosperity will leak through on those below. The Democratic idea, however, has been that if you legislate to make the masses prosperous, their prosperity will find its way up through every class which rests upon them.

You come to us and tell us that the great cities are in favor of the gold standard; we reply that the great cities rest upon our broad and fertile prairies. Burn down your cities and leave our farms, and your cities will spring up again as if by magic; but destroy our farms and the grass will grow in the streets of every city in the country. . . .

. . . Having behind us the producing masses of this nation and the world, supported by the commercial interests, the laboring interests, and the toilers everywhere, we will answer their demand for a gold standard by saying to them: You shall not press down upon the brow of labor this crown of thorns, you shall not crucify mankind upon the cross of gold.

TRUE OR FALSE?

Write the letter T *if the statement is correct; write* F *if it is false.*

_____1. The Populist Party was supported mainly by industrialists.

_____2. In the Presidential election of 1896, the conservatives advocated retention of the gold standard.

_____3. Poor farming methods and bad planning were the causes of the poverty of the farmer after the Civil War.

_____4. The Populists wanted the Government to control the railroads.

_____5. The Republican victory in the election of 1896 was a victory for agriculture over industry, the South and West over the East.

_____6. Bryan and his political party were in favor of an income tax.

_____7. Both political parties in the election campaign of 1896 favored abandonment of the gold standard.

_____8. Bimetalism is the use of gold and silver in a fixed ratio for a nation's currency.

_____9. Bryan believed that legislation to make the rich richer would also bring prosperity to the masses.

_____10. Agriculture is the basic industry of any nation.

THOUGHT QUESTIONS

1. Why did the Populists feel that the Atlantic seaboard states were their political enemies?
2. The position which the Republican Party took in the 1896 election was a *conservative* position. What is meant by *conservative*?

Chinese Exclusion Act
1902

* * * * *The first Chinese immigrants came* to the Pacific Coast after the discovery of gold in 1849, and by 1852 there were about 25,000 Chinese there. When the Central Pacific Railroad began to build eastward after 1860, its labor was supplied by additional thousands of Chinese immigrants. By 1880, there were about 150,000 Chinese in California.

The Chinese, long accustomed to a low standard of living, worked long hours at low pay. This cheap labor threatened the standard of living for which the budding American labor movement was struggling. Racial prejudice was widespread because of the refusal of the Oriental immigrants to adopt American customs. For most of the Chinese, their life in America was just a means to save enough money to return "wealthy" to their homeland.

In 1882, 1892, and finally in 1902, laws were passed to end further Chinese and other Oriental immigration. They were part of the intolerance and discrimination from which Chinese living in the United States suffered for so long. In recent years this exclusion has persisted except for the emergency admission of refugees from the Communist Chinese.

Be it enacted . . . , That all laws now in force prohibiting and regulating the coming of Chinese persons, and persons of Chinese descent, into the United States, and the residence of such persons therein . . . . be, and the same are hereby, reenacted, extended, and continued so far as the same are not inconsistent with treaty obligations, until otherwise provided by law, and said laws shall also apply to the island territory under the jurisdiction of the United States, and prohibit the immigration of Chinese laborers, not citizens of the United States, from such island territory to the mainland territory of the United States, whether in such island territory at the time of cession or not, and from one portion of the island territory of the United States to another portion of said island territory: *Provided, however,* That said laws shall not apply to the transit of Chinese laborers from one island to another island of the same group; and any islands within the jurisdiction of any State or the District of Alaska shall be considered a part of the mainland under this section.

Section 2. That the Secretary of the Treasury is hereby authorized and empowered to make and prescribe, and from time to time to change such rules and regulations not inconsistent with the laws of the land as he may deem necessary and proper to execute the provisions of this Act and of the Acts hereby extended and continued and of the treaty of . . . (December 8, 1894,) . . . between the United States and China, and with the approval of the President to appoint such agents as he may deem necessary for the efficient execution of said treaty and said Acts.

Section 3. That nothing in the provisions of this Act or any other Act shall be construed to prevent, hinder, or restrict any foreign exhibitor, representative, or citizen of any foreign nation, or the holder, who is a citizen of any foreign nation, of any concession or privilege from any fair or exposition authorized by Act of Congress from bringing into the United States, under contract, such mechanics, artisans, agents, or other employees, natives of their respective foreign countries, as they or any of them may deem necessary for the purpose of making preparation for installing or conducting their exhibits or of preparing for installing or conducting any business authorized or permitted under or by virtue of or pertaining to any concession or privilege which may have been or may be granted by any said fair or exposition in connection with such exposition, under such rules and regulations as the Secretary of the Treasury may prescribe, both as to the admission and return of such person or persons.

Section. 4. That it shall be the duty of every Chinese laborer, other than a citizen, rightfully in, and entitled to remain in any of the insular territory of the United States (Hawaii excepted) at the time of the passage of this Act, to obtain within one year thereafter a certificate of residence in the insular territory wherein he resides, which certificate shall entitle him to residence therein, and upon failure to obtain such certificate as herein provided he shall be deported from such insular territory; and the Philippine Commission is authorized and required to make all regulations and provisions necessary for the enforcement of this section in the Philippine Islands, including the form and substance of the certificate of residence so that the same shall clearly and sufficiently identify the holder thereof and enable officials to prevent fraud in the transfer of the same . . .

TRUE OR FALSE?

Write T if the statement is correct; Write F if it is false.

_____1. The law prevented all Asians from immigrating to the United States.

_____2. All Chinese who were citizens were forced to leave.

_____3. A Chinese born in the United States is a citizen of the United States and of the state in which he resides.

_____4. The law was administered by the Secretary of State.

_____5. Chinese who were not citizens were required to obtain permits to remain.

_____6. Chinese workers could be brought to the United States for special listed purposes.

_____7. American worker groups protested this law directed against Chinese laborers.

_____8. Most Chinese in America soon adopted American ways of living.

_____9. All Chinese residents in the Philippine Islands had to be finger-printed.

_____10. Chinese laborers were permitted to transfer their certificates of residence to other members of their immediate families.

THOUGHT QUESTIONS

1. For what reasons did the United States adopt a policy of preventing the immigration of Chinese and other Orientals?
2. What effect can our anti-Asian immigration policies have on the world position of the United States today?

Theodore Roosevelt's Conservation Message 1907

* * * * *In Roosevelt's annual message to* Congress he declared that the conservation of our nation's forests and water supply was the most vital of America's domestic problems. During his presidency he succeeded in setting aside 150 million acres of timber land, and 85 million acres of mineral lands in Alaska as national property. We are all of us, today, grateful for his foresight.

To the Senate and House of Representatives:

. . . The conservation of our natural resources and their proper use constitute the fundamental problem which underlies almost every other problem of our national life . . .

As a nation we not only enjoy a wonderful measure of present prosperity but if this prosperity is used aright it is an earnest of future success such as no other nation will have. The reward of foresight for this nation is great and easily foretold. But there must be the look ahead, there must be the realization of the fact that to waste, to destroy our natural resources, to skin and exhaust the land instead of using it so as to increase its usefulness, will result in undermining in the days of our children the very prosperity which we ought by right to hand down to them amplified and developed.

For the last few years, through several agencies, the government has been endeavoring to get our people to look ahead and to substitute a planned and orderly development of our resources in place of a haphazard striving for immediate profit. . . .

Irrigation should be far more extensively developed than at present, not only in the States of the great plains and the Rocky Mountains, but in many others, as, for instance, in large portions of the South Atlantic and Gulf States, where it should go hand in hand with the reclamation of swampland. The Federal Government should seriously devote itself to this task, realizing that utilization of waterways and waterpower, forestry, irrigation, and the reclamation of lands threatened with overflow, are all interdependent parts of the same problem. The work of the Reclamation Service in developing the larger opportunities of the Western half of our country for irrigation is more important than almost any other movement. . . .

Optimism is a good characteristic, but if carried to an excess it becomes foolishness. We are prone to speak of the resources of this country as inexhaustible; this is not so. The mineral wealth of the country, the coal, iron, oil, gas, and the like, does not reproduce itself, and therefore is certain to be exhausted ultimately; and wastefulness in dealing with it today means that our descendants will feel the exhaustion a generation or two before they otherwise would. But there are certain other forms of waste which could be entirely stopped — the waste of soil by washing, for instance, which is among the most dangerous of all wastes now in progress in the United States, is easily preventable, so that this present enormous loss of fertility is entirely unnecessary. The preservation or replacement of the forests is one of the most important means of preventing this loss. We have made a beginning in forest preservation, but . . . so rapid has been the rate of exhaustion of timber in the United States in the past, and so rapidly is the remainder being exhausted, that the country is unquestionably on the verge of a timber famine which will be felt in every household in the land ... The present annual consumption of lumber is certainly three times as great as the annual growth; and if the consumption and growth continue unchanged, practically all our lumber will be exhausted in another generation, while long before the limit to complete exhaustion is reached the growing scarcity will make itself felt in many blighting ways upon

CONSERVING OUR VALUABLE RESOURCES

WE ARE BLESSED WITH VAST NATURAL RESOURCES . . . BUT

Forests, natural watersheds | Fertile soil | Valuable mineral resources | Fish, game, fowl

WE HAVE USED OUR RESOURCES BADLY . . . THEREFORE

Devastation, floods | Worn out soil | Waste | Wiping out of whole species

WE MUST RECLAIM AND CONSERVE

Plant new forests and prevent floods | Restore soil by scientific methods | Maximum use of our mineral resources | Wild life preserves

our national welfare. About twenty per cent of our forested territory is now reserved in national forests; but these do not include the most valuable timberlands, and in any event the proportion is too small to expect that the reserves can accomplish more than a mitigation of the trouble which is ahead for the nation . . . We should acquire in the Appalachian and White Mountain regions all the forestlands that it is possible to acquire for the use of the nation. These lands, because they form a national asset, are as emphatically national as the rivers which they feed, and which flow through so many States before they reach the ocean. . . .

THOUGHT QUESTIONS

1. Conservation, or wise use of our natural resources, is important to the welfare of the nation.
   (*a*) In what ways has the dumping of sewage and waste into our waterways affected health and recreation?
   (*b*) In what ways has reckless logging destroyed the nation's watersheds?
   (*c*) What steps have been taken to reclaim the desert lands of our Western States?
   (*d*) How has the Forestry Service insured a reasonable supply of timber for the future?
   (*e*) How has the Soil Conservation Service helped farmers use their lands wisely?
2. Americans enjoy the highest standard of living ever attained by man. Explain and illustrate how natural resources helped to bring about this high standard of living in the United States.
3. Present both sides of the following questions:
   (*a*) The fear of a shortage of raw materials has not been justified by the facts of history.
   (*b*) Conservation penalizes the present generation for the doubtful benefit of future generations.
   (*c*) There is no need for conserving coal and oil, for the sun and the tides will supply future generations with unlimited amounts of power. If they don't, atomic energy will.
   (*d*) Synthetic products already known can replace all the wood now used.
   (*e*) Chemists will find out how to restore the fertility of the soil with synthetics.

Woodrow Wilson Documents 1913-1917

* * * *Both President Theodore Roosevelt* and President William Howard Taft launched vigorous campaigns against trusts. More than 100 court cases were started, but they dragged along for years without the courts arriving at a decision.

President Woodrow Wilson promised the nation a New Freedom. He planned to reform the work of the government by laws designed to place tighter controls on business. Three laws of special importance were passed: the Federal Reserve Act; the law creating the Federal Trade Commission, and the Clayton Anti-Trust Act.

The Federal Reserve Act set up a new kind of

banking system. Under this system the power of the federal government was used to make banking practices more uniform, to control credit, and to make the currency more elastic. The Federal Trade Commission was given the task of ensuring fair competition in business, and of publicizing any violations that it found. The Clayton Act defined some of the provisions of the Sherman Act which the courts had found unclear, and prohibited specific monopolistic business practices.

These laws have had a great effect upon American business life. The Federal Reserve system, by its power to set the rate at which commercial paper is discounted, and to change reserve requirements of banks, has lessened, in recent years, the effect of business recessions. The FTC has prevented unfair advertising and other improper business practices. The Clayton Act has helped to wipe out much of the threat of monopoly.

Federal Reserve Act (1913)

Section 2. As soon as practicable, the Secretary of the Treasury, the Secretary of Agriculture and the Comptroller of the Currency, acting as "The Reserve Bank Organization Committee," shall designate not less than eight nor more than twelve cities to be known as Federal reserve cities, and shall divide the continental United States, excluding Alaska, into districts, each district to contain only one of such Federal reserve cities. . . . *Provided,* That the districts shall be apportioned with due regard to the convenience and customary course of business and shall not necessarily be coterminous with any State or States. . . . Such districts shall be known as Federal reserve districts and may be designated by number. . . .

. . . .

. . . When the organization committee shall have designated the cities in which Federal reserve banks are to be organized, and fixed the geographical limits of the Federal reserve districts, every national banking association within that district shall be required within thirty days after notice from the organization committee, to subscribe to the capital stock of such Federal reserve bank in a sum equal to six per centum of the paid-up capital stock and surplus of such bank. . . .

. . . .

Should any national banking association in the United States now organized fail within one year after the passage of this Act to become a member bank or fail to comply with any of the provisions of this Act applicable thereto, all of the rights, privileges, and franchises of such association granted to it under the national-bank Act, or under the provision of this Act, shall be thereby forfeited. . . .

. . . .

Section 3. Each Federal reserve bank shall establish branch banks within the Federal reserve district in which it is located and may do so in the district of any Federal reserve bank which may have been suspended.

. . . .

Section 9. Any bank incorporated by special law of any State, or organized under the general laws of any State or of the United States, may make application to . . . the Federal Reserve Board for the right to subscribe to the stock of the Federal reserve bank organized or to be organized within the Federal reserve district where the applicant is located. . .

Section 10. A Federal Reserve Board is hereby created which shall consist of seven members, including the Secretary of the Treasury and the Comptroller of the Currency, who shall be members ex officio, and five members appointed by the President of the United States, by and with the advice and consent of the Senate. In selecting the five appointive members of the Federal Reserve Board, not more than one of whom shall be selected from any one Federal reserve district, the President shall have due regard to a fair representation of the different commercial, industrial and geographical divisions of the country. The five members of the Federal

Reserve Board appointed by the President and confirmed as aforesaid shall devote their entire time to the business of the Federal Reserve Board. . . .

. . . .

Section 11. The Federal Reserve Board shall be authorized and empowered:

(a) To examine at its discretion the accounts, books and affairs of each Federal reserve bank and of each member bank and to require such statements and reports as it may deem necessary. The said board shall publish once each week a statement showing the condition of each Federal reserve bank and a consolidated statement for all Federal reserve banks. . . .

(b) To permit, or, on the affirmative vote of at least five members of the Reserve Board to require Federal reserve banks to rediscount the discounted paper of other Federal reserve banks at rates of interest to be fixed by the Federal Reserve Board.

. . . .

(j) To exercise general supervision over said Federal reserve banks.

Section 12. There is hereby created a Federal Advisory Council, which shall consist of as many members as there are Federal reserve districts. Each Federal reserve bank by its board of directors shall annually select from its own Federal reserve district one member of said council. . . .

The Federal Advisory Council shall have power, by itself or through its officers, (1) to confer directly with the Federal Reserve Board on general business conditions; (2) to make oral or written representations concerning matters within the jurisdiction of said board; (3) to call for information and to make recommendations in regard to discount rates, rediscount business, note issues, reserve conditions in the various districts, the purchase and sale of gold or securities by reserve banks, open-market operations by said banks, and the general affairs of the reserve banking system.

Section 13. Any Federal reserve bank may receive from any of its member banks, and from the United States, deposits of current funds in lawful money, national-bank notes, Federal reserve notes, or checks and drafts upon solvent member banks, payable upon presentation; or, solely for exchange purposes, may receive from other Federal reserve banks deposits of current funds in lawful money, national-bank notes, or checks and drafts upon solvent member or other Federal reserve banks, payable upon presentation.

Upon the indorsement of any of its member banks, with a waiver of demand, notice and protest by such bank, any Federal reserve bank may discount notes, drafts, and bills of exchange arising out of actual commercial transactions; . . .

Any Federal reserve bank may discount acceptances which are based on the importation or exportation of goods and which have a maturity at time of discount of not more than three months, and indorsed by at least one member bank. The amount of acceptances so discounted shall at no time exceed one-half the paid-up capital stock and surplus of the bank for which the rediscounts are made.

The aggregate of such notes and bills bearing the signature or indorsement of any one person, company, firm, or corporation rediscounted for any one bank shall at no time exceed ten per centum of the unimpaired capital and surplus of said bank; but this restriction shall not apply to the discount of bills of exchange drawn in good faith against actually existing values. . . .

Section 14. Any Federal reserve bank may, under rules and regulations prescribed by the Federal Reserve Board, purchase and sell in the open market, at home or abroad, either from or to domestic or foreign banks, firms, corporations, or individuals, cable transfers and bankers' acceptances and bills of exchange of the kinds and maturities by this Act made eligible for rediscount, with or without the indorsement of a member bank.

Every Federal reserve bank shall have power:

(a) To deal in gold coin and bullion at home or abroad, to make loans thereon, exchange Federal reserve notes for gold, gold coin, or gold certificates, and to contract for loans of gold coin or bullion, giving therefor, when necessary, acceptable security, including the hypothecation of United States bonds or other securities which Federal reserve banks are authorized to hold;

(b) To buy and sell, at home or abroad, bonds and notes of the United States, and bills, notes, revenue bonds, and warrants with a maturity from date of purchase of not exceeding six months, issued in anticipation of the collection of taxes or in anticipation of the receipt of assured revenues by any State, county, district, political subdivision, or municipality in the continental United States, including irrigation, drainage and reclamation districts. . . .

. . . .

(d) To establish from time to time, subject to review and determination of the Federal Reserve Board, rates of discount to be charged by the Federal reserve bank for each class of paper, which shall be fixed with a view of accommodating commerce and business;

(e) To establish accounts with other Federal reserve banks for exchange purposes and, with the consent of the Federal Reserve Board, to open and maintain banking accounts in foreign countries, . . .

Section 15. The moneys held in the general fund of the Treasury, except the five per centum fund for the redemption of outstanding national-bank notes and the funds provided in this Act for the redemption of Federal reserve notes may, upon the direction of the Secretary of the Treasury, be deposited in Federal reserve banks, which banks, when required by the Secretary of the Treasury, shall act as fiscal agents of the United States; and the revenues of the Government or any part thereof may be deposited in such banks, and disbursements may be made by checks drawn against such deposits.

. . . .

Section 16. Federal reserve notes, to be issued at the discretion of the Federal Reserve Board for the purpose of making advances to the Federal reserve banks through the Federal reserve agents hereinafter set forth and for no other purpose, are hereby authorized. The said notes shall be obligations of the United States and shall be receivable by all national and member banks and Federal reserve banks and for all taxes, customs, and other public dues. . . .

Any Federal reserve bank may make application to the local Federal reserve agent for such amount of the Federal reserve notes hereinbefore provided for as it may require.

Every Federal reserve bank shall maintain reserves in gold or lawful money of not less than thirty-five per centum against its deposits and reserves in gold of not less than forty per centum against its Federal reserve notes in actual circulation, and not offset by gold or lawful money deposited with the Federal reserve agent. . . .

. . . .

Section 25. Any national banking association possessing a capital and surplus of $1,000,000 or more may file application with the Federal Reserve Board . . . for the purpose of securing authority to establish branches in foreign countries or dependencies of the United States for the furtherance of the foreign commerce of the United States, and to act, if required to do so, as fiscal agents of the United States. . . . The Federal Reserve Board shall have power to approve or to reject such application if, in its judgment, the amount of capital proposed to be set aside for the conduct of foreign business is inadequate, or if for other reasons the granting of such application is deemed inexpedient. . . .

Federal Trade Commission (1914)

Be it enacted . . . , That a commission is hereby created and established, to be known as the Federal Trade Commission (hereinafter referred to as the commission), which shall be composed of five commissioners, who shall be appointed by the President, by and with the advice and consent of the Senate. Not more than three of the commissioners shall be members of the same political party. The first commissioners appointed shall continue in office for terms of three, four, five, six, and seven years, respectively, from the date of the taking effect of this Act, the term of each to be designated by the President, but their successors shall be appointed for terms of seven years.

. . . The commission shall choose a chairman from its own membership. No commissioner shall engage in any other business, vocation, or employment. Any commissioner may be removed by the President for inefficiency, neglect of duty, or malfeasance in office. A vacancy in the commission shall not impair the right of the remaining commissioners to exercise all the powers of the commission.

. . . .

Section 3. . . . The principal office of the commission shall be in the city of Washington, but it may meet and exercise all its powers at any other place. The commission may, by one or more of its members, or by such examiners as it may designate, prosecute any inquiry necessary to its duties in any part of the United States.

. . . .

Section 5. That unfair methods of competition in commerce are hereby declared unlawful.

The commission is hereby empowered and directed to prevent persons, partnerships, or corporations, except banks, and common carriers subject to the Acts to regulate commerce, from using unfair methods of competition in commerce.

Whenever the commission shall have reason to believe that any such person, partnership, or corporation has been or is using any unfair method of competition in commerce, and if it shall appear to the commission that a proceeding by it in respect thereof would be to the interest of the public, it shall issue and serve upon such person, partnership, or corporation a complaint stating its charges in that respect, and containing a notice of a hearing upon a day and at a place therein fixed at least thirty days after the service of said complaint. The person, partnership, or corporation so complained of shall have the right to appear at the place and time so fixed and show cause why an order should not be entered by the commission requiring such person, partnership, or corporation to cease and desist from the violation of the law so charged in said complaint. . . .

If such person, partnership, or corporation fails or neglects to obey such order of the commission while the same is in effect, the commission may apply to the circuit court of appeals of the United States, within any circuit where the method of competition in question was used or where such person, partnership, or corporation resides or carries on business, for the enforcement of its order, and shall certify and file with its application a transcript of the entire record in the proceeding, including all the testimony taken and the report and order of the commission. . . . The judgment and decree of the court shall be final, except that the same shall be subject to review by the Supreme Court upon certiorari as provided in section two hundred and forty of the Judicial Code.

. . . .

Such proceedings shall be given precedence over other cases pending . . . , and shall be in every way expedited. No order of the commission or judgment of the court to enforce the same shall in any wise relieve or absolve any person, partnership, or corporation from any liability under the antitrust acts. . . .

Section 6. That the commission shall also have power—

(a) To gather and compile information concerning, and to investigate from time to time the organization, business, conduct, practices, and management of any corporation engaged in commerce, excepting banks and common carriers subject to the Act to regulate commerce, and its relation to other corporations and to individuals, associations, and partnerships.

(b) To require, by general or special orders, corporations engaged in commerce, excepting banks, and common carriers subject to the Act to regulate commerce, or any class of them, or any of them, respectively, to file with the commission in such form as the commission may prescribe annual or special, or both annual and special, reports or answers in writing to specific questions, furnishing to the commission such information as it may require as to the organization, business, conduct, practices, management, and relation to other corporations, partnerships, and individuals of the respective corporations filing such reports or answers in writing. . . .

(c) Whenever a final decree has been entered against any defendant corporation in any suit brought by the United States to prevent and restrain any violation of the antitrust Acts, to make investigation, upon its own initiative, of the manner in which the decree has been or is being carried out, and upon the application of the Attorney General it shall be its duty to make such investigation. It shall transmit to the Attorney General a report embodying its findings and recommendations as a result of any such investigation, and the report shall be made public in the discretion of the commission.

(d) Upon the direction of the President or either House of Congress to investigate and report the facts relating to any alleged violations of the antitrust Acts by any corporation.

(e) Upon the application of the Attorney General to investigate and make recommendations for the readjustment of the business of any corporation alleged to be violating the antitrust Acts in order that the corporation may thereafter maintain its organization, management, and conduct of business in accordance with law.

(f) To make public from time to time such portions of the information obtained by it hereunder, except trade secrets and names of customers, as it shall deem expedient in the public interest; and to make annual and special reports to the Congress and to submit therewith recommendations for additional legislation; and to provide for the publication of its reports and decisions in such form and manner as may be adapted for public information and use.

. . . .

(h) To investigate, from time to time, trade conditions in and with foreign countries where associations, combinations, or practices of manufacturers, merchants, or traders, or other conditions, may affect the foreign trade of the United States, and to report to Congress thereon, with such recommendations as it deems advisable.

. . . .

Section 8. That the several departments and bureaus of the Government when directed by the President shall furnish the commission, upon its request, all records, papers, and information in their possession relating to any corporation subject to any of the provisions of this Act, and shall detail from time to time such officials and employees to the commission as he may direct.

Section 9. That for the purposes of this Act the commission or its duly authorized agent or agents, shall at all reasonable times have access to, for the purpose of examination, and the right to copy any documentary evidence of any corporation being investigated or proceeded against; and the commission shall have power to require by subpoena the attendance and testimony of witnesses and the production of all such documentary evidence relating to any matter under investigation. . . .

. . . .

No person shall be excused from attending and testifying or from producing documentary evidence before the commission or in obedience to the subpoena of the commission on the ground or for the reason that the testimony or evidence, documentary or otherwise, required of him may tend to incriminate him or subject him to a penalty or forfeiture.

. . . .

Section 11. Nothing contained in this Act shall be construed to prevent or interfere with the enforcement of the provisions of the antitrust Acts or the Acts to regulate commerce, nor shall anything contained in the Act be construed to alter, modify, or repeal the said antitrust Acts or the Acts to regulate commerce or any part or parts thereof.

Clayton Anti-Trust Act (1914)

Section 2. That it shall be unlawful for any person engaged in commerce, in the course of such commerce, either directly or indirectly to discriminate in price between different purchasers of commodities, which commodities are sold for use, consumption, or resale within the United States or any Territory thereof or the District of Columbia or any insular possession or other place under the jurisdiction of the United States, where the effect of such discrimination may be to substantially lessen competition or tend to create a monopoly in any line of commerce: *Provided,* That nothing herein contained shall prevent discrimination in price between purchasers of commodities on account of differences in the grade, quality, or quantity of the commodity sold, or that makes only due allowance for difference in the cost of selling or transportation, or discrimination in price in the same or different communities made in good faith to meet competition: *And provided further,* That nothing herein contained shall prevent persons engaged in selling goods, wares, or merchandise in commerce from selecting their own customers in bona fide transactions and not in restraint of trade.

Section 3. That it shall be unlawful for any person engaged in commerce, in the course of such commerce, to lease or make a sale or contract for sale of goods, wares, merchandise, machinery, supplies or other commodities, whether patented or unpatented, for use, consumption or resale within the United States or any Territory thereof or the District of Columbia or any insular possession or other place under the jurisdiction of the United States, or fix a price charged therefor, or discount from, or rebate upon, such price, on the condition, agreement or understanding that the lessee or purchaser thereof shall not use or deal in the goods, wares, merchandise, machinery, supplies or other commodities of a competitor or competitors of the lessor or seller, where the effect of such lease, sale, or contract for sale or such condition, agreement or understanding may be to substantially lessen competition or tend to create a monopoly in any line of commerce.

. . . .

Section 7. That no corporation engaged in commerce shall acquire, directly or indirectly, the whole or any part of the stock or other share capital of another corporation engaged also in commerce, where the effect of such acquisition may be to substantially lessen competition between the corporation whose stock is so acquired and the corporation making the acquisition, or to restrain such commerce in any section or community, or tend to create a monopoly of any line of commerce.

. . . .

FILL IN THE ANSWERS

Write the word or phrase which best completes the statement.
1. The number of Federal Reserve districts is limited to _____.
2. The paper money we use today is issued by _____ _____ rather than by the Treasury Department.
3. The letters FTC stand for _____.
4. The orders of the FTC are enforced by the federal _____.
5. The FTC may require a report in writing from any _____ _____.

6. If two customers in the same city wish to buy a commodity from some manufacturer, the price they pay must be _____ _____.

7. The Clayton Act tried to prevent business practices which might lessen _____ or create _____.

8. The money which a bank is required to keep rather than lend is called its _____.

9. Woodrow Wilson called his plan to improve our government _____.

10. The Commissioners of the FTC are appointed by _____ _____.

THOUGHT QUESTIONS

1. In what ways did the FTC and the Clayton Act help our government check the unfair practices of big business?

2. How can the operations of the Federal Reserve system maintain the economic health of the United States?

Woodrow Wilson's War Message to Congress (1917)

* * * * *In the first fourteen years of the 20th* century the countries of Europe drew farther and farther apart until Europe was divided into two armed camps. The shooting of Archduke Francis Ferdinand of Austria-Hungary on June 28, 1914, was the spark that touched off the explosion. One by one the countries of Europe were drawn into war.

President Wilson issued a proclamation of neutrality, hoping thereby to be able to avoid having the United States involved in a European war. But the Germans' unrestricted submarine warfare and the sinking of the *Lusitania* shocked the country. German sabotage in American factories, German efforts to persuade Mexico to declare war on the United States, and Allied stories of German atrocities increased pro-Allied sentiment. Finally, on April 2, 1917, Wilson asked Congress for a declaration of war against Germany.

Gentlemen of the Congress: I have called the Congress into extraordinary session because there are serious, very serious choices of policy to be made, and made immediately, which it was neither right nor constitutionally permissible that I should assume the responsibility of making.

On the third day of February last I officially laid before you the extraordinary announcement of the Imperial German Government that on and after the first day of February it was its purpose to put aside all restraints of law or of humanity and use its submarines to sink every vessel that sought to approach either the ports of Great Britain and Ireland or the western coasts of Europe or any of the ports controlled by the enemies of Germany within the Mediterranean. . . .

When I addressed the Congress on the twenty-sixth of February last I thought that it would suffice to assert our neutral rights with arms, our right to use the seas against unlawful interference, our right to keep our people safe against unlawful violence. But armed neutrality, it now appears, is impracticable. . . .

With a profound sense of the solemn and even tragical character of the step I am taking and of the grave responsibilities which it involves, but in unhesitating obedience to what I deem my constitutional duty, I advise that the Congress declare the recent course of the Imperial German Government to be in fact nothing less than war against the Government and the people of the United States; that it formally accept the status of belligerent which has thus been thrust upon it; and that it take immediate steps not only to put the country in a more thorough state of defense but also to exert all its power and employ all its resources to bring the Government of the German Empire to terms and end the war. . . .

While we do these things, these deeply momentous things, let us be very clear, and make very clear to all the world what our motives and objects are. My own thought has not been driven from its habitual and normal course by the unhappy events of the last two months, and I do not believe that the thought of the nation has been altered or clouded by them. I have exactly the same things in mind now that I had in mind when I addressed the Senate on the twenty-second of January last; the same that I had in mind when I addressed the Congress on the third of February, and on the twenty-sixth of February. Our object now, as then, is to vindicate principles of peace and justice in the life of the world as against selfish and autocratic power and to set up amongst the really free and self-governed peoples of the world such a concert of purpose and of action as will henceforth ensure the observance of those principles. Neutrality is no longer feasible or desirable where the peace of the world is involved and the freedom of its peoples, and the menace of that peace and freedom lies in the existence of autocratic governments backed by organized force which is controlled wholly by their will, not by the will of their people. We have seen the last of neutrality in such circumstances. We are at the beginning of an age in which it will be insisted that the same standards of conduct and of responsibility for wrong done shall be observed among nations and their governments that are observed among the individual citizens of civilized states.

We have no quarrel with the German people. We have no feeling towards them but one of sympathy and friendship. It was not upon their impulse that their government acted in entering the war. It was not with their previous knowledge or approval. It was a war determined upon as wars used to be determined upon in the old, unhappy days when people were nowhere consulted by their rulers and wars were provoked and waged in the interest of dynasties or of little groups of ambitious men who were accustomed to use their fellow men as pawns and tools. Self-governed nations do not fill their neighbor states with spies or set the course of intrigue to bring about some critical posture of affairs which will give them an opportunity to strike and make conquest. Such designs can be successfully worked out only under cover and where no one has the right to ask questions. Cunningly contrived plans of deception or aggression, carried, it may be, from generation to generation, can be worked out and kept from the light only within the privacy of courts or behind the carefully guarded confidences of a narrow and privileged class. They are happily impossible where public opinion commands and insists upon full information concerning all the nation's affairs. . . .

. . .The world must be made safe for democracy. Its peace must be placed upon the tested foundations of political liberty. We have no selfish ends to serve. We desire no conquest, no dominion. We seek no indemnities for ourselves, no material compensation for the sacrifices we shall freely make. We are but one of the champions of the rights of mankind. We shall be satisfied when those rights have been made as secure as the faith and the freedom of nations can make them.

Just because we fight without rancour and without selfish object, seeking nothing for ourselves but what we shall wish to share with all free peoples, we shall, I feel confident, conduct our operations as belligerents without passion and ourselves observe with proud punctilio the principles of right and of fair play we profess to be fighting for. . . .

It is a distressing and oppressive duty, Gentlemen of the Congress, which I have performed in thus addressing you. There are, it may be, many months of fiery trial and sacrifice ahead of us. It is a fearful thing to lead this great peaceful people into war, into the most terrible and disastrous of all wars, civilization itself seeming to be in the balance. But the right is more precious than peace, and we shall fight for the things which we have always carried nearest our hearts — for democracy, for the right of those who submit to authority to have a voice in their own governments, for the rights and liberties of small nations, for a universal dominion of right by such a concert of free peoples as shall bring peace and safety to all nations and make the world itself at last free. To such a task we can dedicate our lives and our fortunes, everything that we are and everything that we have, with the pride of those who know that the day has come when America is privileged to spend her blood and her might for the principles that gave her birth and happiness and the peace which she has treasured. God helping her, she can do no other.

CHOOSE THE CORRECT ANSWER

Write the number that best completes the statement.

1. At the outbreak of war in Europe the people of the United States were (1) ready to go to war, (2) neutral, (3) indifferent, (4) opposed to the war.   1._____

2. American neutrality was abandoned with the sinking of the
   (1) *Europa,* (2) *Queen Mary,* (3) *Normandie,* (4) *Lusitania.*
   2._____

3. One of the aims of the United States in World War I was to
   (1) acquire the new territory, (2) collect debts owed by Germany, (3) regain the freedom of the seas, (4) divide German
   territory among the Allies.   3._____

4. The reason that did *not* lead the United States to declare war
   on Germany was (1) German submarine activities, (2) sabotage activities of German agents in the United States, (3) the
   attempt to get Mexico to attack us, (4) American desire for
   German territory.   4._____

5. President Wilson told the world that the Allies were fighting
   to (1) gain an economic advantage in the world, (2) to enslave Germany, (3) to make the world safe for democracy,
   (4) make a one-nation world. ·   5._____

THOUGHT QUESTIONS

1. The President of the United States cannot declare war at will.
   Explain the procedure necessary before the United States can
   be declared formally at war.

2. Why is it impossible for a self-governing nation to commit
   surprise aggression against another country?

Wilson's Fourteen Points (1918)

* * * *The United States entered World War
I in 1917 but, by January, 1918, the war was still
far from won.* Nevertheless, President Woodrow
Wilson had already thought about the kind of peace
which should end the war, and he presented a four-
teen-point peace proposal for Germany in an address
to Congress.

Wilson wanted to end the causes of wars. He
wanted the peoples of Europe to be free to choose
the governments under which they preferred to
live. He favored a world organization which would
work to prevent war and to improve the conditions
of all peoples.

His plan was successful only in part. The steps which he felt would prevent future wars, chiefly disarmament, were not taken seriously by the world's major powers. Many of the new small nations of Europe, created at the end of the war, did not retain their freedom. The League of Nations, of which Wilson's own country was never a member, was organized but it died when World War II began in 1939.

In recent years, some of Wilson's points have become reality, however. European nations have formed a Common Market to remove economic barriers. The United Nations has become a strong agency for world peace.

What we demand in this war, therefore, is nothing peculiar to ourselves. It is that the world be made fit and safe to live in; and particularly that it be made safe for every peace-loving nation which, like our own, wishes to live its own life, determine its own institutions, be assured of justice and fair dealing by the other peoples of the world as against force and selfish aggression.

All the peoples of the world are in effect partners in this interest, and for our own part we see very clearly that unless justice be done to others it will not be done to us. The program of the world's peace, therefore, is our program; and that program, the only possible program, as we see it, is this:

1. Open covenants of peace, openly arrived at, after which there shall be no private international understandings of any kind but diplomacy shall proceed always frankly and in the public view.

2. Absolute freedom of navigation upon the seas, outside territorial waters, alike in peace and in war, except as the seas may be closed in whole or in part by international action for the enforcement of international covenants.

3. The removal, so far as possible, of all economic barriers and the establishment of an equality of trade conditions among all the nations consenting to the peace and associating themselves for its maintenance.

4. Adequate guarantees given and taken that national armaments will be reduced to the lowest points consistent with domestic safety.

5. A free, open-minded, and absolutely impartial adjustment of all colonial claims, based upon a strict observance of the principle that in determining all such questions of sovereignty the interests of the populations concerned must have equal weight with the equitable claims of the government whose title is to be determined.

6. The evacuation of all Russian territory and such a settlement of all questions affecting Russia as will secure the best and freest co-operation of the other nations of the world in obtaining for her an unhampered and unembarrassed opportunity for the independent determination of her own political development and national policy and assure her of a sincere welcome into the society of free nations under institutions of her own choosing; and, more than a welcome, assistance also of every kind that she may need and may herself desire. The treatment accorded Russia by her sister nations in the months to come will be the acid test of their good will, of their comprehension of her needs as distinguished from their own interests, and of their intelligent and unselfish sympathy.

7. Belgium, the whole world will agree, must be evacuated and restored, without any attempt to limit the sovereignty which she enjoys in common with all other free nations. No other single act will serve as this will serve to restore confidence among the nations in the laws which they have themselves set and determined for the government of their relations with one another. Without this healing act the whole structure and validity of international law is forever impaired.

8. All French territory should be freed and the invaded portions restored, and the wrong done to France by Prussia in 1871 in the matter of Alsace-Lorraine, which has unsettled the peace of the world for nearly fifty years, should be righted, in order that peace may once more be made secure in the interest of all.

9. A readjustment of the frontiers of Italy should be effected along clearly recognizable lines of nationality.

10. The peoples of Austria-Hungary, whose place among

the nations we wish to see safeguarded and assured, should be accorded the freest opportunity of autonomous development.

11. Rumania, Serbia, and Montenegro should be evacuated; occupied territories restored; Serbia accorded free and secure access to the sea; and the relations of the several Balkan states to one another determined by friendly counsel along historically established lines of allegiance and nationality; and international guarantees of the political and economic independence and territorial integrity of the several Balkan states should be entered into.

12. The Turkish portions of the present Ottoman Empire should be assured a secure sovereignty, but the other nationalities which are now under Turkish rule should be assured an undoubted security of life and an absolutely unmolested opportunity of autonomous development, and the Dardanelles should be permanently opened as free passage to the ships and commerce of all nations under international guarantees.

13. An independent Polish state should be erected which should include the territories inhabited by indisputably Polish populations, which should be assured a free and secure access to the sea, and whose political and economic independence and territorial integrity should be guaranteed by international covenant.

14. A general association of nations must be formed under specific covenants for the purpose of affording mutual guarantees of political independence and territorial integrity to great and small states alike.

TRUE OR FALSE?

Write T *if the statement is correct; Write* F *if it is false.*

_____1. A "covenant" of peace, to Wilson, was any open or secret agreement that would prevent future wars.

_____2. Wilson wanted to see the defeated nations disarmed, while the Allies kept their armies and navies as large as they were at the end of the war.

_____3. President Wilson did not wait for the war's end to discuss peace.

_____4. Wilson wanted to see an independent Poland which had free access to the sea.

_____5. The Fourteen Points considered only the nations of Europe and the Americas.

_____6. Wilson believed that the people of Alsace-Lorraine should decide for themselves whether they would be part of France or of Germany.

_____7. The Balkan states of which Wilson spoke were in Southeastern Europe.

_____8. Wilson believed in freedom of the seas.

_____9. Wilson wanted a league of nations which would guarantee all nations their freedom.

_____10. Wilson was ready to force Russia to give up its type of government.

THOUGHT QUESTIONS

1. Compare the aims of those who led the governments of the European democracies with those expressed by Wilson in his Fourteen Points.

2. Explain in detail the ways in which Wilson's peace plan succeeded, and the ways in which it failed.

Indian Citizenship Act 1924

* * * * *The story of the relations between* the United States and its Indian tribes is a tragic account of broken promises, massacres, and humiliation. By the late 1880's the last Indian lands had been taken away from them. The Dawes Act of 1887 firmly placed all Indian tribes upon reservations, most of them west of the Mississippi.

The Fourteenth Amendment, by the Dawes Act, gave every Indian born in the United States the opportunity to become a citizen. To do this, he had to leave the tribe and the reservation. This was not easy for a people with little education and little economic opportunity. Yet the good work of the Bureau of Indian Affairs over the years had so improved their education and skills that by 1924 more than half of the Indian population had received citizenship.

A simple law was passed in 1924 which provided that any Indian who applied for citizenship would receive it.

Be it enacted . . ., That all non-citizen Indians born within the territorial limits of the United States be, and they are hereby, declared to be citizens of the United States: *Provided,* That the granting of such citizenship shall not in any manner impair or otherwise affect the right of any Indian to tribal or other property.

FILL IN THE ANSWERS

Write the word or phrase which best completes the statement.

1. The lands given to Indian tribes are called_____.
2. The law which placed all Indian tribes on reservations was called _____.
3. An Indian who left his reservation in 1900 could become a _____.
4. There were about 250,000 Indians in the United States in 1924. The number who were citizens was about _____ _____.
5. Most of our Indians still live in the _____ part of the United States.

THOUGHT QUESTIONS

1. Describe the treatment accorded Indians between 1789 and 1924.
2. Why did the granting of citizenship to Indians living on reservations have little effect upon the way in which they lived?

The Norris-La Guardia Anti-Injunction Bill 1932

* * * * *Before the Norris-La Guardia Anti-Injunction Bill was passed, courts had the power to issue an "injunction" when workers threatened to strike. This power was based on the argument that strikes violated or endangered property rights.*

An injunction is a court order, often issued to order workers not to strike. If the workers disobeyed and struck anyway, they could be held in contempt of court. The Norris-La Guardia Bill restricted the power of the courts to use injunctions in labor disputes. The following are some of the major points in this bill.

Section 4. No court of the United States shall have the jurisdiction to issue any restraining order or temporary or permanent injunction in any case involving or growing out of any labor dispute to prohibit any person or persons . . . from doing, whether singly or in concert, any of the following acts:

(*a*) Ceasing or refusing to perform any work or to remain in any relation of employment;

(*b*) Becoming or remaining a member of any labor organization or of any employer organization . . .

(*c*) Paying or giving to, or withholding from any person participating or interested in such labor dispute, any strike or employment benefits or insurance, or other moneys or things of value;

(*d*) By all lawful means aiding any person participating or interested in any labor dispute who is being proceeded against in, or is prosecuting any action or suit in any court in the United States or of any state;

(*e*) Giving publicity to the extent of, or the facts involved in any labor dispute whether by advertising, speaking, patrolling, or by any other method not involving fraud or violence;

. . . .

Section 7. No court of the United States shall have jurisdiction to issue a temporary or permanent injunction . . . except after hearing the testimony of witnesses in open court (with opportunity for cross-examination) . . . and except after findings of fact by the court, to the effect:

(*a*) That unlawful acts have been threatened and will be committed and will be continued unless restrained . . .

(*b*) That substantial and irreparable injury to complainant's property will follow;

(*c*) That . . . greater injury will be inflicted upon complainant by the denial of relief than will be inflicted upon defendants by granting of relief;

(*d*) That complainant has no adequate remedy at law;

(*e*) That the public officers charged with the duty to protect complainant's property are unable or unwilling to furnish adequate protection . . .

Section 13. . . . (*c*) The term "labor dispute" includes any controversy concerning terms or conditions of employment, or concerning the association or representation of persons negotiating, fixing, maintaining, changing, or seeking to arrange terms or conditions of employment, regardless of whether or not the disputants stand in approximate relation of employer and employee . . . .

TRUE OR FALSE?

Write the letter T *if the statement is correct; write* F *if it is false.*

_____1. If reliable evidence is produced in court that some strikers are planning to do personal injury as a result of a labor dispute, the court can issue an injunction.

_____2. The Norris-La Guardia Bill extended the power of courts of equity.

_____3. No court of the United States has the power to issue an order prohibiting a worker from refusing to work for an employer.

_____4. A court can issue an injunction in a labor dispute after it has found that the local police are unable to protect an employer's property against striking workers.

_____5. A court has the power to prevent a worker from joining a labor union.

THOUGHT QUESTIONS

1. In recent years there have been strikes against big city newspapers, against public transportation and shipping lines, against telephone companies. When the general public is inconvenienced during such labor disputes, are such strikes justified?

2. What other means besides strikes are available to settle disputes between workers or labor unions and employers?

Franklin D. Roosevelt Documents 1933-1941

* * * * *The stock market failed in 1929, and* the worst depression in the country's history followed. The public lost confidence in the Republican Party which had governed since 1921. Democratic candidate Franklin Delano Roosevelt won the election of 1932, running on a campaign which promised government activity designed to put people back to work.

The depression deepened between Roosevelt's election and his inauguration on March 4, 1933. Banks and small businesses failed, millions were unemployed, emergency soup kitchens and bread lines existed all over the country.

Roosevelt's promise of a "New Deal" for the people in his inauguration address was heard by millions over the radio, giving new hope to people close to despair.

First Inaugural Address
(March 4, 1933)

President Hoover, Mr. Chief Justice, my friends:

This is a day of national consecration, and I am certain that my fellow-Americans expect that on my induction into the Presidency I will address them with a candor and a decision which the present situation of our nation impels.

This is pre-eminently the time to speak the truth, the whole truth, frankly and boldly. Nor need we shrink from honestly facing conditions in our country today. This great nation will endure as it has endured, will revive and will prosper.

So first of all let me assert my firm belief that the only thing we have to fear is fear itself—nameless, unreasoning, unjustified terror which paralyzes needed efforts to convert retreat into advance.

In every dark hour of our national life a leadership of frankness and vigor has met with that understanding and support of the people themselves which is essential to victory. I am convinced that you will again give that support to leadership in these critical days.

In such a spirit on my part and on yours we face our common difficulties. They concern, thank God, only material things. Values have shrunken to fantastic levels; taxes have risen; our ability to pay has fallen, government of all kinds is faced by serious curtailment of income; the means of exchange are frozen in the currents of trade; the withered leaves of industrial enterprise lie on every side; farmers find no markets for their products; the savings of many years in thousands of families are gone.

More important, a host of unemployed citizens face the grim problem of existence, and an equally great number toil with little return. Only a foolish optimist can deny the dark realities of the moment.

Yet our distress comes from no failure of substance. We are stricken by no plague of locusts. Compared with the perils which our forefathers conquered because they believed and were not afraid, we have still much to be thankful for.

Nature still offers her bounty and human efforts have multiplied it. Plenty is at our doorstep, but a generous use of it languishes in the very sight of the supply.

Primarily, this is because the rulers of the exchange of mankind's goods have failed through their own stubbornness and their own incompetence, have admitted their failure and abdicated. Practices of the unscrupulous money changers stand indicted in the court of public opinion, rejected by the hearts and minds of men.

True, they have tried, but their efforts have been cast in the pattern of an outworn tradition. Faced by failure of credit, they have proposed only the lending of more money. Stripped of the lure of profit by which to induce our people to follow their false leadership, they have resorted to exhortation, pleading tearfully for restored confidence. They know only the rules of a generation of self-seekers. They have no vision, and when there is no vision the people perish. The money changers have fled from their high seats in the temple of our civilization. We may now restore that temple to the ancient truths.

The measure of the restoration lies in the extent to which we apply social values more noble than mere monetary profit.

The joy and moral stimulation of work no longer must be forgotten in the mad chase of evanescent profits. These dark days will be worth all they cost us if they teach us that our true destiny is not to be ministered unto but to minister to ourselves and to our fellow-men. . . .

Restoration calls, however, not for changes in ethics alone. This nation asks for action, and action now. Our greatest primary task is to put people to work. This is no unsolvable problem if we face it wisely and courageously. . . .

The task can be helped by definite efforts to raise the values of agricultural products and with this the power to purchase the output of our cities. It can be helped by preventing realistically the tragedy of the growing loss, through foreclosure, of our small homes and our farms.

It can be helped by insistence that the Federal, State and local governments act forthwith on the demand that their cost be drastically reduced.

It can be helped by the unifying of relief activities which

today are often scattered, uneconomical and unequal. It can be helped by national planning for and supervision of all forms of transportation and of communications and other utilities which have a definitely public character.

There are many ways in which it can be helped, but it can never be helped merely by talking about it. We must act, and act quickly.

Finally, in our progress toward a resumption of work we require two safeguards against a return of the evils of the older order; there must be a strict supervision of all banking and credits and investments; there must be an end to speculation with other people's money, and there must be provision for an adequate but sound currency. . . .

The basic thought that guides these specific means of national recovery is not narrowly nationalistic. It is the insistence, as a first consideration, upon the interdependence of the various elements in, and parts of, the United States— a recognition of the old and permanently important manifestation of the American spirit of the pioneer.

It is the way to recovery. It is the immediate way. It is the strongest assurance that the recovery will endure.

In the field of world policy I would dedicate this nation to the policy of the good neighbor—the neighbor who resolutely respects himself and, because he does so, respects the rights of others—the neighbor who respects his obligations and respects the sanctity of his agreements in and with a world of neighbors. . . .

We are, I know, ready and willing to submit our lives and property to such discipline because it makes possible a leadership which aims at a larger good.

This I propose to offer, pledging that the larger purposes will bind upon us all as a sacred obligation with a unity of duty hitherto evoked only in time of armed strife.

With this pledge taken, I assume unhesitatingly the leadership of this great army of our people, dedicated to a disciplined attack upon our common problems.

Action in this image and to this end is feasible under the form of government which we have inherited from our ancestors. Our Constitution is so simple and practical that it is possible always to meet extraordinary needs by changes in emphasis and arrangement without loss of essential form. . . .

It is to be hoped that the normal balance of executive and legislative authority may be wholly adequate to meet the unprecedented task before us. But it may be that an unprecedented demand and need for undelayed action may call for temporary departure from that normal balance of public procedure.

I am prepared under my constitutional duty to recommend the measures that a stricken world may require. These measures, or such other measures as the Congress may build out of its experience and wisdom, I shall seek, within my constitutional authority, to bring to speedy adoption.

But in the event that the Congress shall fail to take one of these two courses, and in the event that the national emergency is still critical, I shall not evade the clear course of duty that will then confront me.

I shall ask the Congress for the one remaining instrument to meet the crisis—broad executive power to wage a war against the emergency as great as the power that would be given me if we were in fact invaded by a foreign foe.

For the trust reposed in me I will return the courage and the devotion that befit the time. I can do no less. . . .

We do not distrust the future of essential democracy. The people of the United States have not failed. In their need they have registered a mandate that they want direct, vigorous action. They have asked for discipline and direction under leadership. They have made me the present instrument of their wishes. In the spirit of the gift I take it.

In this dedication of a nation we humbly ask the blessing of God. May He protect each and every one of us! May He guide me in the days to come!

CHOOSE THE CORRECT ANSWER

Write T *if the statement is correct; Write* F *if it is false.*

1. Roosevelt felt that the only thing people had to fear was (*a*) loss of jobs, (*b*) war, (*c*) fear itself, (*d*) the Republican Party.

    1._____

2. By "money changers" Roosevelt meant (*a*) the banks, (*b*) big business, (*c*) those who supported the gold standard, (*d*) Euro-

pean countries who had not paid their debts to the United States.   2._____

3. The first task facing the nation was (a) to help the farmers, (b) to improve the credit of the government, (c) to amend the Constitution to give the President power to end the depression, (d) to put people to work.   3._____

4. Roosevelt felt that our state, local, and national governments should (a) cut their costs, (b) exchange information about economic troubles, (c) close all banks, (d) raise armies to fight strikers.   4._____

5. Roosevelt promised that, if ordinary methods did not solve the country's problems soon, he would ask for (a) power to borrow money on the credit of the United States, (b) emergency powers, (c) a new election, (d) a law to end unemployment.   5._____

6. In foreign affairs, Roosevelt favored (a) an end to aid to other countries, (b) a good neighbor policy, (c) saving money by closing United States embassies in other lands, (d) use of force to collect debts owed by European nations. 6._____

7. For the farmer, Roosevelt promised action to end (a) fore-closures of small farms, (b) high prices for farm products, (c) government work teams to help with crops, (d) purchases by farmers in the cities.   7._____

8. Roosevelt appealed to (a) the profit motive, (b) the hatred of foreign nations, (c) the pioneer spirit, (d) respect for the banks.   8._____

9. The goal Roosevelt set for all Americans was (a) to help their fellow men, (b) to cut profits, (c) to forget the Constitution, (d) to end government control of transportation and communication.   9._____

10. Roosevelt promised that he would try to regulate (a) state and local governments, (b) neighboring countries, (c) all business activities, (d) public utilities.   10._____

THOUGHT QUESTIONS

1. Discuss the problems faced by the United States early in 1933.
2. State the solutions for these problems offered by Franklin D. Roosevelt in his inaugural address.

Excerpts from Six "New Deal" Laws (1933-1935)

* * * * *The promises made by Franklin D.* Roosevelt in his inaugural address were soon fol-

lowed by a series of laws passed by Congress to deal with the national emergency. By a broad interpretation of the powers of Congress, laws were passed which probably would have been rejected in previous years. They were intended to achieve a new purpose of government — to better the living conditions of large numbers of the American people.

These laws established government control on a scale never before attempted. In so doing, they gave too much power to the executive branch of the government. For this reason, the NRA and AAA Acts were later declared unconstitutional. However, they existed long enough to accomplish much of what they set out to do. The laws dealt with long-range as well as immediate emergency problems and many still function as important parts of American economic life.

Tennessee Valley Act (1933)

* * * * *Senator George W. Norris of* Nebraska had long pleaded with Congress to develop the resources of the Tennessee Valley. Muscle Shoals, on the Tennessee River, was the site of power and munitions plants that the federal government had built as a war measure during World War I. Norris proposed that these plants should be used to provide power for the region, and to produce much-needed fertilizer.

Attempts by Congress to accept Norris' plan had been vetoed by both President Coolidge and President Hoover. President Roosevelt, however, approved the plan, and the Tennessee Valley Act became law in May, 1933.

Under the capable administration of David E. Lilienthal, the TVA Authority proved to the world that an area blighted by poverty, flood and ruined farmland, could become self-sufficient and prosperous. Its production of electric power has been used as a "yardstick" in determining fair rates for private utilities.

Be it enacted, That for the purpose of maintaining and operating the properties now owned by the United States in the vicinity of Muscle Shoals, Alabama, . . . there is hereby created a body corporate by the name of the "Tennessee Valley Authority." . . .

Section 3. All contracts to which the Corporation is a party and which require the employment of laborers and mechanics . . . shall contain a provision that not less than the prevailing rate of wages for work of a similar nature prevailing in the vicinity shall be paid to such laborers or mechanics. . . .

Section 4. Except as otherwise specifically provided in this Act, the Corporation . . .

(f) May purchase or lease and hold such real and personal property as it deems necessary or convenient in the transaction of its business, and may dispose of any such personal property held by it. . . .

(h) Shall have power in the name of the United States of America to exercise the right of eminent domain, . . .

(i) Shall have power to acquire real estate for the construction of dams, reservoirs, transmission lines, power houses, and other structures, and navigation projects at any point along the Tennessee River, or any of its tributaries, . . .

(j) Shall have power to construct dams, reservoirs, power houses, power structures, transmission lines, navigation projects, and incidental works in the Tennessee River and its tributaries, and to unite the various power installations into one or more systems by transmission lines.

Section 5. The board is hereby authorized . . .

(b) To arrange with farmers and farm organizations for large-scale practical use of the new forms of fertilizers under conditions permitting an accurate measure of the economic return they produce. . . .

(d) The board in order to improve and cheapen the production of fertilizer is authorized to manufacture and sell fixed nitrogen, fertilizer, and fertilizer ingredients at Muscle Shoals by the employment of existing facilities, by modernizing existing plants, or by any other process or processes that in its judgment shall appear wise and profitable for the fixation of atmospheric nitrogen or the cheapening of the production of fertilizer.

(e) Under the authority of this Act the board may make donations or sales of the product of the plant or plants operated by it to be fairly and equitably distributed through the agency of county demonstration agents, agricultural colleges, or otherwise as the board may direct, for experimentation, education, and introduction of the use of such products in cooperation with practical farmers so as to obtain information as to the value, effect, and best methods of their use.

(f) The board is authorized to make alterations, modifications, or improvements in existing plants and facilities, and to construct new plants.

(g) In the event it is not used for fixation of nitrogen for agricultural purposes or leased, then the board shall maintain in standby condition nitrate plant numbered 2, or its equivalent, for the fixation of atmospheric nitrogen, for the production of explosives in the event of war or a national emergency, until the Congress shall by joint resolution release the board from this obligation, . . .

(h) To establish, maintain, and operate laboratories and experimental plants, and to undertake experiments for the purpose of enabling the Corporation to furnish nitrogen products for military purposes, and nitrogen and other fertilizer products for agricultural purposes in the most economical manner and at the highest standard of efficiency. . . .

(l) To produce, distribute, and sell electric power, as herein particularly specified. . . .

Section 10. The board is hereby empowered and authorized to sell the surplus power not used in its operations, and for operation of locks and other works generated by it, to States, counties, municipalities, corporations, partnerships, or individuals, according to the policies hereinafter set forth; and to carry out said authority, the board is authorized to enter into contracts for such sale for a term not exceeding twenty years, and in the sale of such current by the board it shall give preference to States, counties, municipalities, and cooperative organizations of citizens or farmers, not organized or doing business for profit, but primarily for the purpose of supplying electricity to its own citizens or members: . . . In order to promote and encourage the fullest possible use of electric light and power on farms within reasonable distance of any of its transmission lines, the board in its discretion shall have power to construct transmission lines to farms and small villages that are not otherwise supplied with electricity at reasonable rates, and to make such rules and regulations governing such sale and distribution of such electric power as in its judgment may be just and equitable: *Provided further,* That the board is hereby authorized and directed to make studies, experiments, and determinations to promote the wider and better use of electric power for agricultural and domestic use, or for small or local industries, and it may cooperate with State governments, or their subdivisions or agencies, with educational or research institutions, and with cooperatives or other organizations, in the application of electric power to the fuller and better balanced development of the resources of the region.

Section 11. It is hereby declared to be the policy of the Government so far as practical to distribute and sell the surplus power generated at Muscle Shoals equitably among the States, counties, and municipalities within transmission distance. This policy is further declared to be that the projects herein provided for shall be considered primarily as for the benefit of the people of the section as a whole and particularly the domestic and rural consumers to whom the power can economically be made available, and accordingly that sale to and use by industry shall be a secondary purpose, to be utilized principally to secure a sufficiently high load factor and revenue returns which will permit domestic and rural use at the lowest possible rates . . .

National Industrial Recovery Act

(1933)

This Act was designed to help small businesses by working out fair practice codes within each industry or form of business. It gave government approval to the further union organization of labor. It gave President Roosevelt power to make the government the nation's largest employer through the creation of a federal agency which hired unemployed workers for a large variety of public works.

Most of the nation responded warmly to the NIRA, and its eagle and lightning bolt symbol appeared all over the country. In 1935, however, the law was declared unconstitutional as having given the President too much power. Meanwhile, the federal government had entered the public works field, and membership in labor unions had grown rapidly.

Section I. A national emergency productive of widespread unemployment and disorganization of industry, which burdens interstate and foreign commerce, affects the public welfare, and undermines the standards of living of the American people, is hereby declared to exist. It is hereby declared to be the policy of Congress to remove obstructions to the free flow of interstate and foreign commerce which tend to diminish the amount thereof; and to provide for the general welfare by promoting the organization of industry for the purpose of cooperative action among trade groups, to induce and maintain united action of labor and management under adequate governmental sanctions and supervision, to eliminate unfair competitive practices, to promote the fullest possible utilization of the present productive capacity of industries, to avoid undue restriction of production (except as may be temporarily required), to increase the consumption of industrial and agricultural products by increasing purchasing power, to reduce and relieve unemployment, to improve standards of labor, and otherwise to rehabilitate industry and to conserve natural resources. . . .

Section 3. (a) Upon the application to the President by one or more trade or industrial associations or groups, the President may approve a code or codes of fair competition for the trade or industry or subdivision thereof, represented by the applicant or applicants . . . The President may, as a condition of his approval of any such code, impose such conditions . . . for the protection of consumers, competitors, employees, and others, and in furtherance of the public interest, and may provide such exceptions to and exemptions from the provisions of such code, as the President in his discretion deems necessary to effectuate the policy herein declared.

(b) After the President shall have approved any such code, the provisions of such code shall be the standards of fair competition for such trade or industry or subdivision thereof. Any violation of such standards in any transaction in or affecting interstate or foreign commerce shall be deemed an unfair method of competition in commerce within the meaning of the Federal Trade Commission Act, as amended; . . .

Section 4. (a) The President is authorized to enter into agreements with, and to approve voluntary agreements between and among, persons engaged in a trade or industry, labor organizations, and trade or industrial organizations, associations, or groups, relating to any trade or industry, if in his judgment such agreements will aid in effectuating the policy of this title with respect to transactions in or affecting interstate or foreign commerce, . . .

(b) Whenever the President shall find that destructive wage or price cutting or other activities contrary to the policy of this title are being practiced in any trade or industry or any subdivision thereof, and . . . shall find it essential to license business enterprises in order to make effective a code of fair competition or an agreement under this title or otherwise to effectuate the policy of this title, and shall publicly so announce, no person shall, after a date fixed in such announcement, engage in or carry on any business, in or affecting interstate or foreign commerce, specified in such announcement, unless he shall have first obtained a license issued pursuant to such regulations as the President shall prescribe. The President may suspend or revoke any such license, after due notice and opportunity for hearing, for violations of the terms or conditions thereof. . . .

Section 7. (a) Every code of fair competition, agreement and license approved, prescribed, or issued under this title shall contain the following conditions: (1) That employees shall have the right to organize and bargain collectively through representatives of their own choosing, and shall be free from the interference, restraint, or coercion of employers of labor, or their agents, in the designation of such representatives or in self-organization or in other concerted activities for the purpose of collective bargaining or other mutual aid or protection; (2) that no employee and no one seeking employment shall be required as a condition of employment to join any company union or to refrain from joining, organizing, or assisting a labor organization of his own choosing; and (3) that employers shall comply with the maximum hours of labor, minimum rates of pay, and other conditions of employment, approved or prescribed by the President. . . .

PUBLIC WORKS AND CONSTRUCTION PROJECTS

Section 201. (a) To effectuate the purposes of this title, the President is hereby authorized to create a Federal Emergency Administration of Public Works, all the powers of which shall be exercised by a Federal Emergency Administrator of Public Works, . . .

Section 202. The Administrator, under the direction of the President, shall prepare a comprehensive program of public works, which shall include among other things the following: (a) Construction, repair, and improvement of public highways and parkways, public buildings, and any publicly owned instrumentalities and facilities; (b) conservation and development of natural resources, including control, utilization, and purification of waters, prevention of soil or coastal erosion, development of water power, transmission of electrical energy, and construction of river and harbor improvements and flood control . . .

Agricultural Adjustment Act (1933)

* * * * *This Act was intended to raise the* purchasing power of the farmers and thereby increase demand for manufactured goods made in the cities. It set up "parity prices" for farm products which would ensure higher total income for each participating farmer. The farmer received special payments for each reduction he made in the production of cotton, wheat, hogs, and other products.

In 1933, cotton farmers cut their acreage by one-fourth; hog farmers killed six million of the pigs they would have otherwise prepared for market. In 1934 and 1935, the government paid out more than one billion dollars to farmers who cut down the number of acres they used for the crops covered by the law.

The law was declared unconstitutional in 1936, for Congress had improperly financed it by a tax on food processors. Meanwhile, total farm production had been cut, farm income had risen considerably, while the prices of farm products had almost doubled. Congress then passed other farm laws which kept the subsidy provisions of the AAA and continued the limits on the total production of certain crops.

That the present acute economic emergency being in part the consequence of a severe and increasing disparity between the prices of agriculture and other commodities, which disparity has largely destroyed the purchasing power of farmers for industrial products . . . and has seriously impaired the agricultural assets supporting the national credit structure, it is hereby declared that these conditions . . . have affected transactions in agricultural commodities with a national public interest . . . and render imperative the immediate enactment of Title I of this Act.

Section 2. It is hereby declared to be the policy of Congress—

(1) To establish and maintain such balance between the production and consumption of agricultural commodities, and such marketing conditions therefor, as will reestablish prices to farmers at a level that will give agricultural commodities a purchasing power with respect to articles that farmers buy, equivalent to the purchasing power of agricultural commodities in the base period. . . .

(2) To approach such equality of purchasing power by gradual correction of the present inequalities therein at as rapid a rate as is deemed feasible in view of the current consumptive demand in domestic and foreign markets.

(3) To protect the consumers' interest by readjusting farm production at such level as will not increase the percentage of the consumers' retail expenditures for agricultural commodities, . . .

COMMODITY BENEFITS

Section 8. The Secretary of Agriculture shall have power—

(1) To provide for reduction in the acreage or reduction in the production for market, or both, of any basic agricultural commodity, through agreements with producers or by other voluntary methods, and to provide for rental or benefit payments in connection therewith or upon that part of the production of any basic agricultural commodity required for domestic consumption, in such amounts as the Secretary deems fair and reasonable, to be paid out of any moneys available for such payments. Under regulations of the Secretary of Agriculture requiring adequate facilities for the storage of any non-perishable agricultural commodity on the farm, inspection and measurement of any such commodity so stored, and the locking and sealing thereof, and such other regulations as may be prescribed by the Secretary of Agriculture for the protection of such commodity and for the marketing thereof, a reasonable percentage of any benefit payment may be advanced on any such com-

modity so stored. In any such case, such deduction may be made from the amount of the benefit payment as the Secretary of Agriculture determines will reasonably compensate for the cost of inspection and sealing, but no deduction may be made for interest.

(2) To enter into marketing agreements with processors, associations of producers, and others engaged in the handling, in the current of interstate or foreign commerce of any agricultural commodity or product thereof, after due notice and opportunity for hearing to interested parties. The making of any such agreement shall not be held to be in violation of any of the antitrust laws of the United States, and any such agreement shall be deemed to be lawful: *Provided,* That no such agreement shall remain in force after the termination of this Act. For the purpose of carrying out any such agreement the parties thereto shall be eligible for loans from the Reconstruction Finance Corporation under section 5 of the Reconstruction Finance Corporation Act. Such loans shall not be in excess of such amounts as may be authorized by the agreements.

(3) To issue licenses permitting processors, associations of producers, and others to engage in the handling, in the current of interstate or foreign commerce, of any agricultural commodity or product thereof, or any competing commodity or product thereof. . . .

Processing Tax

Section 9. (a) To obtain revenue for extraordinary expenses incurred by reason of the national economic emergency, there shall be levied processing taxes as hereinafter provided. When the Secretary of Agriculture determines that rental or benefit payments are to be made with respect to any basic agricultural commodity, he shall proclaim such determination, and a processing tax shall be in effect with respect to such commodity from the beginning of the marketing year therefor next following the date of such proclamation. The processing tax shall be levied, assessed, and collected upon the first domestic processing of the commodity, whether of domestic production or imported, and shall be paid by the processor. . . . The processing tax shall be at such rate as equals the difference between the current average farm price for the commodity and the fair exchange value of the commodity. . . .

National Labor Relations Act (1935)

* * * * *This Act, also known as the Wagner* Act after the New York Senator who sponsored it, set a pattern for the recognition of unions as collective bargaining agents in most kinds of industry. Secret elections were to be held by the National Labor Relations Board to determine whether workers wanted a union, or which union they wanted to represent them. The Board would certify the winning union as the collective bargaining agent for that factory or business, and would then protect it. The Board could prevent employers from certain anti-union activities, and could force the rehiring of workers who had been dismissed because of their union activities.

The chief effect of the law was to triple the size of the organized labor movement. By 1940 there were between nine and ten million workers in unions.

Section 1. The denial by employers of the right of employees to organize and the refusal by employers to accept the procedure of collective bargaining lead to strikes and other forms of industrial strife or unrest, which have the intent or the necessary effect of burdening or obstructing commerce by (a) impairing the efficiency, safety, or operation of the instrumentalities of commerce; (b) occurring in the current of commerce; (c) materially affecting, restraining, or controlling the flow of raw materials or manufactured or processed goods from or into the channels of commerce, or the prices of such materials or goods in commerce; or (d) causing diminution of employment and wages in such volume as substantially to impair or disrupt the market for goods flowing from or into the channels of commerce.

The inequality of bargaining power between employees who do not possess full freedom of association or actual liberty of contract, and employers who are organized in the corporate or other forms of ownership association substantially burdens and affects the flow of commerce, and tends to aggravate recurrent business depressions, by depressing wage rates and the purchasing power of wage earners in industry and by preventing the stabilization of competitive wage rates and working conditions within and between industries.

It is hereby declared to be the policy of the United States to eliminate the causes of certain substantial obstructions to the free flow of commerce and to mitigate and eliminate these obstructions when they have occurred by encouraging the practice and procedure of collective bargaining and by protecting the exercise by workers of full freedom of association, self-organization, and designation of representatives of their own choosing, for the purpose of negotiating the terms and conditions of their employment or other mutual aid or protection. . . .

Rights of Employees

Section 7. Employees shall have the right to self-organization, to form, join, or assist labor organizations, to bargain collectively through representatives of their own choosing, and to engage in concerted activities, for the purpose of collective bargaining or other mutual aid or protection.

Section 8. It shall be an unfair labor practice for an employer—

(1) To interfere with, restrain, or coerce employees in the exercise of the rights guaranteed in section 7.

(2) To dominate or interfere with the formation or administration of any labor organization or contribute financial or other support to it: *Provided,* That subject to rules and regulations made and published by the Board pursuant to section 6 (a), an employer shall not be prohibited from permitting employees to confer with him during working hours without loss of time or pay.

(3) By discrimination in regard to hire or tenure of employment or any term or condition of employment to encourage or discourage membership in any labor organization: *Provided,* That nothing in this Act, or in the National

Industrial Recovery Act (U. S. C., Supp. VII, title 15, secs. 701-712), as amended from time to time, or in any code or agreement approved or prescribed thereunder, or in any other statute of the United States, shall preclude an employer from making an agreement with a labor organization (not established, maintained, or assisted by any action defined in this Act as an unfair labor practice) to require as a condition of employment membership therein, if such labor organization is the representative of the employees as provided in section 9 (a), in the appropriate collective bargaining unit covered by such agreement when made.

(4) To discharge or otherwise discriminate against an employee because he has filed charges or given testimony under this Act.

(5) To refuse to bargain collectively with the representatives of his employees, subject to the provisions of Section 9 (a).

Representatives and Elections

Section 9. (a) Representatives designated or selected for the purposes of collective bargaining by the majority of the employees in a unit appropriate for such purposes, shall be the exclusive representatives of all the employees in such unit for the purposes of collective bargaining in respect to rates of pay, wages, hours of employment, or other conditions of employment: *Provided,* That any individual employee or a group of employees shall have the right at any time to present grievances to their employer.

(c) Whenever a question affecting commerce arises concerning the representation of employees, the Board may investigate such controversy and certify to the parties, in writing, the name or names of the representatives that have been designated or selected. . . .

Prevention of Unfair Labor Practices

Section 10. (a) The Board is empowered, as hereinafter provided, to prevent any person from engaging in any unfair labor practice (listed in section 8) affecting commerce. This power shall be exclusive, and shall not be affected by any other means of adjustment or prevention that has been or may be established by agreement, code, law, or otherwise.

(b) Whenever it is charged that any person has engaged

in or is engaging in any such unfair labor practice, the Board, or any agent or agency designated by the Board for such purposes, shall have power to issue and cause to be served upon such person a complaint stating the charges in that respect, . . . The person so complained of shall have the right to file an answer to the original or amended complaint and to appear in person or otherwise and give testimony at the place and time fixed in the complaint. In the discretion of the member, agent or agency conducting the hearing or the Board, any other person may be allowed to intervene in the said proceeding and to present testimony. In any such proceeding the rules of evidence prevailing in courts of law or equity shall not be controlling. . . .

Social Security Act (1935)

* * * * *The principle of this New Deal law,* also sponsored by New York's Senator Robert F. Wagner, was that it was the responsibility of the state and federal governments to provide for those citizens who are unable to provide for themselves. The states received funds to help them care for dependent children, the crippled, the blind, and those who are not fit to work at all.

Employers were required to pay a special tax to build a fund for unemployment insurance. Old-age pensions would be paid to workers who retire at age 65. The money for such payments was raised through a tax shared by worker and employer on a given annual wage. A Social Security Board was established to supervise the functioning of this complex law.

The law has been expanded year by year since 1935, until today it is a fairly complete system of social insurance. With a few exceptions, it now covers all industrial and domestic labor, some agricultural labor, and self-employed individuals.

FEDERAL OLD-AGE BENEFITS

Old-Age Reserve Account

Section 201. (a) There is hereby created an account in the Treasury of the United States to be known as the "Old-Age Reserve Account" hereinafter in this title called the "Account." There is hereby authorized to be appropriated to the Account for each fiscal year, beginning with the fiscal year ending June 30, 1937, an amount sufficient as an annual premium to provide for the payments required under this title, such amount to be determined on a reserve basis in accordance with accepted actuarial principles, and based upon such tables of mortality as the Secretary of the Treasury shall from time to time adopt, and upon an interest rate of 3 per centum per annum compounded annually. The Secretary of the Treasury shall submit annually to the Bureau of the Budget an estimate of the appropriations to be made to the Account. . . .

Old-Age Benefit Payments

Section 202. (a) Every qualified individual (as defined in section 210) shall be entitled to receive, with respect to the period beginning on the date he attains the age of sixty-five, or on January 1, 1942, whichever is the later, and ending on the date of his death, an old-age benefit (payable as nearly as practicable in equal monthly installments). . . .

GRANTS TO STATES FOR UNEMPLOYMENT COMPENSATION

Section 301. For the purpose of assisting the States in the administration of their unemployment compensation laws, there is hereby authorized to be appropriated, for the fiscal year ending June 30, 1936, the sum of $4,000,000, and for each fiscal year thereafter the sum of $49,000,000, to be used as hereinafter provided. . . .
(There follows a list of rules to be followed by the states.)

GRANTS TO STATES FOR AID TO DEPENDENT CHILDREN

Section 401. For the purpose of enabling each State to

furnish financial assistance, as far as practicable under the conditions in such State, to needy dependent children, there is hereby authorized to be appropriated for the fiscal year ending June 30, 1936, the sum of $24,750,000, and there is hereby authorized to be appropriated for each fiscal year thereafter a sum sufficient to carry out the purposes of this title. The sums made available under this section shall be used for making payments to States which have submitted, and had approved by the Board, State plans for aid to dependent children. . . .

Definitions

Section 811. When used in this title—

(a) The term "wages" means all remuneration for employment, including the cash value of all remuneration paid in any medium other than cash; except that such term shall not include that part of the remuneration which, after remuneration equal to $3,000 has been paid to an individual by an employer with respect to employment during any calendar year, is paid to such individual by such employer with respect to employment during such calendar year.

(b) The term "employment" means any service, of whatever nature, performed within the United States by an employee for his employer, except—

(1) Agricultural labor;

(2) Domestic service in a private home;

(3) Casual labor not in the course of the employer's trade or business;

(4) Service performed by an individual who has attained the age of sixty-five;

(5) Service performed as an officer or member of the crew of a vessel documented under the laws of the United States or of any foreign country;

(6) Service performed in the employ of the United States Government or of an instrumentality of the United States;

(7) Service performed in the employ of a State, a political subdivision thereof, or an instrumentality of one or more States or political subdivisions;

(8) Service performed in the employ of a corporation, community chest, fund, or foundation, organized and operated exclusively for religious, charitable, scientific, literary,

or educational purposes, or for the prevention of cruelty to children or animals, no part of the net earnings of which inures to the benefit of any private shareholder or individual.

TAX ON EMPLOYERS OF EIGHT OR MORE

Imposition of Tax

Section 901. On and after January 1, 1936, every employer ... shall pay for each calendar year an excise tax, with respect to having individuals in his employ, equal to the following percentages of the total wages ... payable by him (regardless of the time of payment) with respect to employment ... during such calendar year:

(1) With respect to employment during the calendar year 1936 the rate shall be 1 per centum;

(2) With respect to employment during the calendar year 1937 the rate shall be 2 per centum;

(3) With respect to employment after December 31, 1937, the rate shall be 3 per centum.

TRUE OR FALSE?

Write T *if the statement is correct; write* F *if it is false.*

_____1.The Tennessee Valley Authority was administered by Senator George W. Norris.

_____2. Muscle Shoals had been built during World War I as a war measure.

_____3. The NLRB tried to prevent labor unions from becoming strong.

_____4. The Social Security Act was at first limited to industrial workers.

_____5. The NIRA and the AAA were declared unconstitutional.

_____6. Today, each stock exchange makes its own "margin" rules.

_____7. The Securities Exchange Act abolished the Clayton Act.

_____8. The cost of old-age pensions under the Social Security Act is divided between the worker and his employer.

_____9. TVA has served as a "yardstick" in determining fair electric rates.

_____10. The AAA tried to get farmers to grow less than they had been growing.

1. Describe three of the problems facing the United States in 1933. Explain the provisions of a specific law designed to solve each problem.
2. "The New Deal introduced welfare state concepts." Explain this statement by specific reference to New Deal thinking and the legislation which resulted from it.

"Quarantine the Aggressors" Speech (October, 1937)

* * * * *It was 1937 — Italy had conquered* Ethiopia. The Spanish Civil War, in which Nazi Germany and Fascist Italy tested their weapons and proved that the democracies would do little in the face of aggression, was under way. Japan was preparing aggression against China. Hitler's speeches and war preparations forecast later moves against Austria and Czechoslovakia.

The first reaction of the United States to these developments was the hope that two oceans and a history of neutrality would keep Americans out of war. In May, 1937, Congress passed a Neutrality Act which prohibited Americans from helping either side in a war.

When Japan began its conquest of China in July, President Roosevelt refused to apply the neutrality law on the grounds that neither side had formally declared war. Then, in October, he delivered a speech in Chicago in which he warned the world of the dangers of aggression, and asked for collective action to halt aggressive wars.

. . . Some fifteen years ago the hopes of mankind for a continuing era of international peace were raised to great heights when more than sixty nations solemnly pledged themselves not to resort to arms in furtherance of their national aims and policies. The high aspirations expressed in the Briand-Kellogg Peace Pact and the hopes for peace thus raised have of late given way to a haunting fear of calamity. The present reign of terror and international lawlessness began a few years ago.

It began through unjustified interference in the internal affairs of other nations or the invasion of alien territory in violation of treaties; and has now reached a stage where the very foundations of civilization are seriously threatened. . . .

How happy we are that the circumstances of the moment permit us to put our money into bridges and boulevards, dams and reforestation, the conservation of our soil and many other kinds of useful works rather than into huge standing armies and vast supplies of implements of war.

I am compelled and you are compelled, nevertheless, to look ahead. The peace, the freedom and the security of ninety percent of the population of the world are being jeopardized by the remaining ten percent who are threatening a breakdown of all international order and law. Surely the ninety percent who want to live in peace under law and in accordance with moral standards that have received almost universal acceptance through the centuries, can and must find some way to make their will prevail. . . .

It seems to be unfortunately true that the epidemic of world lawlessness is spreading.

When an epidemic of physical disease starts to spread, the community approves and joins in a quarantine of the patients in order to protect the health of the community against the spread of the disease. . . .

War is a contagion, whether it be declared or undeclared. It can engulf states and peoples remote from the original scene of the hostilities. We are determined to keep out of war, yet we cannot insure ourselves against the disastrous effects of war and the dangers of involvement. We are adopting such measures as will minimize our risk of involvement, but we cannot have complete protection in a world of disorder in which confidence and security have broken down.

If civilization is to survive the principles of the Prince of Peace must be restored. Trust between nations must be revived.

Most important of all, the will for peace on the part of peace-loving nations must express itself to the end that nations that may be tempted to violate their agreements and the rights of others will desist from such a course. There must be positive endeavors to preserve peace.

America hates war. America hopes for peace. Therefore, America actively engages in the search for peace.

Four Freedoms Speech (January, 1941)

* * * * *From the beginning of World War II* in September, 1939, the United States, led by President Roosevelt, gave moral support to the Western democracies, chiefly England. By January, 1941, the President had decided to give the British the ships and supplies they needed to resist Germany. The suggestions he made in his annual message to Congress became law when Congress passed the Lend-Lease Act.

Roosevelt's words were a statement of his policy, and a lecture to the "isolationists" who felt that the United States could avoid being involved in the war. The speech ended with a call to the world to fight, not for conquest, but for the Four Freedoms which would make all men free.

I address you, the Members of the Seventy-seventh Congress, at a moment unprecedented in the history of the Union. I use the word "unprecedented," because at no previous time has American security been as seriously threatened from without as it is today. . . .

It is true that prior to 1914 the United States often had been disturbed by events in other continents. We had even engaged in two wars with European nations and in a number of undeclared wars in the West Indies, in the Mediterranean, and in the Pacific for the maintenance of American rights and for the principles of peaceful commerce. In no case, however, had a serious threat been raised against our national safety or our independence. . . .

. . . We need not harp on failure of the democracies to deal with problems of world reconstruction. We should remember that the peace of 1919 was far less unjust than the kind of "pacification" which began even before Munich and which is being carried on under the new order of tyranny that seeks to spread over every continent today. The American people have unalterably set their faces against that tyranny.

Every realist knows that the democratic way of life is at this moment being directly assailed in every part of the world—assailed either by arms, or by secret spreading of poisonous propaganda by those who seek to destroy unity and promote discord in nations still at peace.

During 16 months this assault has blotted out the whole pattern of democratic life in an appalling number of independent nations, great and small. The assailants are still on the march, threatening other nations, great and small.

Therefore, as your President, performing my constitutional duty to "give to the Congress information of the state of the Union," I find it necessary to report that the future and the safety of our country and of our democracy are overwhelmingly involved in events far beyond our borders.

Armed defense of democratic existence is now being gallantly waged in four continents. If that defense fails, all the population and all the resources of Europe, Asia, Africa, and Australasia will be dominated by the conquerors. The total of those populations and their resources greatly exceeds the sum total of the population and resources of the whole of the Western Hemisphere—many times over. . . .

No realistic American can expect from a dictator's peace international generosity, or return of true independence, or world disarmament, or freedom of expression, or freedom of religion—or even good business.

Such a peace would bring no security for us or for our neighbors. Those, who would give up essential liberty to purchase a little temporary safety deserve neither liberty nor safety.

.   .   .   .

There is much loose talk of our immunity from immediate and direct invasion from across the seas. Obviously, as long as the British Navy retains its power, no such danger exists. Even if there were no British Navy, it is not probable that any enemy would be stupid enough to attack us by landing troops in the United States from across thousands of miles of ocean, until it had acquired strategic bases from which to operate.

But we learn much from the lessons of the past years in Europe—particularly the lesson of Norway, whose essential seaports were captured by treachery and surprise built up over a series of years. . . .

As long as the aggressor nations maintain the offensive, they, not we, will choose the time and the place and the method of their attack.

. . . .

The need of the moment is that our actions and our policy should be devoted primarily—almost exclusively—to meeting this foreign peril. For all our domestic problems are now a part of the great emergency.

Just as our national policy in internal affairs has been based upon a decent respect for the rights and dignity of all our fellow-men within our gates, so our national policy in foreign affairs has been based on a decent respect for the rights and dignity of all nations, large and small. And the justice of morality must and will win in the end.

Our national policy is this:

First, by an impressive expression of the public will and without regard to partisanship, we are committed to all-inclusive national defense.

Second, by an impressive expression of the public will and without regard to partisanship, we are committed to full support of all those resolute peoples, everywhere, who are resisting aggression and are thereby keeping war away from our hemisphere. By this support, we express our determination that the democratic cause shall prevail, and we strengthen the defense and security of our own Nation.

Third, by an impressive expression of the public will and without regard to partisanship, we are committed to the proposition that principles of morality and considerations for our own security will never permit us to acquiesce in a peace dictated by aggressors and sponsored by appeasers. We know that enduring peace cannot be bought at the cost of other people's freedom. . . .

Our most useful and immediate role is to act as an arsenal for them as well as for ourselves. They do not need manpower. They do need billions of dollars' worth of the weapons of defense. . . .

Let us say to the democracies, "We Americans are vitally concerned in your defense of freedom. We are putting forth our energies, our resources and our organizing powers to give you the strength to regain and maintain a free world. We shall send you, in ever-increasing numbers, ships, planes, tanks, guns. This is our purpose and our pledge."

In fulfillment of this purpose we will not be intimidated by the threats of dictators that they will regard as a breach of international law and as an act of war our aid to the democracies which dare to resist their aggression. Such aid is not an act of war, even if a dictator should unilaterally proclaim it so to be.

When the dictators are ready to make war upon us, they will not wait for an act of war on our part. They did not wait for Norway or Belgium or The Netherlands to commit an act of war.

Their only interest is in a new one-way international law, which lacks mutuality in its observance and, therefore, becomes an instrument of oppression. . . .

As men do not live by bread alone, they do not fight by armaments alone. Those who man our defenses, and those behind them who build our defenses, must have the stamina and courage which come from an unshakable belief in the manner of life which they are defending. The mighty action which we are calling for cannot be based on a disregard of all things worth fighting for.

There is nothing mysterious about the foundations of a healthy and strong democracy. The basic things expected by our people of their political and economic systems are simple. They are:

Equality of opportunity for youth and for others.

Jobs for those who can work.

Security for those who need it.

The ending of special privilege for the few.

The preservation of civil liberties for all.

The enjoyment of the fruits of scientific progress in a wider and constantly rising standard of living.

These are the simple and basic things that must never be lost sight of in the turmoil and unbelievable complexity of our modern world. The inner and abiding strength of our economic and political systems is dependent upon the degree to which they fulfill these expectations. . . .

I have called for personal sacrifice. I am assured of the willingness of almost all Americans to respond to that call.

A part of the sacrifice means the payment of more money in taxes. . . . No person should try, or be allowed to get rich out of this program. . . .

In the future days, which we seek to make secure, we look forward to a world founded upon four essential human freedoms.

The first is freedom of speech and expression, everywhere in the world.

The second is freedom of every person to worship God in his own way, everywhere in the world.

The third is freedom from want, which, translated into world terms, means economic understandings which will secure to every nation a healthy peace time life for its inhabitants, everywhere in the world.

The fourth is freedom from fear—which, translated into world terms, means a world-wide reduction of armaments to such a point and in such a thorough fashion that no nation will be in a position to commit an act of physical aggression against any neighbor—anywhere in the world.

That is no vision of a distant millennium. It is a definite basis for a kind of world attainable in our own time and so-called new order of tyranny which the dictators seek to generation. That kind of world is the very antithesis of the create with the crash of a bomb.

To that new order we oppose the greater conception—the moral order. A good society is able to face schemes of world domination and foreign revolutions alike without fear.

Since the beginning of our American history we have been engaged in change—in a perpetual peaceful revolution—a revolution which goes on steadily, quietly adjusting itself to changing conditions—without the concentration camp or the quicklime in the ditch. The world order which we seek is the cooperation of free countries, working together in a friendly, civilized society.

This Nation has placed its destiny in the hands and heads and hearts of its millions of free men and women; and its faith in freedom under the guidance of God. Freedom means the supremacy of human rights everywhere. Our support goes to those who struggle to gain those rights or keep them. Our strength is in our unity of purpose.

To that high concept there can be no end save victory.

The Atlantic Charter (August, 1941)

* * * * *By the summer of 1941, continued* German bombings by planes and rockets were weakening England's ability to maintain its defense. Meanwhile, Germany had invaded Russia. To stop Germany, aid would have to be sent to the Russians, too.

President Roosevelt and British Prime Minister Winston Churchill met secretly in August aboard the *U.S.S. Augustus* in the North Atlantic. They issued a statement of the principles for which both nations were willing to devote their fullest energies. Fifteen other countries later publicly subscribed to the Atlantic Charter.

Joint declaration of the President of the United States of America and the Prime Minister, Mr. Churchill, representing His Majesty's government in the United Kingdom, being met together, deem it right to make known certain common principles in the national policies of their respective countries on which they base their hopes for a better future for the world.

First, their countries seek no aggrandizement, territorial or other;

Second, they desire to see no territorial changes that do not accord with the freely expressed wishes of the people concerned;

Third, they respect the right of all peoples to choose the form of government under which they will live; and they wish to see sovereign rights and self-government restored to those who have been forcibly deprived of them;

Fourth, they will endeavor, with due respect for their existing obligations, to further the enjoyment by all States, great or small, victor or vanquished, of access, on equal terms, to the trade and to the raw materials of the world which are needed for their economic prosperity;

Fifth, they desire to bring about the fullest collaboration between all nations in the economic field with the object of securing, for all, improved labor standards, economic advancement and social security;

Sixth, after the final destruction of the Nazi tyranny, they hope to see established a peace which will afford to all nations the means of dwelling in safety within their own boundaries, and which will afford assurance that all the men in all the lands may live out their lives in freedom from fear and want;

Seventh, such a peace should enable all men to traverse the high seas and oceans without hindrance;

Eighth, they believe that all of the nations of the world, for realistic as well as spiritual reasons, must come to the abandonment of the use of force. Since no future peace can be maintained if land, sea or air armaments continue to be employed by nations which threaten, or may threaten, aggression outside of their frontiers, they believe, pending the establishment of a wider and permanent system of general security, that the disarmament of such nations is essential. They will likewise aid and encourage all other practicable measures which will lighten for peace-loving peoples the crushing burden of armaments.

FRANKLIN D. ROOSEVELT
WINSTON S. CHURCHILL

War Message (December, 1941)

* * * * *While Japan's envoys were negotiat-*ing with the State Department to ease the tensions in the Far East, Japan launched a sneak attack on Pearl Harbor. On December 7, 1941, "a day that will live in infamy," the United States was thrust into World War II, a war toward which it had inevitably moved since 1939.

On December 8, Roosevelt asked Congress to declare war against Japan. Germany and Italy declared war on the United States two days later.

In his radio address, President Roosevelt assured the nation, shocked by the sudden turn of events, that victory would come, victory over not only Japan but Japan's allies as well. He promised that the nation would win the war and the peace to follow.

The sudden criminal attacks perpetrated by the Japanese in the Pacific provide the climax of a decade of international immorality.

Powerful and resourceful gangsters have banded together to make war upon the whole human race. Their challenge has now been flung at the United States of America. The Japanese have treacherously violated the long-standing peace between us. Many American soldiers and sailors have been killed by enemy action. American ships have been sunk; American airplanes have been destroyed.

The Congress and the people of the United States have accepted that challenge.

Together with other free peoples, we are now fighting to maintain our right to live among our world neighbors in freedom and in common decency, without fear of assault. . . .

The course that Japan has followed for the past 10 years in Asia has paralleled the course of Hitler and Mussolini in Europe and Africa. Today, it has become far more than a parallel. It is collaboration so well calculated that all the continents of the world, and all the oceans, are now considered by the Axis strategists as one gigantic battlefield. . . .

In these past few years—and, most violently, in the past few days—we have learned a terrible lesson. It is our obligation to our dead—it is our sacred obligation to their children and our children—that we must never forget what we have learned. And what we all have learned is this:

There is no such thing as security for any nation—or any individual—in a world ruled by the principles of gangsterism. There is no such thing as impregnable defense against powerful aggressors who sneak up in the dark and strike without warning. We have learned that our ocean-girt hemisphere is not immune from severe attack—that we cannot measure our safety in terms of miles on any map. . . .

Your Government knows that for weeks Germany has been telling Japan that if Japan did not attack the United States, Japan would not share in dividing the spoils with Germany when peace came. . . .

We also know that Germany and Japan are conducting their military and naval operations in accordance with a joint plan. That plan considers all peoples and nations which are not helping the Axis powers as common enemies of each and every one of the Axis powers.

That is their simple and obvious grand strategy. That is why the American people must realize that it can be matched only with similar grand strategy. We must realize for example that Japanese successes against the United States in the Pacific are helpful to German operations in Libya; that any German success against the Caucasus is inevitably an assistance to Japan in her operations against the Dutch East Indies; that a German attack against Algiers or Morocco opens the way to a German attack against South America. . .

Remember always that Germany and Italy, regardless of any formal declaration of war, consider themselves at war with the United States at this moment just as much as they consider themselves at war with Britain and Russia. And Germany puts all the other republics of the Americas into the category of enemies. The people of the hemisphere can be honored by that. . . .

We are now in the midst of a war, not for conquest, not for vengeance, but for a world in which this Nation, and all that this Nation represents, will be safe for our children. We expect to eliminate the danger from Japan, but it would serve us ill if we accomplished that and found that the rest of the world was dominated by Hitler and Mussolini.

We are going to win the war and we are going to win the peace that follows.

And in the dark hours of this day—and through dark days that may be yet to come—we will know that the vast majority of the members of the human race are on our side. Many of them are fighting with us. All of them are praying for us. For, in representing our cause, we represent theirs as well—our hope and their hope for liberty under God.

CHOOSE THE CORRECT ANSWERS

Write the letter that best completes the statement or answers the question.

1. President Roosevelt, in 1937, warned that the United States must (*a*) declare war on Japan, (*b*) strengthen England, (*c*) quarantine aggressor nations, (*d*) refuse to involve itself further in world affairs.   1._____

2. In the Atlantic Charter, England and the United States promised (*a*) to divide up Germany, (*b*) to support self-government for all peoples, (*c*) to end the trade of the defeated Fascist nations, (*d*) to build powerful armies in the future to prevent future wars.   2._____

3. In the Atlantic Charter, Roosevelt and Churchill assured the world that England and the United States did not seek (*a*) new colonies, (*b*) a change of government anywhere in the world, (*c*) world disarmament, (*d*) the right of all to travel freely on the seas.   3._____

4. In his war message, Roosevelt blamed the coming of war on (*a*) our lack of defensive preparation, (*b*) Germany's attack on England, (*c*) Japan's treachery, (*d*) German and Japanese attacks on religion.   4._____

5. Before 1941, the United States had helped (*a*) England, (*b*) Russia, (*c*) all nations which had asked for aid, (*d*) none of the nations in World War II.   5._____

6. An aggressor is a nation that (*a*) attacks another nation, (*b*) tries to win a war, (*c*) refuses to discuss peace terms, (*d*) will not fight.   6._____

7. A quarantine is used when there is (*a*) a war, (*b*) a disagreement between nations, (*c*) a contagious disease, (*d*) death from disease.   7._____

8. Among the Four Freedoms Roosevelt listed (*a*) freedom to vote, (*b*) freedom of speech, (*c*) freedom from punishment, (*d*) freedom of trade.   8._____

9. The speech made before World War II began was (*a*) the Quarantine the Aggressors speech, (*b*) the Four Freedoms speech, (*c*) announcement of the Atlantic Charter, (*d*) announcement of Lend-Lease.   9._____

THOUGHT QUESTIONS

1. How did the Atlantic Charter express the basic differences between the philosophies of democracy and totalitarianism?

2. Express your reasons for agreeing or disagreeing with the statement that United States involvement in World War II could not be avoided.

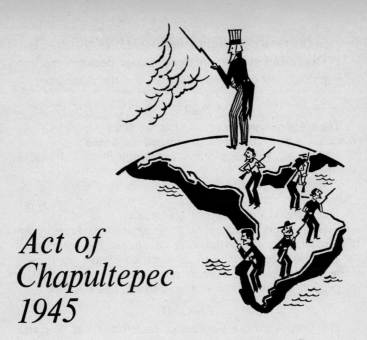

Act of Chapultepec 1945

* * * * *In 1938, at the Pan American Con-*
ference in Lima, Peru, the Declaration of Lima
announced the general unity of the American
nations "against all foreign intervention or activity." The United States thus gave up its role as
the enforcer of the Monroe Doctrine, and agreed
to a regional mutual defense alliance.

When the United States was drawn into World
War II, the Act of Havana, 1940, declared that the
Pan-American nations would stand together to pre-
vent the Axis powers from taking any land in the
Americas. During 1942, one Latin-American coun-
try after another became an ally of the United
States.

As the war drew to its close, an Inter-American
Conference was called in Mexico City, in 1945. It
was agreed that the defense of the Americas would

in the future be mutual defense. Later, in 1948, the Organization of American States became the regional collective security plan for the Americas

PART I

The Governments represented at the Inter-American Conference on Problems of War and Peace *declare:*

1. That all sovereign States are juridically equal among themselves.

2. That every State has the right to the respect of its individuality and independence, on the part of the other members of the international community.

3. That every attack of a State against the integrity or the inviolability of the territory or against the sovereignty or political independence of an American State, shall, conformably to Part III hereof, be considered as an act of aggression against the other States which sign this Act. . . .

PART II

The Inter-American Conference on Problems of War and Peace *recommends:*

That for the purpose of meeting threats or acts of aggression against any American Republic following the establishment of peace, the Governments of the American Republics consider the conclusion, in accordance with their constitutional processes, of a treaty establishing procedures whereby such threats or acts may be met by the use, by all or some of the signatories of said treaty, of any one or more of the following measures; recall of chiefs of diplomatic missions; breaking of diplomatic relations, breaking of consular relations; breaking of postal, telegraphic, telephonic, radio-telephonic relations; interruption of economic, commercial and financial relations; use of armed force to prevent or repel aggression.

PART III

The above Declaration and Recommendation constitute a regional arrangement for dealing with such matters relating to the maintenance of international peace and security as are appropriate for regional action in this Hemisphere. The said arrangement, and the pertinent activities and procedures, shall be consistent with the purposes and principles of the general international organization, when established. This agreement shall be known as the ACT OF CHAPULTEPEC.

TRUE OR FALSE?

Write T *if the statement is correct; write* F *if it is false.*

_____1. The United States had long considered itself the guardian of the Americas.

_____2. The other American nations agreed at Chapultepec that the United States was their proper leader.

_____3. An attack on one nation in the Americas is regarded as an attack on all.

_____4. If any American nation attacks a European nation, it is assured of the military support of all other American nations.

_____5. The Act of Chapultepec later led to the Organization of American States.

_____6. The Declaration of Lima had kept South American nations out of World War II.

_____7. By the Act of Chapultepec the United States renounced the Monroe Doctrine.

_____8. In 1945, the American nations agreed to respect one another's independence.

THOUGHT QUESTIONS

1. How did the Pan-Americanization of the Monroe Doctrine reflect a new policy of inter-American relations?
2. How did the Act of Chapultepec illustrate the nature of a regional agreement for collective security?

Excerpts from the United Nations Charter 1945

* * * * *Out of such declarations of principle* as the Four Freedoms speech of Franklin D. Roosevelt, the Atlantic Charter, and the Declaration of the United Nations, came an international determination to win the peace through the creation of a worldwide organization — the United Nations. On June 26, 1945, after years of preliminary discussions, the Charter of the United Nations was adopted in San Francisco. During the years which followed, the United Nations struggled to achieve its objectives despite the continuing "Cold War" between nations led by the United States on one side and the Soviet Union on the other. These sections from the long Charter illustrate the purposes, basic organization, and specialized goals of the United Nations.

We, the peoples of the United Nations, determined

to save succeeding generations from the scourge of war, which twice in our lifetime has brought untold sorrow to mankind, and

to reaffirm faith in fundamental human rights, in the dignity and worth of the human person, in the equal rights of men and women and of nations large and small, and

to establish conditions under which justice and respect for the obligations arising from treaties and other sources of international law can be maintained, and

to promote social progress and better standards of life in larger freedom,

And for these ends

to practice tolerance and live together in peace with one another as good neighbors, and

to unite our strength to maintain international peace and security, and

to ensure, by the acceptance of principles and the institution of methods, that armed force shall not be used, save in the common interest, and

to employ international machinery for the promotion of the economic and social advancement of all peoples,

Have resolved to combine our efforts to accomplish these aims.

Accordingly, our respective Governments, through representatives assembled in the city of San Francisco, who have exhibited their full powers found to be in good and due form, have agreed to the present Charter of the United Nations and do hereby establish an international organization to be known as the United Nations.

PURPOSES AND PRINCIPLES

Article 1

The Purposes of the United Nations are:

1. To maintain international peace and security, and to that end: to take effective collective measures for the prevention and removal of threats to the peace, and for the suppression of acts of aggression or other breaches of the peace, and to bring about by peaceful means, and in conformity with the principles of justice and international law,

THE UNITED NATIONS AND RELATED AGENCIES

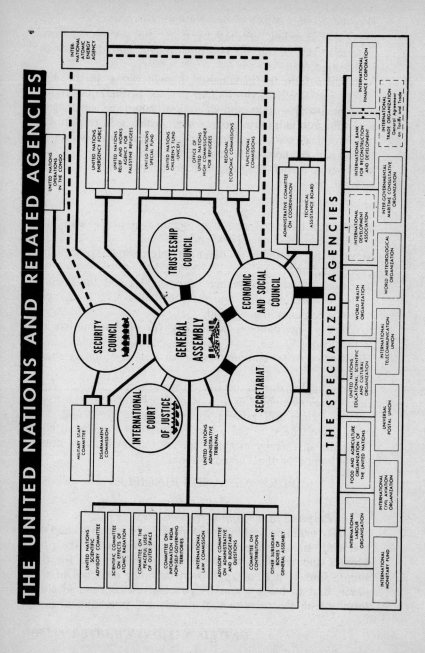

THE SPECIALIZED AGENCIES

INTER-NATIONAL ATOMIC ENERGY AGENCY

UNITED NATIONS OPERATIONS IN THE CONGO

SECURITY COUNCIL

GENERAL ASSEMBLY

TRUSTEESHIP COUNCIL

ECONOMIC AND SOCIAL COUNCIL

INTERNATIONAL COURT OF JUSTICE

SECRETARIAT

UNITED NATIONS EMERGENCY FORCE
UNITED NATIONS RELIEF AND WORKS AGENCY FOR PALESTINE REFUGEES
UNITED NATIONS SPECIAL FUND
UNITED NATIONS CHILDREN'S FUND (UNICEF)
OFFICE OF UNITED NATIONS HIGH COMMISSIONER FOR REFUGEES
REGIONAL ECONOMIC COMMISSIONS
FUNCTIONAL COMMISSIONS

ADMINISTRATIVE COMMITTEE ON COORDINATION
TECHNICAL ASSISTANCE BOARD

MILITARY STAFF COMMITTEE
DISARMAMENT COMMISSION

UNITED NATIONS ADMINISTRATIVE TRIBUNAL

UNITED NATIONS SCIENTIFIC ADVISORY COMMITTEE
SCIENTIFIC COMMITTEE ON EFFECTS OF ATOMIC RADIATION
COMMITTEE ON THE PEACEFUL USES OF OUTER SPACE
COMMITTEE ON INFORMATION FROM NON-SELF-GOVERNING TERRITORIES
INTERNATIONAL LAW COMMISSION
ADVISORY COMMITTEE ON ADMINISTRATIVE AND BUDGETARY QUESTIONS
COMMITTEE ON CONTRIBUTIONS
OTHER SUBSIDIARY BODIES OF GENERAL ASSEMBLY

INTERNATIONAL FINANCE CORPORATION
INTERNATIONAL BANK FOR RECONSTRUCTION AND DEVELOPMENT
INTERNATIONAL TRADE ORGANIZATION General Agreement on Tariffs and Trade
INTER-GOVERNMENTAL MARITIME CONSULTATIVE ORGANIZATION
INTERNATIONAL DEVELOPMENT ASSOCIATION
WORLD METEOROLOGICAL ORGANIZATION
WORLD HEALTH ORGANIZATION
INTERNATIONAL TELECOMMUNICATION UNION
UNITED NATIONS EDUCATIONAL, SCIENTIFIC AND CULTURAL ORGANIZATION
UNIVERSAL POSTAL UNION
FOOD AND AGRICULTURE ORGANIZATION OF THE UNITED NATIONS
INTERNATIONAL CIVIL AVIATION ORGANIZATION
INTERNATIONAL LABOUR ORGANISATION
INTERNATIONAL MONETARY FUND

adjustment or settlement of international disputes or situations which might lead to a breach of the peace;

2. To develop friendly relations among nations based on respect for the principle of equal rights and self-determination of peoples, and to take other appropriate measures to strengthen universal peace;

3. To achieve international cooperation in solving international problems of an economic, social, cultural, or humanitarian character, and in promoting and encouraging respect for human rights and for fundamental freedoms for all without distinction as to race, sex, language, or religion; and

4. To be a center for harmonizing the actions of nations in the attainment of these common ends.

Article 2

The Organization and its Members, in pursuit of the Purposes stated in Article 1, shall act in accordance with the following Principles:

1. The Organization is based on the principle of the sovereign equality of all its Members.

2. All Members, in order to ensure to all of them the rights and benefits resulting from membership, shall fulfill in good faith the obligations assumed by them in accordance with the present Charter.

3. All Members shall settle their international disputes by peaceful means in such a manner that international peace and security, and justice, are not endangered.

4. All Members shall refrain in their international relations from the threat or use of force against the territorial integrity or political independence of any state, or in any other manner inconsistent with the Purposes of the United Nations.

5. All Members shall give the United Nations every assistance in any action it takes in accordance with the present Charter, and shall refrain from giving assistance to any state against which the United Nations is taking preventive or enforcement action.

6. The Organization shall ensure that states which are not Members of the United Nations act in accordance with these

Principles so far as may be necessary for the maintenance of international peace and security.

7. Nothing contained in the present Charter shall authorize the United Nations to intervene in matters which are essentially within the domestic jurisdiction of any state or shall require the Members to submit such matters to settlement under the present Charter; but this principle shall not prejudice the application of enforcement measures under Chapter VII.

MEMBERSHIP
Article 4

1. Membership in the United Nations is open to all other peace-loving states which accept the obligations contained in the present Charter and, in the judgment of the Organization, are able and willing to carry out these obligations.

2. The admission of any such state to membership in the United Nations will be effected by a decision of the General Assembly upon the recommendation of the Security Council.

Article 5

A Member of the United Nations against which preventive or enforcement action has been taken by the Security Council may be suspended from the exercise of the rights and privileges of membership by the General Assembly upon the recommendation of the Security Council. The exercise of these rights and privileges may be restored by the Security Council.

Article 6

A Member of the United Nations which has persistently violated the Principles contained in the present Charter may be expelled from the Organization by the General Assembly upon the recommendation of the Security Council.

ORGANS
Article 7

1. There are established as the principal organs of the United Nations: a General Assembly, a Security Council, an Economic and Social Council, a Trusteeship Council, an International Court of Justice, and a Secretariat.

2. Such subsidiary organs as may be found necessary may be established in accordance with the present Charter.

Article 8

The United Nations shall place no restrictions on the eligibility of men and women to participate in any capacity and under conditions of equality in its principal and subsidiary organs.

THE GENERAL ASSEMBLY

Article 9

1. The General Assembly shall consist of all the Members of the United Nations.

2. Each Member shall have not more than five representatives in the General Assembly.

Article 11

1. The General Assembly may consider the general principles of cooperation in the maintenance of international peace and security, including the principles governing disarmament and the regulation of armaments, and may make recommendations with regard to such principles to the Members or to the Security Council or to both.

2. The General Assembly may discuss any questions relating to the maintenance of international peace and security brought before it by any Member of the United Nations, or by the Security Council, or by a state which is not a Member of the United Nations. . . .

3. The General Assembly may call the attention of the Security Council to situations which are likely to endanger international peace and security.

Article 18

1. Each member of the General Assembly shall have one vote.

2. Decisions of the General Assembly on important questions shall be made by a two-thirds majority of the members present and voting. . . .

THE SECURITY COUNCIL

Article 23

1. The Security Council shall consist of eleven Members of the United Nations. The Republic of China, France, the Union of Soviet Socialist Republics, the United Kingdom of

Great Britain and Northern Ireland, and the United States of America shall be permanent members of the Security Council. The General Assembly shall elect six other Members of the United Nations to be non-permanent members of the Security Council, due regard being specially paid, in the first instance to the contribution of Members of the United Nations to the maintenance of international peace and security and to the other purposes of the Organization, and also to equitable geographical distribution.

2. The non-permanent members of the Security Council shall be elected for a term of two years.

Article 24

1. In order to ensure prompt and effective action by the United Nations, its Members confer on the Security Council primary responsibility for the maintenance of international peace and security, and agree that in carrying out its duties under this responsibility the Security Council acts on their behalf.

Article 27

1. Each member of the Security Council shall have one vote.

2. Decisions of the Security Council on procedural matters shall be made by an affirmative vote of seven members.

Article 34

The Security Council may investigate any dispute, or any situation which might lead to international friction or give rise to a dispute, in order to determine whether the continuance of the dispute or situation is likely to endanger the maintenance of international peace and security.

Article 41

The Security Council may decide what measures not involving the use of armed force are to be employed to give effect to its decisions, and it may call upon the Members of the United Nations to apply such measures. These may include complete or partial interruption of economic relations and of rail, sea, air, postal, telegraphic, radio, and other means of communication, and the severance of diplomatic relations.

Article 42

Should the Security Council consider that measures provided for in Article 41 would be inadequate or have proved to be inadequate, it may take such action by air, sea, or land forces as may be necessary to maintain or restore international peace and security. Such action may include demonstrations, blockade, and other operations by air, sea, or land forces of Members of the United Nations.

Article 43

1. All Members of the United Nations, in order to contribute to the maintenance of international peace and security, undertake to make available to the Security Council, on its call and in accordance with a special agreement or agreements, armed forces, assistance, and facilities, including rights of passage, necessary for the purpose of maintaining international peace and security.

Article 51

Nothing in the present Charter shall impair the inherent right of individual or collective self-defense if an armed attack occurs against a Member of the United Nations, until the Security Council has taken measures necessary to maintain international peace and security. Measures taken by Members in the exercise of this right of self-defense shall be immediately reported to the Security Council and shall not in any way affect the authority and responsibility of the Security Council under the present Charter to take at any time such action as it deems necessary in order to maintain or restore international peace and security.

REGIONAL ARRANGEMENTS

Article 52

1. Nothing in the present Charter precludes the existence of regional arrangements or agencies for dealing with such matters relating to the maintenance of international peace and security as are appropriate for regional action, provided that such arrangements or agencies and their activities are consistent with the Purposes and Principles of the United Nations.

INTERNATIONAL ECONOMIC
AND SOCIAL COOPERATION

Article 55

With a view to the creation of conditions of stability and well-being which are necessary for peaceful and friendly relations among nations based on respect for the principle of equal rights and self-determination of peoples, the United Nations shall promote:

a. higher standards of living, full employment, and conditions of economic and social progress and development;

b. solutions of international economic, social, health, and related problems; and international cultural and educational cooperation; and

c. universal respect for, and observance of, human rights and fundamental freedoms for all without distinction as to race, sex, language, or religion.

THE ECONOMIC AND SOCIAL COUNCIL

Article 62

1. The Economic and Social Council may make . . . recommendations for the purpose of promoting respect for, and observance of, human rights and fundamental freedoms for all.

DECLARATION REGARDING
NON-SELF-GOVERNING TERRITORIES

Article 73

Members of the United Nations which have or assume responsibilities for the administration of territories whose peoples have not yet attained a full measure of self-government recognize the principle that the interests of the inhabitants of these territories are paramount, and accept as a sacred trust the obligation to promote to the utmost, within the system of international peace and security established by the present Charter, the well-being of the inhabitants of these territories, and, to this end:

a. to ensure, with due respect for the culture of the peoples concerned, their political, economic, social, and educational advancement, their just treatment, and their protection against abuses;

b. to develop self-government, to take due account of the political aspirations of the peoples, and to assist them in the progressive development of their free political institutions, according to the particular circumstances of each territory and its peoples and their varying stages of advancement;

c. to further international peace and security;

d. to promote constructive measures of development, to encourage research, and to cooperate with one another and, when and where appropriate, with specialized international bodies with a view to the practical achievement of the social, economic, and scientific purposes set forth in this Article; . . .

INTERNATIONAL TRUSTEESHIP SYSTEM

Article 75

The United Nations shall establish under its authority an international trusteeship system for the administration and supervision of such territories as may be placed thereunder by subsequent individual agreements. These territories are hereinafter referred to as trust territories.

Article 76

The basic objectives of the trusteeship system, in accordance with the Purposes of the United Nations laid down in Article 1 of the present Charter, shall be:

a. to further international peace and security;

b. to promote the political, economic, social, and educational advancement of the inhabitants of the trust territories, and their progressive development towards self-government or independence as may be appropriate to the particular circumstances of each territory and its peoples and the freely expressed wishes of the peoples concerned, and as may be provided by the terms of each trusteeship agreement;

c. to encourage respect for human rights and for fundamental freedoms for all without distinction as to race, sex, language, or religion, and to encourage recognition of the interdependence of the peoples of the world; . . .

Article 81

The trusteeship agreement shall in each case include the terms under which the trust territory will be administered and designate the authority which will exercise the administration of the trust territory. Such authority, hereinafter called the administering authority, may be one or more states or the Organization itself.

THE INTERNATIONAL COURT OF JUSTICE

Article 92

The International Court of Justice shall be the principal judicial organ of the United Nations. It shall function in accordance with the annexed Statute, which is based upon the Statute of the Permanent Court of International Justice and forms an integral part of the present Charter.

Article 93

1. All Members of the United Nations are *ipso facto* parties to the Statute of the International Court of Justice.

2. A state which is not a Member of the United Nations may become a party to the Statute of the International Court of Justice on condition to be determined in each case by the General Assembly upon the recommendation of the Security Council.

Article 94

1. Each Member of the United Nations undertakes to comply with the decision of the International Court of Justice in any case to which it is a party.

2. If any party to a case fails to perform the obligations incumbent upon it under a judgment rendered by the Court, the other party may have recourse to the Security Council, which may, if it deems necessary, make recommendations or decide upon measures to be taken to give effect to the judgment.

Article 95

Nothing in the present Charter shall prevent Members of the United Nations from entrusting the solution of their differences to other tribunals by virtue of agreements already in existence or which may be concluded in the future.

THE SECRETARIAT

Article 97

The Secretariat shall comprise a Secretary-General and such staff as the Organization may require. The Secretary-General shall be appointed by the General Assembly upon the recommendation of the Security Council. He shall be the chief administrative officer of the Organization.

Article 99

The Secretary-General may bring to the attention of the Security Council any matter which in his opinion may threaten the maintenance of international peace and security.

Article 101

3. The paramount consideration in the employment of the staff and in the determination of the conditions of service shall be the necessity of securing the highest standards of efficiency, competence, and integrity. Due regard shall be paid to the importance of recruiting the staff on as wide a geographical basis as possible.

Declaration of Human Rights

Preamble

Whereas recognition of the inherent dignity and of the equal and inalienable rights of all members of the human family is the foundation of freedom, justice and peace in the world,

Whereas disregard and contempt for human rights have resulted in barbarous acts which have outraged the conscience of mankind, and the advent of a world in which human beings shall enjoy freedom of speech and belief and freedom from fear and want has been proclaimed as the highest aspiration of the common people,

Whereas it is essential, if man is not to be compelled to have recourse, as a last resort, to rebellion against tyranny and oppression, that human rights should be protected by the rule of law,

Whereas it is essential to promote the development of friendly relations between nations,

Whereas the peoples of the United Nations have in the Charter reaffirmed their faith in fundamental human rights, in the dignity and worth of the human person and in the equal rights of men and women and have determined to promote social progress and better standards of life in larger freedom,

Whereas Member States have pledged themselves to achieve, in co-operation with the United Nations, the promotion of universal respect for and observance of human rights and fundamental freedoms,

Whereas a common understanding of these rights and freedoms is of the greatest importance for the full realization of this pledge,

Now, Therefore,
The General Assembly
Proclaims the Universal Declaration of Human Rights as a common standard of achievement for all peoples and all nations, to the end that every individual and every organ of society, keeping this Declaration constantly in mind, shall strive by teaching and education to promote respect for these rights and freedoms and by progressive measures, national and international, to secure their universal and effective recognition and observance, both among the peoples of Member States themselves and among the peoples of territories under their jurisdiction.

Article 1. All human beings are born free and equal in dignity and rights. They are endowed with reason and conscience and should act towards one another in a spirit of brotherhood.

Article 2. Everyone is entitled to all the rights and freedoms set forth in this Declaration without distinction of any kind, such as race, color, sex, language, religion, political or other opinion, national or social origin, property, birth or other status.

Furthermore, no distinction shall be made on the basis of the political, jurisdictional or international status of the country or territory to which a person belongs, whether it be independent, trust, non-self-governing or under any other limitation of sovereignty.

Article 3. Everyone has the right to life, liberty and security of person.

Article 4. No one shall be held in slavery or servitude; slavery and the slave trade shall be prohibited in all their forms.

Article 5. No one shall be subjected to torture or to cruel, inhuman or degrading treatment or punishment.

Article 6. Everyone has the right to recognition everywhere as a person before the law.

Article 7. All are equal before the law and are entitled without any discrimination to equal protection of the law. All are entitled to equal protection against any discrimination in violation of this Declaration and against any incitement to such discrimination.

Article 8. Everyone has the right to an effective remedy by the competent national tribunals for acts violating the fundamental rights granted him by the constitution or by law.

Article 9. No one shall be subjected to arbitrary arrest, detention, or exile.

Article 10. Everyone is entitled in full equality to a fair and public hearing by an independent and impartial tribunal, in the determination of his rights and obligations and of any criminal charge against him.

Article 11.

1. Everyone charged with a penal offense has the right to be presumed innocent until proved guilty according to the law in a public trial at which he has had all the guarantees necessary for his defense.

2. No one shall be held guilty of any penal offense on account of any act or omission which did not constitute a penal offense, under national or international law, at the time when it was committed. Nor shall a heavier penalty be imposed than the one that was applicable at the time the penal offense was committed.

Article 12. No one shall be subjected to arbitrary interference with his privacy, family, home or correspondence nor to attacks upon his honor and reputation.

Everyone has the right to the protection of the law against such interference or attacks.

Article 13

1. Everyone has the right to freedom of movement and residence within the borders of each state.

2. Everyone has the right to leave any country, including his own, and to return to his country.

Article 14

1. Everyone has the right to seek and to enjoy in other countries asylum from persecution.

2. This right may not be invoked in the case of prosecutions genuinely arising from non-political crimes or from acts contrary to the purposes and principles of the United Nations.

Article 15.

1. Everyone has the right to a nationality.

2. No one shall be arbitrarily deprived of his nationality nor denied the right to change his nationality.

Article 16

1. Men and women of full age, without limitation due to race, nationality or religion, have the right to marry and to found a family. They are entitled to equal rights as to marriage, during marriage and at its dissolution.

2. Marriage shall be entered into only with the free and full consent of the intending spouses.

3. The family is the natural and fundamental group unit of society and is entitled to protection by society and the state.

Article 17

1. Everyone has the right to own property alone as well as in association with others.

2. No one shall be arbitrarily deprived of his property.

Article 18. Everyone has the right to freedom of thought, conscience and religion; this right includes freedom to change his religion or belief, and freedom, either alone or in community with others and in public or private, to manifest his religion or belief in teaching, practice, worship and observance.

Article 19. Everyone has the right to freedom of opinion and expression; this right includes freedom to hold opinions without interference and to seek, receive and impart information and ideas through any media and regardless of frontiers.

Article 20

1. Everyone has the right to freedom of peaceful assembly and association.

2. No one may be compelled to belong to an association.

Article 21.

1. Everyone has the right to take part in the government of his country, directly or through freely chosen representatives.

2. Everyone has the right of equal access to public service in his country.

3. The will of the people shall be the basis of the authority of government; this will shall be expressed in periodic and genuine elections which shall be by universal and equal suffrage and shall be held by secret vote or by equivalent free voting procedures.

Article 22. Everyone, as a member of society, has the right to social security and is entitled to realization, through national effort and international cooperation and in accordance with the organization and resources of each state, of the economic, social and cultural rights indispensable for his dignity and the free development of his personality.

Article 23.

1. Everyone has the right to work, to free choice of employment, to just and favorable conditions of work and to protection against unemployment.

2. Everyone, without any discrimination, has the right to equal pay for equal work.

3. Everyone who works has the right to just and favorable remuneration ensuring for himself and his family an existence worthy of human dignity, and supplemented, if necessary, by other means of social protection.

4. Everyone has the right to form and to join trade unions for the protection of his interests.

Article 24. Everyone has the right to rest and leisure, including reasonable limitation of working hours and periodic holidays with pay.

Article 25.

1. Everyone has the right to a standard of living adequate for the health and well-being of himself and of his family, including food, clothing, housing and medical care and necessary social services, and the right to security in the event of unemployment, sickness, disability, widowhood, old age or other lack of livelihood in circumstances beyond his control.

2. Motherhood and childhood are entitled to special care and assistance. All children, whether born in or out of wedlock, shall enjoy the same social protection.

Article 26.

1. Everyone has the right to education. Education shall be free, at least in the elementary and fundamental stages. Elementary education shall be compulsory. Technical and professional education shall be made generally available and higher education shall be made equally accessible to all on the basis of merit.

2. Education shall be directed to the full development of the human personality and to the strengthening of respect for human rights and fundamental freedoms. It shall promote understanding, tolerance and friendship among all nations, racial or religious groups, and shall further the activities of the United Nations for the maintenance of peace.

3. Parents have a prior right to choose the kind of education that shall be given to their children.

Article 27.

1. Everyone has the right freely to participate in the cultural life of the community, to enjoy the arts and to share in scientific advancement and its benefits.

2. Everyone has the right to the protection of the moral and material interests resulting from any scientific, literary, or artistic production of which he is the author.

Article 28. Everyone is entitled to a social and international order in which the rights and freedoms set forth in this Declaration can be fully realized.

Article 29.

1. Everyone has duties to the community, in which alone the free and full development of his personality is possible.

2. In the exercise of his rights and freedoms, everyone shall be subject only to such limitations as are determined by law solely for the purpose of securing due recognition and respect for the rights and freedoms of others and of meeting the just requirements of morality, public order and the general welfare in a democratic society.

3. These rights and freedoms may in no case be exercised contrary to the purposes and principles of the United Nations.

Article 30. Nothing in this Declaration may be interpreted as implying for any state, group or person any right to engage in any activity or to perform any act aimed at the destruction of any of the rights and freedoms set forth herein.

CHOOSE THE CORRECT ANSWER

Write the letter that best completes the statement or answers the question.

1. The veto can prevent action in (*a*) the General Assembly, (*b*) the Security Council, (*c*) the Secretariat, (*d*) all parts of the UN. 1._____

2. The members of the United Nations promised not to (*a*) vote in blocs, (*b*) use force in international affairs, (*c*) vote against the majority, (*d*) follow the ideas of communism. 2._____

3. The organ of the United Nations with the chief responsibility to prevent wars is (*a*) the Secretariat, (*b*) the General Assembly, (*c*) the Social and Economic Council, (*d*) the Security Council. 3._____

4. A trust territory is one which is (*a*) being prepared for independence, (*b*) under the permanent control of another nation, (*c*) unable to educate its own people, (*d*) too deeply in debt to be independent. 4._____

5. The International Court of Justice makes decisions which the members of the United Nations (*a*) agree to enforce, (*b*) agree to discuss, but without any promise to accept them, (*c*) agree to accept if they are parties to the issue that has been decided, (*d*) may ignore whenever they wish. 5._____

6. The part of the United Nations which works most closely with the specialized agencies is (*a*) the Security Council, (*b*) the Social and Economic Council, (*c*) the International Court of Justice, (*d*) the Military Staff Committee. 6._____

7. The Secretariat employs people from (*a*) all countries, (*b*) only democratic countries, (*c*) any country where English is spoken, (*d*) only the "Big Five" countries.

8. The Declaration of Human Rights states that everyone has the right to all of the following *except* (*a*) equal protection of the law, (*b*) social security, (*c*) a college education, (*d*) privacy.   8._____

9. According to the United Nations Charter human rights should be protected by (*a*) force, (*b*) law, (*c*) the Church, (*d*) a special committee on human rights.   9._____

10. According to the Declaration of Human Rights all human beings are endowed with (*a*) intelligence and emotion, (*b*) responsibility and freedom of choice, (*c*) reason and conscience, (*d*) original sin and guilt.   10._____

THOUGHT QUESTIONS

1. List the four chief aims of the United Nations, and explain how it is organized to achieve each of the selected aims.

2. Explain one special problem facing each of the six chief organs of the United Nations and discuss how it can be resolved.

3. Explain why you agree or disagree with the statement that "Regional organizations are as important as the United Nations today, and have brought more important changes to the world."

The North Atlantic Treaty 1949

* * * * *It was hoped that the United Nations* would solve the outstanding problems after World War II. But when it became clear that the Soviet Union was spreading its ideology, the United States saw that it would have to rebuild and defend Europe.

In March, 1947, the Truman Doctrine provided aid to Greece and Turkey to crush Communist-inspired internal revolts. In the next few years, under the Marshall Plan, the United States spent more than 14 billion dollars to rebuild the war-torn industries of Europe's democracies. In 1949, President Truman added the Point Four Program, through which special technical assistance was made available to nations requesting it.

Meanwhile, Russian expansion continued. Czechoslovakia became a puppet state in 1948, and Russian troops remained in the satellite nations. With

Russian assistance, the Chinese Communists took over China. Western and Russian forces were ready to clash over access routes to Berlin. For the next eleven months the United States and Britain, in the famous airlift, flew in all necessary supplies to keep Berlin free.

The United States then decided to join in the active defense of Western Europe and, in April, 1949, the North Atlantic Treaty Organization was created. NATO extended to the countries of Europe the kind of defense agreement made by the Organization of American States in Latin America.

PREAMBLE. The parties to this treaty reaffirm their faith in the purposes and principles of the Charter of the United Nations and their desire to live in peace with all peoples and all governments.

They are determined to safeguard the freedom, common heritage and civilization of their peoples, founded on the principles of democracy, individual liberty and the rule of law.

They seek to promote stability and well-being in the North Atlantic area.

They are resolved to unite their efforts for collective defense and for the preservation of peace and security.

They therefore agree to this North Atlantic Treaty:

Article 1. The parties undertake, as set forth in the Charter of the United Nations, to settle any international disputes in which they may be involved by peaceful means in such a manner that international peace and security, and justice, are not endangered, and to refrain in their international relations from the threat or use of force in any manner inconsistent with the purposes of the United Nations.

Article 2. The parties will contribute toward the further development of peaceful and friendly international relations by strengthening their free institutions, by bringing about a better understanding of the principles upon which these

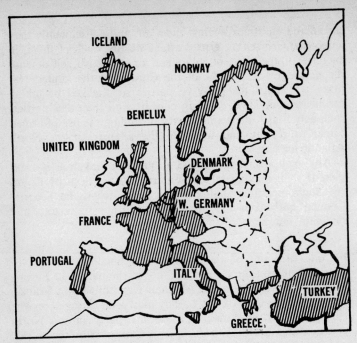

ICELAND

NORWAY

BENELUX

UNITED KINGDOM

DENMARK

W. GERMANY

FRANCE

PORTUGAL

ITALY

TURKEY

GREECE

MEMBERS OF NATO

institutions are founded, and by promoting conditions of stability and well-being. They will seek to eliminate conflict in their international economic policies and will encourage economic collaboration between any or all of them.

Article 3. In order more effectively to achieve the objectives of this treaty, the parties, separately and jointly, by means of continuous and effective self-help and mutual aid, will maintain and develop their individual and collective capacity to resist armed attack.

Article 4. The parties will consult together whenever, in the opinion of any of them, the territorial integrity, political independence or security of any of the parties is threatened.

Article 5. The parties agree that an armed attack against one or more of them in Europe or North America shall be considered an attack against them all; and consequently they agree that, if such an armed attack occurs, each of them, in exercise of the right of individual or collective self-defense recognized by Article 51 of the Charter of the United Nations, will assist the party or parties so attacked by taking forthwith, individually and in concert with the other parties, such action as it deems necessary, including the use of armed force, to restore and maintain the security of the North Atlantic area.

Any such armed attack and all measures taken as a result thereof shall immediately be reported to the Security Council. Such measures shall be terminated when the Security Council has taken the measures necessary to restore and maintain international peace and security.

Article 6. For the purpose of Article 5 an armed attack on one or more of the parties is deemed to include an armed attack on the territory of any of the parties in Europe or North America, on the Algerian Departments of France, on the occupation forces of any party in Europe, on the islands under the jurisdiction of any party in the North Atlantic area north of the Tropic of Cancer or on the vessels or aircraft in this area of any of the parties.

Article 7. This treaty does not affect, and shall not be interpreted as affecting, in any way the rights and obligations under the Charter of the parties which are members of the United Nations, or the primary responsibility of the Security Council for the maintenance of international peace and security.

Article 8. Each party declares that none of the international engagements now in force between it and any other of the parties or any third state is in conflict with the provisions of this treaty, and undertakes not to enter into any international engagement in conflict with this treaty.

Article 9. The parties hereby establish a Council, on which each of them shall be represented, to consider matters concerning the implementation of this treaty. The Council shall be so organized as to be able to meet promptly at any time. The Council shall set up such subsidiary bodies as may be necessary; in particular it shall establish immediately a defense committee which shall recommend measures for the implementation of Articles 3 and 5.

Article 10. The parties may, by unanimous agreement, invite any other European state in a position to further the principles of this treaty and to contribute to the security of the North Atlantic area to accede to this treaty. Any state so invited may become a party to the treaty by depositing its instrument of accession with the Government of the United States of America. The Government of the United States of America will inform each of the parties of the deposit of each such instrument of accession.

Article 11. This treaty shall be ratified and its provisions carried out by the parties in accordance with their respective constitutional processes. The instruments of ratification shall be deposited as soon as possible with the Government of the United States of America, which will notify all the other signatories of each deposit. The treaty shall enter into force between the states which have ratified it as soon as the ratifications of the majority of the signatories, including the ratifications of Belgium, Canada, France, Luxembourg, the Netherlands, the United Kingdom and the United States, have been deposited and shall come into effect with respect to other states on the date of the deposit of their ratifications.

Article 12. After the treaty has been in force for ten years, or at any time thereafter, the parties shall, if any of them so requests, consult together for the purpose of reviewing the treaty, having regard for the factors then affecting peace and security in the North Atlantic area, including the development of universal as well as regional arrangements under the Charter of the United Nations for the maintenance of international peace and security.

Article 13. After the treaty has been in force for twenty years, any party may cease to be a party one year after its notice of denunciation has been given to the Government of the United States of America, which will inform the Governments of the other parties of the deposit of each notice of denunciation.

Article 14. This treaty, of which the English and French texts are equally authentic, shall be deposited in the archives of the Government of the United States of America. Duly certified copies thereof will be transmitted by that Government to the Governments of the other signatories.

FILL IN THE ANSWERS

Write the word or phrase which best completes the statement.

1. The non-European countries in NATO are _____ and _____.

2. The two members of NATO which were formerly enemies of the other members are _____ and _____.

3. The man who led NATO, and later became President of the United States, was _____.

4. The international organization which the NATO powers agree to support is _____.

5. The NATO members agreed to review their treaty after a period of _____.

6. The most powerful nation in NATO is _____.

7. The group within NATO which serves as its governing body is called the _____.

8. NATO is a defense organization directed against aggression by the _____.

9. The headquarters of NATO have been established in the city of _____.

10. The number of times NATO has had to go to war to halt aggression against its members is _____.

THOUGHT QUESTIONS

1. Describe the actions that would be taken by the members of NATO when any one of them was threatened by aggression from a non-member.

2. What problems have been created by the membership of West Germany in NATO?

The Immigration Law 1952

* * * * *In early years millions of people* emigrated to the United States without any serious restrictions. Limitations were put on the immigration of the Chinese and other Orientals in 1902. In 1924 and 1927, a quota system based on national origins was adopted. People from each foreign country could come in stated numbers to the United States to keep the same percentage of different foreigners as lived here in 1890.

The immigration laws were widely attacked as discriminating against those groups from southern and eastern Europe which emigrated to the United States in large numbers between 1890 and 1924. Instead, countries such as England and Germany, large numbers of whose people do not wish to emigrate, were permitted the largest quotas.

These excerpts from the 1952 law illustrate the immigration rules in effect today. Significant restrictions apply to members of Communist organizations.

Section 201. (a) The annual quota of any quota area shall be one-sixth of 1 per centum of the number of inhabitants in the continental United States in 1920, which number, except for the purpose of computing quotas for quota areas within the Asia-Pacific triangle, shall be the same number heretofore determined under the provisions of section 11 of the Immigration Act of 1924, attributable by national origin to such quota area: *Provided,* That the quota existing for Chinese persons prior to the date of enactment of this Act shall be continued, and, except as otherwise provided in section 202 (e), the minimum quota for any quota area shall be one hundred.

Allocation of Immigrant Visas Within Quotas

Section 203. (a) Immigrant visas to quota immigrants shall be allotted in each fiscal year as follows:

(1) The first 50 per centum of the quota of each quota area for such year, plus any portion of such quota not required for the issuance of immigrant visas to the classes specified in paragraphs (2) and (3), shall be made available for the issuance of immigrant visas (A) to qualified quota immigrants whose services are determined by the Attorney General to be needed urgently in the United States because of the high education, technical training, specialized experience, or exceptional ability of such immigrants and to be substantially beneficial prospectively to the national economy, cultural interests, or welfare of the United States, and (B) to qualified quota immigrants who are the spouse or children of any immigrant described in clause (A) if accompanying him.

(2) The next 30 per centum of the quota for each quota area for such year, plus any portion of such quota not required for the issuance of immigrant visas to the classes specified in paragraphs (1) and (3), shall be made available for the issuance of immigrant visas to qualified quota immigrants who are the parents of citizens of the United States, such citizens being at least twenty-one years of age.

(3) The remaining 20 per centum of the quota for each quota area for such year, plus any portion of such quota not required for the issuance of immigrant visas to the classes specified in paragraphs (1) and (2), shall be made available for the issuance of immigrant visas to qualified quota immi-

grants who are the spouses or the children of aliens lawfully admitted for permanent residence.

(4) Any portion of the quota for each quota area for such year not required for the issuance of immigrant visas to the classes specified in paragraphs (1), (2), and (3) shall be made available for the issuance of immigrant visas to other qualified quota immigrants chargeable to such quota. Qualified quota immigrants of each quota area who are the brothers, sisters, sons, or daughters of citizens of the United States shall be entitled to a preference of not exceeding 25 per centum of the immigrant visas available for issuance for each quota area under this paragraph.

Unused Quota Immigrant Visas

Section 207. If a quota immigrant having an immigrant visa is excluded from admission to the United States and deported, or does not apply for admission to the United States before the expiration of the validity of the immigrant visa, or if an alien having an immigrant visa issued to him as a quota immigrant is found not to be a quota immigrant, no immigrant visa shall be issued in lieu thereof to any other immigrant.

General Classes of Deportable Aliens

Section 241. (a) Any alien in the United States (including an alien crewman) shall, upon the order of the Attorney General, be deported who—

(1) At the time of entry was within one or more of the classes of aliens excludable by the law existing at the time of such entry;

(2) entered the United States without inspection or at any time or place other than as designated by the Attorney General or is in the United States in violation of this Act or in violation of any other law of the United States;

(3) hereafter, within five years after entry, becomes institutionalized at public expense because of mental disease, defect, or deficiency, unless the alien can show that such disease, defect, or deficiency did not exist prior to his admission to the United States; . . .

(6) is or at any time has been, after entry, a member of any of the following classes of aliens:

(A) Aliens who are anarchists;

(B) Aliens who advocate or teach, or who are members of or affiliated with any organization that advocates or teaches, opposition to all organized government;

(C) Aliens who are members of or affiliated with (i) the Communist Party of the United States; (ii) any other totalitarian party of the United States; (iii) the Communist Political Association; (iv) the Communist or any other totalitarian party of any State of the United States, of any foreign state, or of any political or geographical subdivision of any foreign state; (v) any section, subsidiary, branch, affiliate, or subdivision of any such association or party; or (vi) the direct predecessors or successors of any such association or party, regardless of what name such group or organization may have used, may now bear, or may hereafter adopt: *Provided,* That nothing in this paragraph, or in any other provision of this Act, shall be construed as declaring that the Communist Party does not advocate the overthrow of the Government of the United States by force, violence, or other unconstitutional means;

(D) Aliens not within any of the other provisions of this paragraph who advocate the economic, international, and governmental doctrines of world communism or the establishment in the United States of a totalitarian dictatorship, or who are members of or affiliated with any organization that advocates the economic, international, and governmental doctrines of world communism or the establishment in the United States of a totalitarian dictatorship, either through its own utterances or through any written or printed publications issued or published by or with the permission or consent of or under the authority of such organization or paid for by the funds of, or funds furnished by, such organization;

Notices of Change of Address

Section 265. Every alien required to be registered under this title, or who was required to be registered under the Alien Registration Act, 1940, as amended, who is within the United States on the first day of January following the effective date of this Act, or on the first day of January of each succeeding year shall, within thirty days following such dates, notify the Attorney General in writing of his current address and furnish such additional information as may by regulations be required by the Attorney General. Any such alien shall likewise notify the Attorney General in writing of each change of address and new address within ten days from the date of such change. Any such alien who is temporarily absent from the United States on the first day of January following the effective date of this Act, or on the first day of January of any succeeding year shall furnish his current address and other information as required by this section within ten days after his return. Any such alien in the United States in a lawful temporary residence status shall in like manner also notify the Attorney General in writing of his address at the expiration of each three-month period during which he remains in the United States, regardless of whether there has been any change of address. In the case of an alien for whom a parent or legal guardian is required to apply for registration, the notice required by this section shall be given by such parent or legal guardian.

Penalties

Section 312. No person except as otherwise provided in this title shall hereafter be naturalized as a citizen of the United States upon his own petition who cannot demonstrate—

(1) an understanding of the English language, including an ability to read, write, and speak words in ordinary usage in the English language: *Provided,* That this requirement shall not apply to any person physically unable to comply therewith, if otherwise qualified to be naturalized, or to any person who, on the effective date of this Act, is over fifty years of age and has been living in the United States for periods totaling at least twenty years: *Provided further,* That the requirements of this section relating to ability to read and write shall be met if the applicant can read or write simple words and phrases to the end that a reasonable test of his literacy shall be made and that no extraordinary or unreasonable condition shall be imposed upon the applicant; and

(2) a knowledge and understanding of the fundamentals of the history, and of the principles and form of government, of the United States.

Section 328. (a) A person who has served honorably at any time in the armed forces of the United States for a period or periods aggregating three years, and who, if separated from such service, was never separated except under honorable conditions, may be naturalized without having resided, continuously immediately preceding the date of filing such person's petition, in the United States for at least five years, and in the State in which the petition for naturalization is filed for at least six months, and without having been physically present in the United States for any specified period, if such petition is filed while the petitioner is still in the service or within six months after the termination of such service.

TRUE OR FALSE?

Write T *if the statement is correct; write* F *if it is false.*

_____1. Any unused numbers of quota visas may be used in the next year.

_____2. Immigrants to the United States must pass a physical examination.

_____3. Foreign visitors to the United States must be approved in advance.

_____4. An alien who serves three years in the armed services of the United States becomes eligible for citizenship outside of any quota.

_____5. An alien is one who was born in another country, but who later learned English.

_____6. The chief requirement for naturalization is the ability to read and write English.

_____7. All aliens must register their address once a year.

_____8. Communists who promise to support the Constitution may become citizens.

_____9. An alien who is not a Communist, but who is opposed to organized government, may be forced to leave the United States.

_____10. An alien who wants to set up a dictatorship in the United States cannot be deported, for he is protected by the Bill of Rights.

THOUGHT QUESTIONS

1. How have immigrants to the United States since the Civil War contributed to the growth and development of our country?
2. Explain why the immigration law provides for the barring of:
   a. People with certain political beliefs;
   b. People with certain disabilities.

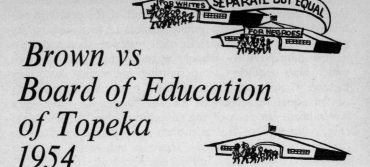

Brown vs Board of Education of Topeka 1954

* * * * *The United States Supreme Court in* its decision in the case of *Plessy vs Ferguson, 1896,* held that the Fourteenth Amendment, in demanding equal protection for all, under the laws did not require that the same treatment be given to all. Instead, the Court held that "separate but equal accommodations" were permitted.

This decision was one of the legal bases for discrimination against Negroes in the South. The "separate but equal" doctrine was used over the years to justify separate school systems for whites and Negroes.

In 1954 a number of cases dealing with segregation in the public schools were argued before the Supreme Court. In the case of *Brown vs Board of Education of Topeka, 1954,* the Court unanimously supported the decision by Chief Justice Warren that the segregation of Negro children in schools was a violation of the equal protection clause of the Fourteenth Amendment, and that all states must end such separation.

WARREN, C. J., These cases come to us from the States of Kansas, South Carolina, Virginia, and Delaware. They are premised on different facts and different local conditions, but a common legal question justifies their consideration together in this consolidated opinion.

In each of the cases, minors of the Negro race, through their legal representatives, seek the aid of the courts in obtaining admission to the public schools of their community on a nonsegregated basis. In each instance, they had been denied admission to schools attended by white children under laws requiring or permitting segregation according to race. This segregation was alleged to deprive the plaintiffs of the equal protection of the laws under the Fourteenth Amendment. In each of the cases other than the Delaware case, a three-judge federal district court denied relief to the plaintiffs on the so-called "separate but equal" doctrine announced by this Court in *Plessy* v. *Ferguson,* 163 U.S. 537. Under that doctrine, equality of treatment is accorded when the races are provided substantially equal facilities, even though these facilities be separate. In the Delaware case, the Supreme Court of Delaware adhered to that doctrine, but ordered that the plaintiffs be admitted to the white schools because of their superiority to the Negro schools.

The plaintiffs contend that segregated public schools are not "equal" and cannot be made "equal," and that hence they are deprived of the equal protection of the laws. Because of the obvious importance of the question presented, the Court took jurisdiction. Argument was heard in the 1952 Term, and reargument was heard this Term on certain questions propounded by the Court.

Reargument was largely devoted to the circumstances surrounding the adoption of the Fourteenth Amendment in 1868. It covered exhaustively consideration of the Amendment in Congress, ratification by the states, then existing practices in racial segregation, and the views of proponents and opponents of the Amendment. This discussion and our own investigation convince us that, although these sources cast some light, it is not enough to resolve the problem with which we are faced. At best, they are inconclusive. The most avid proponents of the post-War Amendments undoubtedly intended them to remove all legal distinctions among "all persons born or naturalized in the United States." Their opponents, just as certainly, were antagonistic to both the letter and the spirit of the Amendments and wished them to have the most limited effect. What others in Congress and the state legislatures had in mind cannot be determined with any degree of certainty.

An additional reason for the inconclusive nature of the Amendment's history, with respect to segregated schools, is the status of public education at that time. In the South, the movement toward free common schools, supported by general taxation, had not yet taken hold. Education of white children was largely in the hands of private groups. Education of Negroes was almost non-existent, and practically all of the race were illiterate. In fact, any education of Negroes was forbidden by law in some states. Today, in contrast, many Negroes have achieved outstanding success in the arts and sciences as well as in the business and professional world. It is true that public school education at the time of the Amendment had advanced further in the North, but the effect of the Amendment on Northern States was generally ignored in the congressional debates. Even in the North, the conditions of public education did not approximate those existing today. The curriculum was usually rudimentary; ungraded schools were common in rural areas; the school term was but three months a year in many states; and compulsory school attendance was virtually unknown. As a consequence, it is not surprising that there should be so little in the history of the Fourteenth Amendment relating to its intended effect on public education.

In the first cases in this Court construing the Fourteenth Amendment, decided shortly after its adoption, the Court interpreted it as proscribing all state-imposed discriminations against the Negro race. The doctrine of "separate but equal" did not make its appearance in this Court until 1896 in the case of *Plessy* v. *Ferguson, supra,* involving not education but transportation. American courts have since labored with the doctrine for over half a century. In this Court, there have been six cases involving the "separate but equal" doctrine in the field of public education. In *Cumming* v. *County Board of Education,* 175 U. S. 528, and *Gong Lum* v. *Rice,* 275 U.S. 78, the validity of the doctrine itself was not challenged. In more recent cases, all on the graduate school level, inequality was found in that specific benefits enjoyed by white students were denied to Negro students of the same educational qualifications. *Missouri ex rel. Gaines* v. *Canada,* 305 U. S. 337; *Sipuel* v. *Oklahoma,* 332 U.S. 631; *Sweatt* v. *Painter,* 339 U.S. 629; *McLaurin* v. *Oklahoma State Regents,* 339 U.S. 637. In none of these cases was it necessary to re-examine the doctrine to grant relief to the Negro plaintiff. And in *Sweatt* v. *Painter, supra,* the Court expressly reserved decision on the question whether *Plessy* v. *Ferguson* should be held inapplicable to public education.

In the instant cases, that question is directly presented. Here, unlike *Sweatt* v. *Painter,* there are findings below that the Negro and white schools involved have been equalized, or are being equalized, with respect to buildings, curricula, qualifications and salaries of teachers, and other "tangible" factors. Our decision, therefore, cannot turn on merely a comparison of these tangible factors in the Negro and white schools involved in each of the cases. We must look instead to the effect of segregation itself on public education.

In approaching this problem, we cannot turn the clock back to 1868 when the Amendment was adopted, or even to 1896 when *Plessy* v. *Ferguson* was written. We must consider public education in the light of its full development and its present place in American life throughout the Nation. Only in this way can it be determined if segregation in public schools deprives these plaintiffs of the equal protection of the laws.

Today, education is perhaps the most important function of state and local governments. Compulsory school attendance laws and the great expenditures for education both demonstrate our recognition of the importance of education to our democratic society. It is required in the performance of our most basic public responsibilities, even service in the armed forces. It is the very foundation of good citizenship. Today it is a principal instrument in awakening the child to cultural values, in preparing him for later professional training, and in helping him to adjust normally to his environment. In these days, it is doubtful that any child may reasonably be expected to succeed in life if he is denied the opportunity of an education. Such an opportunity, where the state has undertaken to provide it, is a right which must be made available to all on equal terms.

We come then to the question presented: Does segregation of children in public schools solely on the basis of race, even though the physical facilities and other "tangible" factors may be equal, deprive the children of the minority group of equal educational opportunities? We believe that it does.

In *Sweatt* v. *Painter, supra,* in finding that a segregated law school for Negroes could not provide them equal educational opportunities, this Court relied in large part on "those equalities which are incapable of objective measurement but which make for greatness in a law school." In *McLaurin* v. *Oklahoma State Regents, supra,* the Court, in requiring that a Negro admitted to a white graduate school be treated like all other students, again resorted to intangible considerations: ". . . his ability to study, to engage in discussions and exchange views with other students, and, in general, to learn his profession." Such considerations apply with added force to children in grade and high schools. To separate them from others of similar age and qualifications solely because of their race generates a feeling of inferiority as to their status in the community that may affect their hearts and minds in a way unlikely ever to be undone. The effect of this separation on their educational opportunities was well stated by a finding in the Kansas case by a court which nevertheless felt compelled to rule against the Negro plaintiffs:

"Segregation of white and colored children in public schools has a detrimental effect upon the colored children. The impact is greater when it has the sanction of the law; for the policy of separating the races is usually interpreted as denoting the inferiority of the Negro group. A sense of inferiority affects the motivation of a child to learn. Segregation with the sanction of law, therefore has a tendency to retard the educational and mental development of Negro children and to deprive them of some of the benefits they would receive in a racially integrated school system."

Whatever may have been the extent of psychological knowledge at the time of *Plessy* v. *Ferguson,* this finding is amply supported by modern authority. Any language in *Plessy* v. *Ferguson* contrary to this finding is rejected. We conclude that in the field of public education the doctrine of "separate but equal" has no place. Separate educational facilities are inherently unequal. Therefore, we hold that the plaintiffs and others similarly situated for whom the actions have been brought are, by reason of the segregation complained of, deprived of the equal protection of the laws guaranteed by the Fourteenth Amendment. This disposition makes unnecessary any discussion whether such segregation also violates the Due Process Clause of the Fourteenth Amendment.

Because these are class actions, because of the wide applicability of this decision, and because of the great variety of local conditions, the formulation of decrees in these cases presents problems of considerable complexity. On reargument, the consideration of appropriate relief was necessarily subordinated to the primary question—the constitutionality of segregation in public education. We have now announced that such segregation is a denial of the equal protection of the laws. In order that we may have the full assistance of the parties in formulating decrees, the cases will be restored to the docket, and the parties are requested to present further argument on Questions 4 and 5 [dealing with detailed implementation of the decision] previously propounded by the Court for the reargument of this Term.

TRUE OR FALSE?

Write T if the statement is correct; write F if it is false.

_____1. The Supreme Court decision in the desegregation case was by a 5-4 vote.

_____2. All of our states have taken steps to carry out the decision.

_____3. The Court held that "separate but equal" facilities were not enough to satisfy the requirements of the Fourteenth Amendment.

_____4. The Court held that the fact that Negro schools might be as good as white schools could not enter into its decision.

_____5. The Court gave all segregated school systems one year to merge with one another.

_____6. In some cases, federal troops have been needed to enforce desegregation.

_____7. In earlier cases, the Court had already decided that Negroes should be admitted to graduate schools on an equal basis with white students.

_____8. The Court held that it made children in Negro schools feel inferior just to be in such schools.

_____9. The Court also held that private schools could not be segregated.

_____10. All of the segregation cases came to the Supreme Court from the state of Kansas.

THOUGHT QUESTIONS

1. Explain with specific references to places and events how at least three Southern states have reacted to the desegregation decision.

2. Identify each of the following: (*a*) integration, (*b*) Freedom Riders (*c*) White Citizens Councils (*d*) NAACP (*e*) Little Rock incident (*f*) Meredith Case (*g*) sit-in demonstrations (*h*) March on Washington.

3. In what ways did the Supreme Court decision in *Brown* v. *Board of Education of Topeka* affect the world position of the United States?

John F. Kennedy's Inaugural Address 1961

*   *   *   *   *An inaugural address permits a new* President to present his evaluation of the state of the nation and the world. It also serves to make known the plans he hopes to carry through in his administration.

When John F. Kennedy was inaugurated, the Cold War was still a world problem. The new states of Asia and Africa were torn between the desire for neutrality and the need for the economic assistance of the more advanced nations. The domestic problems of desegregation and economic growth remained unsolved. The nuclear race with Russia was going on unchecked by any true agreement on disarmament. President Kennedy dealt with these problems in his address, launching what he called "The New Frontier."

Mr. Chief Justice, President Eisenhower, Vice President Nixon, President Truman, reverend clergy, fellow citizens, we observe today not a victory of party, but a celebration of freedom—symbolizing an end, as well as a beginning—signifying renewal, as well as change. For I have sworn before you and Almighty God the same solemn oath our forebears prescribed nearly a century and three quarters ago.

The world is very different now. For man holds in his mortal hands the power to abolish all forms of human poverty and all forms of human life. And yet the same revolutionary beliefs for which our forebears fought are still at issue around the globe—the belief that the rights of man come not from the generosity of the state, but from the hand of God.

We dare not forget today that we are the heirs of that first revolution. Let the word go forth from this time and place, to friend and foe alike, that the torch has been passed to a new generation of Americans—born in this century, tempered by war, disciplined by a hard and bitter peace, proud of our ancient heritage—and unwilling to witness or permit the slow undoing of those human rights to which this Nation has always been committed, and to which we are committed today at home and around the world.

Let every nation know, whether it wishes us well or ill, that we shall pay any price, bear any burden, meet any hardship, support any friend, oppose any foe, in order to assure the survival and the success of liberty.

This much we pledge—and more.

To those old allies whose cultural and spiritual origins we share, we pledge the loyalty of faithful friends. United, there is little we cannot do in a host of cooperative ventures. Divided, there is little we can do—for we dare not meet a powerful challenge at odds and split asunder.

To those new States whom we welcome to the ranks of the free, we pledge our words that one form of colonial control shall not have passed away merely to be replaced by a far greater iron tyranny. We shall not always expect to find them supporting our view. But we shall always hope to find them strongly supporting their own freedom—and to remember that, in the past, those who foolishly sought power by riding the back of the tiger ended up inside.

To those peoples in the huts and villages across the globe struggling to break the bonds of mass misery, we pledge our best efforts to help them help themselves, for whatever period is required—not because the Communists may be doing it, not because we seek their votes, but because it is right. If a free society cannot help the many who are poor, it cannot save the few who are rich.

To our sister republics south of our border, we offer a special pledge—to convert our good words into good deeds, in a new alliance for progress, to assist free men and free governments in casting off the chains of poverty. But this peaceful revolution of hope cannot become the prey of hostile powers. Let all our neighbors know that we shall join with them to oppose aggression or subversion anywhere in the Americas. And let every other power know that this hemisphere intends to remain the master of its own house.

To that world assembly of sovereign states, the United Nations, our last best hope in an age where the instruments of war have far outpaced the instruments of peace, we renew our pledge of support—to prevent it from becoming merely a forum for invective—to strengthen its shield of the new and the weak—and to enlarge the area in which its writ may run.

Finally, to those nations who would make themselves our adversary, we offer not a pledge but a request: that both sides begin anew the quest for peace, before the dark powers of destruction unleashed by science engulf all humanity in planned or accidental self-destruction.

We dare not tempt them with weakness. For only when our arms are sufficient beyond doubt can we be certain beyond doubt that they will never be employed.

But neither can two great and powerful groups of nations take comfort from our present course—both sides overburdened by the cost of modern weapons, both rightly alarmed by the steady spread of the deadly atom, yet both racing to alter that uncertain balance of terror that stays the hand of mankind's final war.

So let us begin anew—remembering on both sides that civility is not a sign of weakness, and sincerity is always subject to proof. *Let us never negotiate out of fear. But let us never fear to negotiate.*

Let both sides explore what problems unite us instead of laboring those problems which divide us.

Let both sides, for the first time, formulate serious and precise proposals for the inspection and control of arms—and bring the absolute power to destroy other nations under the absolute control of all nations.

Let both sides seek to invoke the wonders of science instead of its terrors. Together let us explore the stars, conquer the deserts, eradicate disease, tap the ocean depths, and encourage the arts and commerce.

Let both sides unite to heed in all corners of the earth the command of Isaiah—to "undo the heavy burdens and to let the oppressed go free."

And if a beachhead of cooperation may push back the jungle of suspicion, let both sides join in creating a new endeavor, not a new balance of power, but a new world of law, where the strong are just and the weak secure and the peace preserved.

All this will not be finished in the first 100 days. Nor will it be finished in the first 1,000 days, nor in the life of this administration, nor even perhaps in our lifetime on this planet. But let us begin.

In your hands, my fellow citizens, more than in mine, will rest the final success or failure of our course. Since this country was founded, each generation of Americans has been summoned to give testimony to its national loyalty. The graves of young Americans who answered the call to service are found around the globe.

Now the trumpet summons us again—not as a call to bear arms, though arms we need; not as a call to battle, though embattled we are; but a call to bear the burden of a long twilight struggle, year in, and year out, "rejoicing in hope, patient in tribulation"—a struggle against the common enemies of man: tyranny, poverty, disease, and war itself.

Can we forge against these enemies a grand and global alliance, North and South, East and West, that can assure a more fruitful life for all mankind? Will you join in that historic effort?

In the long history of the world, only a few generations have been granted the role of defending freedom in its hour of maximum danger. I do not shrink from this responsibility

—I welcome it. I do not believe that any of us would exchange places with any other people or any other generation. The energy, the faith, the devotion which we bring to this endeavor will light our country and all who serve it—and the glow from that fire can truly light the world.

And so, my fellow Americans, ask not what your country can do for you: Ask what you can do for your country.

My fellow citizens of the world: Ask not what America will do for you, but what together we can do for the freedom of man.

Finally, whether you are citizens of America or citizens of the world, ask of us the same high standards of strength and sacrifice which we ask of you. With a good conscience our only sure reward, with history the final judge of our deeds, let us go forth to lead the land we love, asking His blessing and His help, but knowing that here on earth God's work must truly be our own.

CHOOSE THE CORRECT ANSWER

Write the letter that best completes the statement or answers the question.

1. To John F. Kennedy, the world's great goal was (*a*) the freedom of all men, (*b*) free trade to build up all countries, (*c*) the conquest of space, (*d*) achieving peace in the next 100 days.

   1._____

2. President Kennedy promised to support (*a*) the United Nations, (*b*) the country's bank, (*c*) all unemployed people, (*d*) any poor nation.

   2._____

3. The promised "alliance for progress" was to be with (*a*) Canada, (*b*) the United Nations, (*c*) Latin America, (*d*) NATO.

   3._____

4. Kennedy promised the people of the world's poor nations that we would (*a*) help them, (*b*) help them help themselves, (*c*) get the United Nations to help them, (*d*) let them work out their own problems.

   4._____

5. President Kennedy promised that the United States would try to protect (*a*) American business rights all over the world, (*b*) human rights all over the world, (*c*) the right of each man to become rich, (*d*) any country attacked by another country.

   5._____

Lyndon B. Johnson's Address to the U.N. 1963

Excerpts from President Johnson's speech to the United Nations General Assembly on December 17, 1963.

* * * * We meet in a time of mourning but in a moment of dedication . . . the assassin's bullet which took his [President Kennedy] life did not alter his nation's purpose. We are more than ever opposed to the doctrines of hate and violence in our own land and around the world.

We are more than ever committed to the rule of law — in our own land and around the world.

We believe more than ever in the rights of man, all men of every color — in our own land and around the world.

And more than ever we support the United Nations, as the best instrument yet devised to promote the peace of the world and to promote the well-being of mankind.

. . . the full power and partnership of the United States is committed to our joint effort to eliminate war and the threat of war, aggression and the danger of violence, and to lift from all people everywhere the blight of disease and poverty and illiteracy.

I know that vast problems remain: conflicts between great powers, conflicts between small neighbors, disagreements over disarmament, persistence of ancient wrongs in the area of human rights, residual problems of colonialism and all the rest.

But men and nations, working apart, created these problems. And men and nations, working together, must solve them.

. . . I have seen too much of misery and despair in Africa, in Asia, in Latin America. I have seen too often the ravages of hunger and tapeworm and tuberculosis, and the scabs and the scars on too many children who have too little health and no hope.

I think that you and I and our countries and this organization can — and must — do something about these conditions . . . .

We favor the steady improvement of collective machinery for helping the less-developed nations build modern societies.

We favor an international aid program that is international in practice as well as in purpose. Every nation must do its share . . . we can build, together, a much better world.

The greatest of human problems — and the greatest of our common tasks — is to keep the peace and save the future.

All that we have built in the wealth of nations, and all that we plan to do toward a better life for all, will be in vain if our feet should slip or our vision falter, and our hopes ended in another world-wide war.

If there is one commitment more than any other that I would like to leave with you today, it is my unswerving commitment to the keeping and to the strengthening of the peace. Peace is a journey of a thousand miles and it must be taken one step at a time.

The United States of America wants to see the cold war end; . . . wants to prevent the dissemination of nuclear weapons to nations not now possessing them . . . wants to press on with arms control and reduction . . . wants to cooperate with all the members of this organization to conquer everywhere the ancient enemies of mankind — hunger, and disease and ignorance . . . wants sanity and security and peace for all, and above all.

Man's age-old hopes remain our goal — that this world, under God, can be safe from diversity and free from hostility, and a better place for our children and for all generations in the years to come.

And therefore any man and any nation that seeks peace — and hates war — and is willing to fight the good fight against hunger, and disease, and ignorance and misery will find the United States of America by their side, willing to walk with them — walk with them every step of the way.

Lyndon B. Johnson's Inaugural Address, 1965

* * * * *Although faced with enormous international as well as national problems, President Johnson, in his Inaugural Address, chose to emphasize his plans, hopes and desires for changes and improvement on the domestic level. In October, 1964, he originally outlined his idea of "The Great Society" and at his inauguration he reiterated the goals he had set. These goals included the continuation of the struggle for equal rights as well as an attack against the scourge of poverty and the improvement of educational and economic opportunity for all of our citizens. Of equal importance, was the President's desire for the development of a unity of national purpose throughout our nation.*

. . . Our destiny in the midst of change will rest on the unchanged character of our people, and on their faith.

They came here — the exile and the stranger, brave but frightened — to find a place where a man could be his own man.

They made a covenant with this land. Conceived in justice, written in liberty, bound in union, it was meant one day to inspire the hopes of all mankind, and it binds us still. If we keep its terms we shall flourish.

First, justice was the promise that all who made the journey would share in the fruits of the land. . . . Liberty was the second article of our covenant. It was self-government. It was our Bill of Rights. But it was more. . . . [It] called on us to help show the way for the liberation of man. And that is today our goal.

. . . If American lives must end, and American treasure be spilled, in countries that we barely know, then that is the price that change has demanded of conviction and of our enduring covenant.

. . . And our nation's course is abundantly clear. We aspire to nothing that belongs to others. We seek no domination over our fellow man, but man's dominion over tyranny and misery.

. . . The third article is union. . . . By working shoulder to shoulder together we can increase the bounty of all.

. . . Under this covenant of justice, liberty and union, we have become a nation; prosperous, great and mighty. And we have kept our freedom. . . . In each generation — with toil and tears — we have had to earn our heritage again. . . . freedom asks more than it gives and the judgment of God is harshest on those most favored.

. . . For this is what America is all about. It is the uncrossed desert and the unclimbed ridge. It is the star that is not reached and the harvest that's sleeping in the unplowed ground.

TRUE OR FALSE

Write the letter T *if the statement is correct; write* F *if it is false.*

_____1. In his inaugural address, President Johnson expressed his desire to increase educational opportunity.

_____2. The three articles of the covenant mentioned in the inaugural address are justice, liberty and prosperity.

_____3. Freedom is an inherent right that Americans will always enjoy.

THOUGHT QUESTIONS

1. What were some of the major domestic problems that President Johnson stressed in his speech?
2. Explain the statement "freedom asks more than it gives."